HONDURAS
SAN SALVADOR
JALAPA
NEW SEGOVIA
Dept of New Segovia
SOMOLO GRANDE
PUEBLO NUEVO
BAY OF FONSECA
SAUCE
VOL. VIEJO
Dept of Leon
Dept of Granada
CHINENDEGA
REALEJO
LAKE MANAGUA
LEON
PORT OF REALEJO
ESTERO PANALOVA
PUEBLO NUEVO
MATEARAS
MANAGUA
NACAROTE
VOL. MASAYA
GRANADA
SAN RAFAEL
JINOTEPEC
STEAMSHIPS to CALIFORNIA
Dept of Rivas
RIVAS
THE TRANSIT ROAD
SAN JUAN DEL SUR
Pacific Ocean

Gold R.
Wanks or
Dept. of Matagalpa
"The Mosquito Kingdom"
BLUEFIELDS R.
Pearl R.
PEARL LAKE
Chontales
ACOYAPA
BLUEFIELD BLUFF
BLUEFIELDS
SAN MIGULITO
STEAMSHIPS to NEW YORK
Atlantic Ocean
SAN CARLOS
GREYTOWN or SAN JUAN DEL NORTE
ROUTE OF THE TRANSIT
Guanacaste
CASTILLO VIEJO
River San Juan
HIPP'S POINT
SAN CARLOS R.
SARAPIQUI R.
GULF OF NICOYA
COSTA RICA

THE FILIBUSTER

To this effete generation a filibuster means a legislative maneuver to defeat action, as by talking it to death. One thinks of Huey Long.

To what weak uses words descend! Consider the original meaning: a freebooter or soldier-of-fortune who aids a revolution in a foreign country in order to enrich himself; first applied to buccaneers, and later to adventurers in a hostile expedition to some country with which their own is at peace. The classic example is WILLIAM WALKER and his expedition to Nicaragua.

In his day his name was on every tongue. There had been nothing to compare with the magnitude of his story since the discovery of gold. In five years (1855-1860) he rose to the heights of fame, repeated the exploits of Cortez, became the darling of the mob. Admiring throngs carried him on their shoulders. America was swept with dreams of Manifest Destiny and here was a gray-eyed Man of Destiny. But before that lustrum was over, the "renowned Walker" had sunk to ignominy, and a firing squad of barefooted brown men at Truxillo had put an end to all the grandiose hopes of El Presidente.

Had he been successful, the Civil War might have been postponed, might never have been fought, or might have had another result. Because he was not successful, and because he immediately preceded the rebellion into the arena, what he did and what he tried to do have been almost overlooked by the historian. To the world at large his name is a strange one.

But now he is alive again.

For Laurence Greene, who wrote *America Goes to Press,* has rescued his story from the limited, scattered and often inaccurate sources and told it in brilliant fashion. He writes with the sharp impressions of an eye-witness, combined with the vision and perspective that only time and distance can lend. He deals with action, action, action, but never loses sight of the trend and purport. He has a lively sense of the dramatic, a keen eye for the bizarre, the dash and fluency of the gifted story-teller.

In a new age of dictators, this biography of a nineteenth century dictator is not only an amazing tale in itself, but a peculiarly meaningful one. Is it not often the obscure chapters of history that make the most exciting—and the most enlightening—reading?

ILIBUSTER
✗ ✗ ✗

BUSTER

aradoxical little Napoleon,
restless ambition.

ded as effeminate. Yet in
ed callously the execution

as thirty, a doctor, lawyer
ave been successful in any
because of his peculiar in-
ession—arms. He plagued
ts, and at last came to dis-

eir own charge, with tyran-
w liked him and none was
him with a loyalty that no
ger could shake, and they
ithout question.

h a stubborn disregard of
sion of failures could con-

plottings of an unhung
ench, "because he might
senselessly with Cornelius
oting Commodore had the
f his stature.

nent from his adversaries
chery.

tune" implies swashbuck-
edible achievement. They
r fitted his deeds no better
d, but not for plunder. He
idealism that led him to
t throats.

egoist, executioner, plotter.
his own infallibility, suffi-
ke it almost plausible even
oughts and deeds three-
rd. Doing wrong, prating
god.

After an engraving by I. C. Buttre; from *The Story of the Filibusters,* by J. J. Roche.

WILLIAM WALKER

THE FILIBUSTER

The Career of William Walker

BY LAURENCE GREENE
Author of *America Goes to Press*

ILLUSTRATED

THE BOBBS-MERRILL COMPANY
PUBLISHERS
INDIANAPOLIS   NEW YORK

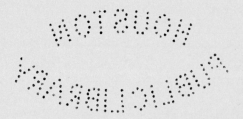

For

KATHERINE BOSWORTH GREENE

CONTENTS...

ILLUSTRATIONS...

ACKNOWLEDGMENT . . .

OF THE many persons who have taken a helpful interest in this book, the author is most deeply indebted to:

Mr. Lynn Carrick, of New York; Mr. Samuel Crowther, of Sunapee, N. H.; Dr. W. O. Scroggs, of New York; Colonel Guy R. Molony, of San Pedro Sula, Honduras; Mr. Paul J. Veith, of New Orleans; Mr. L. S. Rowe, Pan-American Union, Washington; and the staffs of the Enoch Pratt and Peabody Institute Libraries, Baltimore, the Library of Congress, Washington, the New York Public Library and the Department of Middle American Research Tulane University, New Orleans.

NOTE ...

Webster traces the noun filibuster to the Dutch *vrijbuiter* (*vrij*, free; *buit*, booty) and gives this definition: "A freebooter or soldier-of-fortune who aids a revolution in a foreign country in order to enrich himself; first applied to buccaneers in the West Indies, who preyed on the Spanish commerce to South America, and later to such adventurers as followed Lopez to Cuba, and Walker to Nicaragua, in their expeditions of conquest."

BOOK ONE

Rehearsal in Sonora

THE FILIBUSTER

BOOK ONE:

Rehearsal in Sonora ...

---

*Any social organization, no matter how secured, is preferable
to that in which individuals and families are altogether at the
mercy of savages. . . .*

I

WILLIAM WALKER came to his thirtieth birthday in God knows
what desolation of spirit, bitterly aware of the completeness of his
failure, of the enormity of his remaining responsibility, and of the
probability that he would be violently dead before night.

For seven months, with a handful of followers, he had pursued
a hopeless cause in an alien country. For the last twenty-one days,
since the full fact of defeat had been accepted, he had led a desperate band in northward retreat up the peninsula of Lower California. Desertion and death, since a point midway in his adventure,
had reduced his army from three hundred to thirty-four men.

They camped three miles from the border, in the Hacienda Tiajuanna, on the eighth of May, 1854. Around the hacienda, as they
had on all of the long march from San Vicente, hovered the Mexicans who called themselves soldiers and who were so remote from
the central government in Mexico City as to be no more than brigands. Walker's men, who lay in all attitudes in the courtyard trying
to forget that they were starved and exhausted and frantically afraid
of dying, cursed in whispers. They cursed, not because they were in

17

rags or because their feet were bleeding from the cuts of sharp stones, or because they had not eaten for forty-eight hours: those burdens they could carry. But there was something appalling about the tactics of the Mexicans. They declined to fight, because they feared the thirty-four weak wretches and because it better pleased them to torment, by riding on the flanks and harassing the march. And now, within three miles of the blessed security of the United States, the thirty-four and their leader could not yet be sure that they would be allowed to cross the border. Waiting in the courtyard for the commander, who was thirty years old that day, to order them on, they pulled nervously at their beards and at the tatters which they kept on their bodies with cactus spines and their own ingeniousness. Their eyes were bright and staring in the tangle of hair the months had grown and their lips so cracked that it was painful to move them; they spoke little among themselves.

Into this idiot's dream walked two spruce figures in the blue of the United States cavalry—Captain H. S. Burton and Major J. McKinstry, of the post at San Diego. The ones who lay like dogs in the courtyard watched with a deep despair the conference which took place in the corner where the commander crouched. They heard the officers speak of Melendrez, the Mexican who had so relentlessly pursued them, and of his promise of free passage over the border if they laid down their arms; and they heard less distinctly the soft voice of Walker refuse. In the presence of the cavalrymen, who served somewhat illegally as arbiters on the soil of another country, Walker was calm, not angry, and in no appearance the desperate man circumstance had made him. The discussion continued, politely and gravely: the officers promised food and assistance if the remnants of Walker's army could get across the border, but they could pledge no co-operation to achieve that end. Presently they went away, the heels of their good boots sounding crisply on the pavement of the court. Their horses were wheeled in the road; they became the bottom of a cloud of dust moving swiftly toward the north.

The commander stood up. The men watched him, like a circle of rats. He was tiny, less than five and a half feet tall, and his weight could not have been more than a hundred. One of his boots had worn completely away and the other looked like a sandal. His pantaloons were without straps and torn to the knee; he wore a short blue jacket with all but two of its brass buttons gone. His hat was an extraordinary hat, of white beaver, high crowned and with a long nap that fluttered in the breeze. Beneath it showed the ragged edges of straight, tow-colored hair. His face was the thin face of the Scottish preacher: a sharp nose, a line where the lips were, eyes of a clear and icy gray. His expression, as he looked upon his men, was no heavier than usual, and no one of the thirty-four could remember ever having seen an emotion reflected in the face. He walked to the center of the courtyard with precise and almost mincing steps, his single boot heel clattering unevenly. "All right, you men," he said.

They lurched to their feet, the seventeen who still had rifles carrying them with no regard for the positions in the manual of arms. They formed into a semblance of a line and passed out of the courtyard, onto the road for San Diego. The commander went ahead, moving with his parade-ground step, his eyes aimed steadfastly at safety three miles away. Dust rose about the column as it advanced along the road, making the dry lips drier and stirring up a little chorus of sepulchral coughs. The Mexicans, watching with their black eyes, turned their horses and paralleled the march. There was no firing.

They needed a full hour to travel two miles and a half. Then they came to the top of a hill and could see, in the distance, another hilltop, crowded with the people from San Diego, who had come out to see (they hoped) a battle.

The Mexicans whooped suddenly and galloped ahead of the line of walking men, reining up a few hundred feet distant to command and block the road. The man in the beaver hat halted his column with an upraised hand and called to his side Timothy Crocker, a red-haired, slim and powerful youth, who glided up on bare feet soundless in the dust.

When Crocker had heard his orders, he asked for volunteers to clear the road. Nine men responded. The red-haired youth nodded toward the Mexicans and, summoning the energy from some miraculous reserve, the ten moved forward at a trot. When they had gone halfway they began to shrill an ancestor of the rebel yell; after another ten paces they paused at a word from Crocker and fired a deliberate volley. Two Mexicans fell from their horses and lay still. The others wavered, turned; and then, with an unexpectedness that looked rehearsed, galloped off southward. The commander watched them go. It had been like that from the beginning. Opposition had not defeated him; the country itself had. Never a decent fight, never a town worth the taking, never an advantage that could be consolidated into a position. He shrugged a little and lifted his womanlike hand again and his wretches moved. In fifteen minutes they were across the border, lying in the road much as they had lain in the courtyard of the Hacienda Tiajuanna, too dispirited and weary to answer or to resent the curious who had come sixteen miles to look at freaks.

Walker went to where the two cavalry officers waited. He stood before them, looking upward (they were mounted) and announced formally, "I am Colonel William Walker, late President of the Republic of Sonora. I wish to surrender my force to the United States."

In a little while one of the officers carried a document from man to man for signatures. It read:

PAROLE OF HONOR

The undersigned, Officers and Privates of the (so called) "Republic of Sonora," do solemnly pledge their word of honor to report themselves at San Francisco, Cal., to Major General Wool, of the United States Army, charged with having violated the Neutrality Laws of the United States. San Diego, Cal., May 8, 1854.

Thus ended the first expedition of the Filibuster.

II

THIS is the chronicle of a paradoxical little man who was inspired by a desperation of restless ambition.

In boyhood he was regarded by those who knew him as effeminate—a friend of his mother, writing long afterward, remarked, "He was as refined in his feelings as a girl."* Yet in five of his most

* Jane H. Thomas, *Old Days in Nashville, Tennessee.*

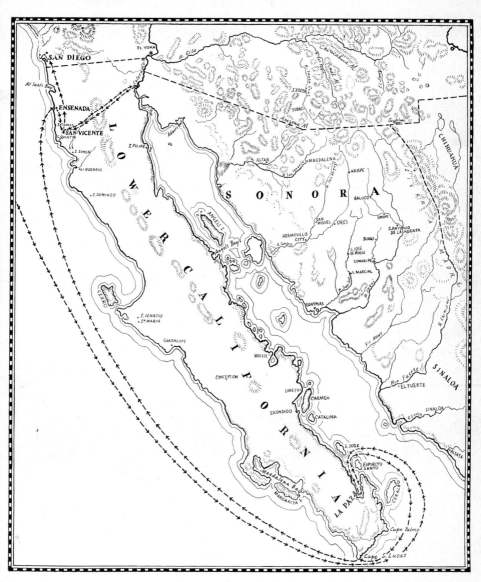

SONORA

crowded years, he ordered callously the execution of at least a dozen men, some of whom had neither done him hurt nor intruded upon his objects.

He became, before he was thirty, doctor, lawyer and journalist, and might have been successful in any one of his professions; but because of his peculiar insanity, he chose a fourth profession—arms. He plagued and terrified ten governments, and at last came to dismal failure.

He treated his men, by their own charge, with tyranny, stiff unfriendliness and a dignified demand for military etiquette in its most exact form. Many admired him, some liked him and none was his friend; but with very few exceptions they served him with a loyalty that no amount of suffering or danger could shake and they obeyed his maddest orders without question.

He believed himself to be ruthlessly fair. In a country where prisoners of war were universally butchered, he treated them as he treated his own wounded and would permit no harm to come to them. And yet, because they were driven to a project of robbery by starvation, he caused to be flogged and driven into a desert two men who had served him well.

He followed a course of action with the stubbornest disregard for consequences and no succession of failures could convince him he was wrong.

Had he been successful, the Civil War might have been postponed, might never have been fought, or might have had another result. Because he was not successful and because he immediately preceded the rebellion into the arena, what he did and what he tried to do have been almost overlooked by the historian: to the world at large, his name is a strange one.

He tolerated the greedy plottings of an unhung scoundrel named Parker French, "because he might have value," and he fought senselessly with Cornelius Vanderbilt when the Commodore had the power to crush a thousand of his stature.

He demanded fair treatment from his adversaries and was a past master of treachery.

He was biased, egocentric, monominded, quite possibly the victim of a sexual disorder, utterly unfair in his motives, acts and conclusions. And yet he wrote a book* about his experiences so honest with the facts that hostile Central American historians have accepted its statements in preference to conflicting ones of their own countrymen.

He was born in Nashville, in 1824, to a Scot named James Walker and to Mary Norvell, of Kentucky. The Filibuster was the first of four children. His parents called him William and saw for him a career in the ministry (making no allowance, it proved, for the family's dark strain, which he so clearly possessed). Their second son, Norvell, grew to be a glossy blood, given to cards and other dissipation, and their third, James, is described by the friend of the family heretofore mentioned as "a little silly at times." Only the daughter, Alice, showed worth and sanity: she married a man named Richardson and went to live in Louisville, where the record has nothing to say of her except that she was a genteel lady.

William Walker studied at the University of Nashville and was graduated when he was fourteen. He appeared to deplore the rougher aspects of boyhood and played seldom with his schoolmates, instead sitting for hours every day at the bedside of his invalid mother to read to her. Because the university was a puritanical school, Walker grew up into an austerity strangely at variance with his ultimate end as a professional killer. Throughout his life, even when he moved among the roughest men of a rough era, he did not drink, smoke or seduce, and was unique for the extreme chastity of his speech. The university, it is safe to say, helped to set him in his mould: it was neither gay nor southern, as novels recall southern colleges, for the students were not allowed to attend balls, horse-races, cockfights or the theatre, and they could own no slaves, no horses and no dogs. They might learn fencing or music only upon the specific request of parents or guardians. They studied much theology, prayed at least eight times a day and were required to attend church. From this beginning, William Walker went into the world: he inclined in adolescence toward the church and, by deciding not to become a minister, may have turned from his true vocation to pursue a false and dishonorable one.

In the beginning though, he could not see his end, and so, influenced by his parents and by his own asceticism, he began a tenta-

---

* The War in Nicaragua.

tive study of the Scriptures, joining the Christian Disciples' Church. He learned little enough because he changed his course so soon; in a matter of weeks he began to spend his days in an old chair in the shabby office of the town's best practitioner, Doctor Jennings, reading medical books, studying charts of the anatomy and soon astonishing his mother's visitors by discussing simple diseases in the professional argot.

He learned a very great deal from the books of Doctor Jennings and he went off in 1838 to the University of Pennsylvania, where five years of study earned him a degree.

Medicine, to this man of nineteen, was his vocation. He returned to Nashville, persuaded his parents that he needed training in Europe and spent a year abroad, in Paris and Heidelberg. When he returned to Tennessee in 1845, a contemporary called him "one of the most accomplished surgeons that ever visited the city." Normally, he was a finished product and his future a neat graph; but because inconsistency was his one constant characteristic, he decided that he was not meant to be a doctor. Coolly and against the wishes of his family and friends, he threw into oblivion six years of work and turned to the bar.

Thence, his career follows no pattern. He read a little law in the office of Edwin Ewing, in Nashville. He went, again on impulse, to New Orleans, where he studied the Code Napoleon and was admitted to the bar. He opened an office at 4 Canal Street and waited for clients. And he met his first and only friend.

His slim practice brought him into contact with Edmund Randolph, a grandson and namesake of the Virginia statesman who was Washington's Attorney General. Randolph, five years older than Walker, had practiced for a time in New Orleans and later served as clerk of the United States Circuit Court. The two were often together, for they had much in common: an intellectual parity, a feeling for their national traditions and a passion for behavior according to the rules. Throughout his life Walker leaned on Edmund Randolph; long afterward, when success had blunted him and he would listen to no advisers, he received gladly whatever opinions Randolph cared to offer.

To his contemporaries, he must have seemed in the New Orleans period at last to have found his niche. He enjoyed little law practice, it is true, because his was an unfortunate personality and prospective clients found it hard to be confidential with a man so damnably self-possessed. But he must have known some happiness. He had New Orleans, by all odds the most civilized city on the continent; he had Edmund Randolph, with whom he could dine and talk and devise the grandiose plans so much the portion of youth. And, when he had been in New Orleans for several months, he had Helen Martin.

III

IT IS more than likely that Edmund Randolph, who knew everyone of consequence in New Orleans, brought the two together. They were in love in the first instant. Helen Martin was a woman of beauty and her handicap (she was deaf) seems to have served only to urge tenderness upon Walker. He learned sign language and they conversed in it, their hands making a ghostly chatter. He began to work harder at his law, so that they might be married soon. Presently, when he saw that the bar would not afford him the sort of living Helen Martin should have, he entered a new profession, his third—journalism.

With J. C. Larue and W. F. Wilson, he founded the New Orleans *Crescent*. He was its editor, an idealistic editor and not a wise one, for he wrote articles on the slavery question so conservative in tone that other Southern journals denounced his for a "Yankee paper." In passing, it should be mentioned that among the editorials he wrote were several condemning the expeditions being formed in the United States at that time to win Cuba her freedom. Narciso Lopez and General John A. Quitman,* to William Walker, the New Orleans editor, were cursed and dangerous filibusters, operating altogether without the pale of law or reason.

---

* Born in Venezuela, Lopez early became interested in Cuban independence. He headed three expeditions against the Spaniards: one to Round Island in 1849, the second to Cardenas in 1851 and the last to Bahia Honda in 1851. Lopez, when the natives failed to rise up and support him, fled to the mountains, was captured and was garrotted in Havana on September 1, 1851. Quitman, a Mississippian, who had fought for Texas independence and in the war against Mexico, was associated with Lopez in the second expedition and earned great fame later when as a member of Congress he fought for the repeal of the neutrality laws.

Then, in his own paper there appeared scattered notices of yellow fever. The plague was a New Orleans perennial, so well expected that as soon as summer came the well-to-do moved away from the city and left the poor to die. The epidemic of 1849 varied little from the others: at first there were rumors of yellow fever cases in the slum districts, then there was a spreading to homes occupied by those who could not, for one reason or another, leave the city, and at last the Board of Health confessed to peril on banners bearing the word "EPIDEMIC" in huge type. Black-bordered cards, announcing in French the details of the funeral, appeared on the doors behind which lay the dead. Business all but stopped, theatres and stores closed, the hotel bars lost their convivial crowds and gained instead morose and solitary drinkers. The city took on the appearance of siege, with block upon block of houses closely shuttered; all day processions of hearses moved out Girod and Julia Streets and the Rue de Conti, carrying bodies to the Protestant Yard, or the Cypress Grove, or the Cemetery of St. Louis. No one was safe. William Walker was appalled by the long lists of dead brought to him in galley proofs; desolated when at last the name of Helen Martin had to be added.

A reporter who worked for him remembered him before Helen Martin died as a man "very silent and very kind, with the look of one bent upon a hard course of study and almost always poring over a book." Now his entire attitude changed, as did his philosophy. He became melancholy and obsessed with the notion of clearing his mind of its sorrow by some deed of violent daring. His ambition changed from one for material success to a force impelling him to seek an outlet in recklessness. The *Crescent,* shortly after Helen Martin died, ceased publication for lack of support. So, with nothing more to bind him, Walker paid his fare and began the tedious journey across the Plains. The year was 1849 and he thought California might be a place from which he·could start again.

IV

THE restless indecision which had sent him from profession to profession forever after dominated his life. He joined the staff of the

San Francisco *Daily Herald* upon his arrival in that city early in 1850. He wrote editorials about the prevalence of crime so bitingly critical of the bench that he was arrested, fined for contempt of court and imprisoned when he refused to pay. He defied the judge, one Levi Parsons, and became a public hero; mass meetings were held for him; he was set free by a superior court. In the midst of this fight he seems to have achieved a certain peace of mind, but when his effort to gain the impeachment of Judge Parsons failed and he was left with nothing to occupy him but the memories of his life in New Orleans, he drifted again. He abandoned San Francisco, for the city of Marysville and a return to the law.

For two years he was in, but not of, Marysville: it was a time of open-handed heartiness and he was too aloof to be successful. What practice his law firm enjoyed was brought in by his partner, Henry P. Watkins. The year 1853 came, to find him ready, at twenty-nine, for what he was to be.

He had come, without in any degree intending it, to his beginnings as a soldier-of-fortune. Colleges and the association of good minds in the law, medicine and journalism had fitted him, after a fashion, for this change: he had the surgeon's steadiness, the journalist's enterprise and the lawyer's cunning. The two women he had loved—the only women he would ever love—his mother and Helen Martin, were dead, and there was no need to prepare for the future. California had received him well and for a brief time he had been a notable. His sleeping ego awakened. He had the habit of courage, inherited and learned. He was discontented with Marysville and the bar and eager for anything that might come.

Californians, in 1850, were the most headlong breed of men the United States had ever known. Drawn from every country in the world by a multitude of hopes and greeds, they lived solely in the present and by a moral code which may be called, for want of a more satisfactory definition, one of expediency. Some were driven to California by an individual sorrow, such as William Walker's. Nearly all wanted gold, as much as they could accumulate. Others wanted the life and excitement of the camps and the gambling and brothels to be found in the towns. And still others were tough and went to California because it was the toughest place there was.

These men, fighters and killers, could not long be satisfied with the routine of San Francisco's normal brawling. They looked about for a broader stage upon which to perform, and found it in the removal of filibustering activity from the Gulf Coast, where Lopez and the other assailants against Spain in Cuba had been operating, to the Pacific. The union of the filibuster chiefs and the men in California who could not find enough fighting to soothe their souls was a natural and inevitable one. Filibusterism fitted these men, for it was, of all the endeavors of the period, the one least possible to classify.

Whether it was wrong or right was a question answerable only after the filibuster had failed or succeeded. Successful, he was a hero; unsuccessful, he was an outlaw contemned by all his fellows.

The United States had stopped growing physically, but its citizens could not be made to realize it. The expansions south and west since the formation of the Republic had been so sweeping and so swift that few observers in the Fifties could believe the march of what they mistakenly called progress was at an end. Visionary statesmen and journalists looked northward to Canada, a little timidly and very wistfully, or—more boldly—southward to Mexico and Cuba and Central America. The phrase of the hour was an attractive one—men spoke of the "manifest destiny" of the United States, as justifying whatever crimes were committed in its name. Typical of the thought of the period is a paragraph in a chronology, *The Annals of San Francisco,* written and published in 1855 by Messrs. Soulé, Gihon and Nisbet:

It is the fate of America ever to "go ahead." She is like the rod of Aaron that became a serpent and swallowed up the other rods. So will America conquer or annex all lands. That is her "manifest destiny." Only give her time for the process. To swallow up every few years a province as large as most European kingdoms is her present rate of progress. Sometimes she purchases the mighty morsel, sometimes she forms it out of waste territory by the natural increase of her own people, sometimes she "annexes" and sometimes she conquers it. Her progress is still steadily onward. Pioneers clear the way. There are political agents with money bags, or settlers in neglected parts of the continent, or peaceable American citizens who happen to reside in the desired countries and who wish to dwell under the old "Stars and Stripes," or they may be only proper filibusters, who steal and fight gratuitously for their own fast-following Uncle Sam. When they fail in their schemes they are certainly scoundrels, and are commonly so termed; when they succeed, though they be dubbed heroes, they are still the old rogues. Meanwhile, AMERICA (that is the true title of our country) secures the spoils won to her hand, however dishonestly they may have come. That is her only destiny, and perhaps she is not so blamable as a nation in bearing it so willingly. One may profit by treason, and yet hate the traitor. America must round her territories by the sea.

This extraordinary philosophy was not, as might be supposed from reading it, the declaration of hoodlums. William Walker subscribed to it and he was an intelligent man. He had a flair for leadership and he had been absorbing, from childhood, the arrogant confidence of the United States. To him she was a country not yet done with her growth and with a "manifest destiny" to fulfill. He could not see, any more than most of his contemporaries could see, that the United States was the lucky bumpkin at the fair, whose finger had happened to point out the shell beneath which lay the little pea.

Infected with the germ that was to blight his life, he studied with more than casual interest the accounts of the mines in Sonora, lying idle because the Apache Indians were so active. He read and discussed the reports of two French expeditions: one led by a Marquis de Pindray, who was shot by a follower in Sonora, and the others conducted by Count Gaston Raoul de Raousset-Boulbon, a prodigal who had not been able to make a second fortune in the California mines and who was executed while trying to steal it from Mexico.

Therefore, when a group of men from Placer County came to William Walker to ask his co-operation in colonizing Sonora, he agreed eagerly. In an instant, the doctor-lawyer became a chief.

V

THE Apache Indians ran wild throughout Sonora and Lower California. Their wandering and well-directed bands crossed the borders from Arizona, descending upon the huts of the peons, killing lustily, burning systematically and retreating with what horses and cattle there were. Mexico City was a long way from its States to the north and the alarm its officials displayed was, at best, abstracted.

Occasionally, the central government sent a regiment or two into the area to subdue the savages. These expeditions were mere gestures: the companies would quarter in a pleasant interior town and remain there while scouts hunted for the Indians. When a band of Apaches was located, the scouts would report, the commandant would buckle on his arms and the troops would march as rapidly as possible away from where the Indians had been seen last. After a reasonable time, the soldiers would return to Mexico City, where the commandant submitted a glowing report of brave battles and everyone concerned received medals.

The country itself offered little surface excuse for occupation. It was infested with centipedes, tarantulas, snakes and insects. Children were the great sufferers from the bites of these creatures; if they lived to adulthood, they learned to avoid the perils of crawling and slithering life. Except to the natives, Sonora was a desolation, but the reports of rich gold and silver deposits made the territory important. Mining companies had worked the region, but had been forced to leave it because of the connivance of Mexican officialdom or the efficiency of the Apaches. The press of California, therefore, began to grieve for the poor peons of Sonora. It was said that the United States, as a humanitarian gesture, should occupy the area and protect the people. Generally, this was accepted as a worthy thought; as responsible and conservative a journal as the *Alta California*, for instance, in September of 1853 discussed the reported murder of eighty persons by Indians in one week and said editorially, "They cannot protect themselves and the government cannot protect them. Their only hope is a war and the occupation of their territory by United States troops."

As his first move to colonize this region, William Walker traveled to Guaymas, on the Gulf of California. The scheme he proposed there met with no encouragement and in a few days he realized that whatever promises he might obtain from the Mexican officials would be immediately broken because of their hostility toward all Americans. He returned to California, where he found that his backers had provided ammunition, supplies and a ship to transport his forces. He needed no more than this; true to the new creed he had adopted, the unwillingness of Mexico to open her lands to him became no more than an indication of foreign whimsicality.

VI

THE FILIBUSTER's first expedition was ill-conceived and executed with all the clumsiness of a Quixote.

A brig, the *Caroline,* sailed on October 16, 1853. She carried forty-five men, the rag-tag and bobtail of all the Coast. In command was a man not yet thirty, with no acquaintance with the country he was invading. He had no maps. His knowledge of military matters was less than elementary, gleaned from a book or two on tactics and some conversation with soldiers. In the hold of the *Caroline* were supplies insufficient to support even the few she carried.

The sailing was achieved through the support of public opinion and Walker's guile. General Ethan Allen Hitchcock, in command of the army's Pacific Department, concluding rightly that Walker's project was a violation of the neutrality laws, tried to uphold them. When his writs failed, Hitchcock seized the brig and would not give it up until he was threatened with citation for contempt of court. Walker, revealing an impatience which should never be present in a man dedicated to so precarious a business as filibustering, sailed stealthily, leaving behind him on the pier the bulk of his foodstuff and ammunition. Hitchcock won little sympathy for what San Francisco considered his quaint conservatism about the neutrality laws, because the public believed that such laws could not be applied to backward countries like Mexico. (As an example of this feeling, consider that the ship which transported Walker was owned by the son of the United States consul in Guaymas.)

Later in his career Walker was ashamed of the Sonora rehearsal and his shame was not misplaced. He was guilty of a sin he did not commit again: amateurism. His original objective—Sonora, whose northern borders ran from Fort Yuma on the Colorado River to what is now New Mexico—was abandoned before the *Caroline* was fairly at sea. Walker decided that his force was too small to attempt the greater conquest and should be used to take Lower California first. With that as a base, he reasoned that the capture of Sonora would be simplicity itself—and, if he succeeded, he would be in control of two States of Mexico instead of one.

The *Caroline* traveled like a bobbin. She touched at Cape San Lucas, on the extreme tip of the peninsula of Lower California. She went to La Paz, south and across the Gulf of Lower California from Guaymas. She returned to San Lucas and then beat her way back up the coast, to Ensenada, sixty miles from the border. Her commander ordered changes of base almost as quickly as the ship came to rest. His reason was uneasiness; with the exception of a brush at La Paz he met with no resistance, but his imagination peopled the interior with an enormous force of Mexicans, which might at any moment fall upon and annihilate him.

His arrival at La Paz was undramatic. The *Caroline* anchored off the town and a landing party under the command of Charles Gilman, a Baltimorean who like Walker had abandoned the law for warfare, went ashore. The seizure of the place was the work of thirty minutes. Gilman, returning to the ship, reported no resistance and the capture of the Governor, one Espanoza.

When he went ashore, Walker carried two articles: a new flag of his own designing and a decree. The standard of Mexico on the Governor's house was hauled down and Walker's flag—a red star on a blue field—hoisted in its place. The decree, first of several, was published:

> The Republic of Lower California is hereby declared Free, Sovereign and Independent and all allegiance to the Republic of Mexico is forever renounced.

With forty-five men and a decree of twenty-three words, William Walker, educated and accounted sane, believed himself, on November 3, 1853, to be master of an entire Mexican State. Here is a paradox difficult to explain. Some of his faith was the faith of all Americans in "manifest destiny"; some ego; some confidence in the vigorous stalwarts at his back; some contempt of the weak Mexican. But added together, such reasons are not enough. There was something more to this man, some feeling within him that lent him mad conviction and blinded him to all possible consequence.

He waited in La Paz for three days. Then he ordered a return to Cape San Lucas, away from Sonora, which was his objective. The hapless and bewildered governor, Espanoza, and his successor, one Colonel Robellero, who was so unfortunate as to arrive in the moment of William Walker's going, were held prisoner. And, before they left, the First Independence Battalion, the fine name by which William Walker's dregs were known, received its baptism of fire.

As the company was embarking at La Paz, a detail of six remained ashore to gather wood for the galley stove. The natives, emboldened by the likelihood of the invaders' retreat, fired on them. Walker, hearing the shots, led thirty men to the rescue and for nearly two hours there was a glorified brawl in the streets and alleys of La Paz. The natives retired at last, into the chaparral, and the *Caroline* sailed way. A month later San Francisco read of this absurd encounter, in a dispatch forwarded by the *Alta California's* San Diego correspondent. He described and exaggerated the fight, concluding: "Thus ended the battle of La Paz, crowning our efforts with victory, releasing Lower California from the tyrannous yoke of declining Mexico, and establishing a new Republic!"

The expedition, until then an *opéra bouffe,* took on a grim tone. Walker kept running from an enemy that did not exist while continuing to make his futile gestures toward Sonora. Food for his forty-five men was getting low and the country was a poor one for foraging. The many recruits he had expected to come from San Francisco did not arrive. There was dissension in the ranks of his undisciplined villains. And yet he retained what a traveler who had seen him in Guaymas described as his "insane confidence."* He contended that he had a mission to protect the border dwellers from the Indians and he meant to fulfill it with or without the sanction of Mexico. He believed that once he had entered Sonora he would be justified in forming an independent government.

At Ensenada he attempted to put his mythical Republic in order. He issued additional decrees, lifting all customs duties and making the Code Napoleon the law of the land. He appointed his cabinet: Frederick Emory, who had preceded him to Guaymas as the first

* *Dust and Foam.*

agent for the Placer County syndicate, was Secretary of State, and John M. Jarnigan Secretary of War. Although there was no navy of Lower California, there was a Secretary—Howard M. Snow. Charles Gilman, Timothy Crocker and John McKibben were the ranking officers of the army. In all, there were eleven functionaries, a ratio true to filibustering tradition: one to every four privates.

The President, now that he had a government, issued an address to the people of the United States, which for its audacity alone is worthy of preservation among history's documents:

> In declaring the Republic of Lower California Free, Sovereign and Independent, I deem it proper to give the people of the United States the reasons for the course I have taken. It is due to the nationality which has most jealously guarded the Independence of the American States to declare why another Republic is created on the immediate confines of the Great Union.
>
> The Mexican Government has for a long time failed to perform its duties in the Province of Lower California. Cut off, as the territory was by the treaty of Guadaloupe-Hidalgo* from all direct communication with the rest of Mexico, the central authorities have manifested little or no interest in the affairs of the California Peninsula. The geographical position of the Province is such as to make it entirely separate and distinct in its interests from the other portions of the Mexican Republic. But the moral and social ties which bound it to Mexico have been even weaker and more dissoluble than the physical. Hence, to develop the resources of Lower California, and to effect a proper social organization thereon, it was necessary to make it Independent.
>
> On such considerations have I and my companions in arms acted in the course we have pursued. And for the success of our enterprise we put our trust in Him Who controls the destiny of nations, and guides them in the way of progress and improvement.

The argument and the facts make this address seem today the veriest nonsense: No man in his right mind could take seriously the declarations of the leader of a handful, who was cut off from all except casual support and who must, in the natural order of things, ultimately be defeated. But an astonishing number of Americans read the address and nodded their heads gravely in agreement with it. If those backward countries would not come along with America,

---

* Ending the Mexican War and ceding to the United States California and New Mexico.

they must be dragged—this was a destiny too manifest to be disputed. This ·Walker fellow, now, had the right idea—if they wouldn't take care of themselves, it was up to us to take care of them. Look at what Sam Houston did for Texas!

The whole country murmured such sentiments; San Francisco shouted them. Recruits of good and bad repute flocked to the office at Kearny and Sacramento Streets, where Henry Watkins, now become a recruiting officer, boldly flew the red-starred flag. The day after the story of the battle of La Paz was published in the *Alta California* fifty men enlisted at a mass meeting held in one of the fire houses. They were of all stamps: failures, gold seekers who had not found, or who had found and spent, saloon loafers, wharf rats, killers, and boys meant by their mothers to be ministers. The authorities were carried along in the stream of public opinion; they were politicians and knew better than to swim against the current. General Hitchcock, whose opinion of filibustering had all but halted the sailing of the *Caroline,* had been transferred, and the army, for the moment, was without a regular commander on the Pacific. Securities of the new Republic were openly sold, bringing ten cents on the dollar.

Reinforcements left on December 7, 1853. Shortly after midnight on that date, a door in a Front Street building was opened cautiously. It was raining hard and the streets were innocent of strollers. Carts and men materialized and, with surprising quiet, loads of guns and ammunition and food were moved from a warehouse to the dock where lay the ship *Anita.* The authorities were suspicious and the *Anita* got off in poor order, as had the *Caroline,* leaving the boxes of food on the pier. There were two hundred and thirty men aboard the ship, including Watkins and George R. Davidson, a veteran of the Mexican War.

VII

WHILE the *Anita* was at sea, the bravos of the First Independence Battalion fought for the second time. Mexicans, outnumbering them several to one, attacked Ensenada. For days the Americans were besieged in the adobe houses. On the morning of December fourteenth, no longer willing to waste ammunition, Walker called for volunteers to break the siege. He sought to lead the charge himself, but Timothy Crocker would not hear of it. The slim young Irishman, inspired as much by adoration of the Filibuster as by his native love of conflict, argued well enough to persuade Walker that the army without its commander would be a doomed rabble.

Crocker was the first of Walker's aides to give him that obedience which, weighed against the Filibuster's personality, is one of the major incongruities of his story. Of Crocker's origins nothing is known. Historically, he appears suddenly at Walker's right hand and in all of the Sonora campaign stands out almost as clearly as the commander himself. He was very boyish in his manner, tall, with a sinuous slimness that made his strength an unobtrusive asset. His military experience was either lacking or limited and of book knowledge he had none. But he believed in Walker utterly. Hero-worship, the eagerness of twenty to defer to thirty, the desire to win approbation from a man more reserved than other men—such impulses made Crocker. Walker called him invaluable and so he was; the Filibuster, in Sonora, required military help not nearly so much as he needed unquestioning approval of his conceptions by the men who were to execute them.

Crocker took twenty men for his charge. They poured out of the adobe house, yelling with the volume of a hundred. After fifteen minutes of brisk firing in the streets, the Mexicans retired and Crocker and the survivors returned, to report the cost of the attack. The body of Lieutenant McKibben, third in command, lay in the street, its chest blown in with a point-blank charge from a musket. Two privates were killed. Captain Gilman, who had gone along because he could not bear to be left out of a fight, had been hit in the leg.

The adobe house in whose defense the lieutenant had died was named Fort McKibben in his honor. Gilman's leg swelled and Richardson, the one doctor with the expedition, decided to amputate. Six men held Gilman down while he set his teeth upon a rifle barrel, and the surgery of the hacksaw and the hot iron was performed.

When it was learned that the Mexican force had retired from the area, the First Independence Battalion went to the beach to get from the *Caroline* what few resources she had. They found no sign of the ship; the harbor was bare, the horizon held no sail. Walker, when this report was brought to him, looked bleak, wondering whether his captain had fled in fright or had been bought by the two captive Mexican governors who had been left aboard.

The *Anita* appeared two weeks later. The entire force, excepting casualties, lined the beach and watched her come in. They spoke of the meal they would have when she had anchored and the boxes and casks in her hold were ashore. They looked upon the decks, crowded with hundreds of men, and rejoiced at the fate they now could dictate for the "Greasers." They were happy and relieved for the first time since they had come to the country.

But when the *Anita's* anchor was down and Watkins came ashore to report that she carried men and guns and powder, but nothing to eat, the expedition lost all its fire. From that moment every man but Walker knew that only one question could be asked about the Republic of Lower California: How many days before it ends?

The necessity of feeding the enlarged army created a situation requiring quick action. Scouts brought in reports of a gifted Mexican cutthroat named Melendrez, whose band served the purposes of an army in this forgotten State, levying tribute on the inhabitants and infrequently fighting the Indians. Melendrez was based at San Vicente, a village thirty miles distant, and he had many cattle. Walker, never at a loss for justification, concluded and maintained that the attack in which McKibben died had been directed by the Mexican, and therefore whatever Melendrez owned became, because of his rebellion, the property of the Republic. Sixty-five men went to San Vicente and met little resistance, returning with a large herd of cattle and horses.

Watkins returned to San Francisco on the *Anita,* to enlist still more men and to send necessities. The army was now unwieldy and, to be kept from disintegrating, must be given tasks. Despite the lack of equipment and supplies, Walker decided to go on to Sonora. For several weeks he prepared for his march, his foragers ranging the countryside and taking what cattle they could seize for butchering and drying. At last with the men divided into companies and enough rough food to sustain them for a considerable period, he made the last move. As had been the case with his others, it came in the form of proclamations—four, this time, covering much ground at once. They were, in order:

REPUBLIC OF SONORA

Decree No. 1

All decrees of a general nature heretofore published as Decrees of the Republic of Lower California are republished as decrees of the Republic of Sonora.

Decree No. 2

1. The Republic of Sonora is hereby divided into two States, to be styled respectively the "State of Sonora" and the "State of Lower California."
2. The State of Sonora comprises all the territories within the following boundaries, to wit: Beginning at a point in the Colorado River, opposite its mouth, and in the middle of the stream thereof; running thence along a line midway between the banks of said river to the boundary line between the United States and Mexico, as established by the treaty of Guadaloupe-Hidalgo; thence along said line until it strikes the summit of the Sierra de los Mimores; thence along the summits of said Sierra to the head-waters of the river Fuerte; thence down the middle of the stream of said river Fuerte, to its mouth.
3. The State of Lower California comprises all the territory south of the boundary line between the United States and Mexico, as established by the treaty of Guadaloupe-Hidalgo, and lying west of the river Colorado and the Gulf of California.
4. All islands in the Gulf of California lying opposite the coasts of the states of Sonora and Lower California, are attached to one of these States respectively, according as said islands be nearer the coasts of one State than to those of the other.

Decree No. 3

The name of the Republic (of Lower California) is hereby changed, and henceforth all decrees, laws and processes issued shall run in the name of the "Republic of Sonora."

Decree No. 4

The State of Sonora, lately declared by the President of Mexico a Department of the Mexican Republic, is hereby constituted a portion of the Republic of Lower California.

All four proclamations concluded: "Given under my hand at Fort McKibben, this eighteenth day of January, in the year of our Lord one thousand eight hundred and fifty-four," and were signed "William Walker, President of Sonora."

When the decrees had been published, the flag was hauled down and one with two red stars against a field of blue substituted.

VIII

THE decrees cost Walker something of his popularity in San Francisco, at least in its articulate part. The return of Watkins from Lower California preceded by only a few weeks the annexation of Sonora. The lack of suitable action to give body to the sweeping proclamations was received poorly by the editors of San Francisco; on January 30, 1854, the *Alta California* ridiculed the addition of Sonora to the "conquered" Lower California, and likened William Walker to Napoleon: "Of [him] it might be said, as of the mighty Corsican, 'he disposes of courts and crowns and camps as mere titulary dignitaries on a chessboard.' Santa Ana must feel obliged to the new President that he has not annexed any more of his territory than Sonora. It would have been just as cheap and easy to have annexed the whole of Mexico at once, and would have saved the trouble of making future proclamations."

Whether Walker ever read this editorial cannot be said, but if he did it had no effect on him. He was President of Sonora, come hell or high water, desertion or disease, scorn or starvation. Why he did nothing to prove his right to his claims, however, remains a mystery. Instead of moving at once into Sonora and subduing (or being subdued by) whatever force he found there, he waited in Ensenada. His men occupied their time by catching and breaking wild horses for the march and by drying beef. The poor generalship he had shown throughout his campaign did not improve. He was too new to his business, as were most of his officers, to see that drill and other occupations were provided, and as a result he faced a growing threat of mutiny. Late in January this came to a head.

The horses which had been caught and broken were assigned to the army as a whole, to be used as pack transport. Certain members of a company commanded by Captain Davidson went into the sagebrush and captured several animals. They stole equipment for their mounts from neighboring ranch houses and became, in their own eyes, cavalrymen. But Walker ordered otherwise. The horses were taken away and placed in the general corral. There were murmurings which Davidson tried vainly to quiet. Walker appeared before the men and demanded an oath of allegiance. When forty refused to give it he ordered them to leave camp within two hours. Soon Crocker came to him to report that the men were leaving, with their guns.

Walker went quickly to the throng of sullen ones in the middle of the street. He found them drawn up in opposition to a handful of loyal troops, both sides spoiling for a fight. One of the two brass cannon the *Anita* had brought was manned and ready. It was all Walker could do to prevent both sides from firing, but he at last restored quiet. The rebels started in the direction of San Diego. He followed them. He is reported to have "spoken kindly to them, to have urged them to return for rations and leave their guns behind, as they were badly needed." Two men gave up their rifles. Several smashed the stocks of theirs against rocks. The rest disregarded their erstwhile leader and the whole company went on to San Diego and thence to San Francisco.

He knew then that he could no longer delay until help came. Within a few days of the mutiny, two gunboats, one Mexican and the other of the United States Navy, anchored off the harbor. Walker waited not upon the order of his going: spiking his guns, with the exception of a small field-piece which he took along, he led one hundred and thirty men to San Tomas, twenty miles east and south. The fragments of the army passed through San Tomas on February sixteenth and occupied San Vicente, ten miles farther south, on the following day. The latter town had once been a proud place, with a gigantic mission built by the fathers; now it was a ghost. The fields for miles around it lay fallow, for the peons had abandoned them when the combination of such scoundrels as Melendrez, the avaricious tax collectors of Mexico City and the Apaches had persuaded them that sustenance was not to be had in the place. Walker's men searched the town and found no sign of Melendrez's bandits; they went then to the roofless, ruined Mission of San Vicente and placed their blankets within the walls of the old monastery and beneath the arches of the crumbling chapel.

While at Ensenada, Walker had been busy with still another set of lines for his impossible drama. Now, again moving to the center of a stage too big for him, he went through motions intended to convince Mexico and the United States (and perhaps himself) that he was the president of a new Republic. He ordered a convention of the natives to be held. Sixty-two persons attended.

In the center of the courtyard of the old mission a table was set, with two of the red-starred flags crossed before it in an arch. Behind this table stood the President and his Cabinet. Arrayed in a long double line leading from it to the street was a full force of the Americans, all armed and, to the natives, a sinister and powerful gathering. The Mexicans walked up to this table, told their names and took an oath of allegiance. Leaving, they walked under the arch of flags. When the last of the sixty-two had declared his loyalty to the new regime (in all probability wondering why he was there, and to what he had given oath) there were cheers and a salute from the single field piece.

On the following day, March first, there was issued, for the consumption of the United States, a "Declaration or Representation of the Inhabitants of the State of Lower California, of the Republic of Sonora, to His Excellency, the President." The document, undoubtedly written by Walker himself, praised the conduct of the Americans, asserted that the delegates to the convention had attended voluntarily and promised loyalty unto death to the new government. Walker probably had learned somehow of his loss of prestige in California and the convention and the declaration must have been aimed particularly at his own countrymen, to persuade them that his mission was both successful and acceptable to the inhabitants.

Since Walker's departure, however, a new commander of the Department of the Pacific had taken up his duties in San Francisco. Brevet Major General John E. Wool, even before leaving Washington, had asked for instructions about filibusters, and had been told in a letter from Jefferson Davis, then Secretary of War, "You will detect the fitting out of armed expeditions against countries with which the United States is at peace, and will zealously co-operate

GENERAL WALKER REVIEWING HIS TROOPS

with the civil authorities in maintaining the neutrality laws." Arriving on the Pacific Coast on February fourteenth, Wool acted within a fortnight. The day after the convention in San Vicente, the headquarters established by Henry Watkins was raided by troops, and Watkins arrested. Other arrests followed. Captain Davidson, sent from Mexico to recruit, was indicted, as were a Major Baird and a Doctor Hoge. Frederick Emory, Secretary of State in Walker's cabinet, was captured as he entered San Diego from Mexico and taken to San Francisco to stand trial. Immediately, the disintegration of the campaign which was to have equaled Sam Houston's began to spread.

Walker was aware only that his support in the press of the north had weakened. The actions of the government were kept from him by lack of communication until he surrendered to Captain Burton in May, two months later. He did not weaken meanwhile, but he must have known that the mark of failure was upon the whole enterprise. It is hard to understand why he did not give up his bad job for what it was and leave the country; but he hung on, ruling his men inflexibly and convincing himself that he controlled and would continue to control the two States of his Republic.

On March 3, 1854, a loyal private came to him to report that four men were marshaling the malcontents into a unit which would leave the army and go north alone. They had decided, this nameless worthy told his chief, to steal what horses and cattle they could and make for Fort Yuma, north and east of the present position. Whatever fell to their hand on the journey they would take along; they expected to arrive in the United States rich with booty.

Walker, now or ever, was no man to hesitate. He listened to this story and sent out squads to bring the four men before him. Two of them—T. F. Nelson and Arthur Morrison, both of Illinois—were exposed as ringleaders in the plot. Walker listened to the charges, his thin lips tight. He ordered Nelson and Morrison executed at once. The two others were flogged and driven into the desert as they came from beneath the whip, without food or arms. Theodore Ryan went into oblivion sore from fifty lashes: Edward Barnes' punishment was half that. How they made their way back to civilization, if they did, is not clear.

There was no court-martial, no defense for the prisoners, nothing but the summary justice of the commander himself. The other members of the First Independence Battalion demurred, among themselves, against acting as whipping and firing squads. But they obeyed orders. Everyone did, who served Walker. In his own account of his career, written a few months before his death, he is pleased to recall this incident:

A military execution is a good test of military discipline, for no duty is so repulsive to the soldier as that of taking life from the comrade who has shared the perils and privations of his arduous service. On this occasion, too, the duty was more difficult, because the number of Americans was small and was daily diminishing. But painful as was their duty, the men charged with the execution did not shrink from the performance of it; and the very field where the unfortunate victims of the law expiated their offense with their lives, was suggestive of comparison between the manner in which the expeditionists and the Mexican Government severally performed the duties of protection to society. . . . Those engaged in the Lower California expedition gave proof of their desire not to destroy, but to reorganize society wherever they went. They were all young men, and youth is apt to err in pulling down before it is ready to build up. But they were men, also, full of military fire and thirsting for military reputation; and the soldier's instinct leads him to construct rather than to destroy. . . .

IX

SEVENTEEN days after the executions, on March twentieth, the march to Sonora began. In the corral at San Vicente were one hundred cattle, gathered over a period of weeks from various ranches; these, an animated food supply, were driven before the troops. The objective was the Colorado River, two hundred miles east.

Upon its departure from San Vicente, where twenty men were left as garrison, the army was as unmartial a rabble as has ever been assembled. The men wore clothing and shoes in a state of imminent collapse. They were neither strong nor happy, for their diet in the weeks since Ensenada was taken had been a monotonous one of corn and beef. They had rifles and a little ammunition, some pack animals and virtually no baggage.

It was Walker's intention to cross the Colorado River a few miles north of its mouth and proceed thence to Arispe, nearly six hundred miles beyond. Arispe was in the center of the region reported to be rich in gold, and there, if he could reach it, he would fortify and make good his seizure of another nation's lands. The Sierra de los Mimores had to be crossed on the march. The men teetered along narrow mountain paths, driving their half wild cattle before them. It was two weeks before they reached the Colorado. On the march two more men deserted, twenty head of cattle died or were killed in falls from the trail. Thirty Cocopa Indians appeared in the middle of the second week and declared themselves willing to help the expedition; they were taken along and within a day had stolen thirty of the precious cattle. Five of the Indians, who failed to move as quickly as the balance of the band, were captured as hostages; three subsequently were shot—in attempting to escape, according to Walker's men.

The march became more dogged and more senseless with the days. At its beginning the men were in no condition to attempt to cross a mountain range, and by the time they reached the river they were far gone, from exhaustion and privation. The Indians hovered at their rear, undiscouraged by the deaths of their fellows and with their little black eyes greedily watching the cattle. And always, with an indomitable will no less admirable for having been so unwise, the tiny commander walked in the van. His clothing was torn and dirty and already the grinding against the rocks of the mountain paths had reduced his boots to shreds. But he did not waver, he did not unbend. To the men he remained aloof, dignified and always the leader. He was penalized for this stiffness: with the exception of the handful intelligent enough to appreciate the iron in his soul there was no cohesion in the ranks.

The army reached the Colorado and halted on the bank, stunned by the same dismay it had known when the *Caroline* sailed away. The river was no trivial stream, but wide, deep and rushing. Of them all, only Walker looked upon this new enemy implacably; and he, after a glance, turned to the faithful Crocker and ordered rafts built for the men. He hoped to swim the cattle.

They spent a day or two building the rafts. The first took across, among others, a Captain Douglass and an Englishman named Smith. Douglass had been saving a little corn from his daily portion and now, with the rest of the army lacking any food but fresh-killed beef, he owned a pint of it, boiled into a hard porridge. This went with him, more carefully handled than his own person. The crude raft was swept for four hundred yards in a vicious current. When it reached the other shore, Douglass set down his can of corn. Smith fell upon it, kneeling to scoop out and wolf handfuls of the stuff.

Douglass, coming up behind him, looked at his back, cursed him briefly and killed him with a shot through the back of his skull.

The murder struck the note of the expedition. There was no more law, little discipline. William Walker's Republic was only ninety-odd starving men, in the midst of a desert waste, faced with a precarious crossing of a river, thinking: When the crossing is accomplished—then what? They could all see it, the stupidest of them could see it. More damned days of dragging themselves along in the sun, more griping pains from the unchanging diet of beef, more quarrels among themselves. More Indians, and fiercer ones than the miserable Cocopas who hovered at the rear. Death in the desert as the only certainty for the remainder of the First Independence Battalion. It might come from starvation, or thirst, or bullets, or the knives of the Indians . . . but if they went on, as much as another league, it would come.

Fifty deserted there. They went off without a word to the Filibuster and appeared at the gates of Fort Yuma, where they were fed by the United States Army and allowed to go back to whatever lives they felt able to reclaim.

The others remained at the Colorado for three days. They tried to swim the cattle and the currents caught the bawling beasts and swirled them downstream. The Cocopas, watching wisely the dwindling of the force and the condition of the men who stayed, became bolder and stole more of the cattle; a battle was fought then and seven Indians died.

It was over. Fort Yuma and the hospitality of the United States Cavalry lay seventy miles to the north: three days' journey and the logical course. But the President of Sonora retraced his steps, instead of turning to the safety of his own country.

He had thirty-four men. What men they must have been! They had watched a grandiloquent idea degenerate into a farce. They had seen Gilman's leg cut off with a hacksaw and the stump cauterized with a hot iron. They had executed two of their fellows; they had met with nothing in the country to which they had come but the harshness of the desert and the bleakness of rocky mountains; they had crossed, with more luck than skill, a fierce river. Nearly three hundred at Ensenada, they now were reduced to a tenth of that number. Under the orders of an egotist who had not unbent an inch and who strutted in his rags as though he were a field marshall in braid, they must have marched with absolutely no hope— but they marched. Back along the way they had come, faster this time because there were only a dozen cattle to hinder them. Through silent San Tomas, where the natives watched them with the impassiveness of all oppressed peoples. At last into San Vicente.

There they had left a garrison of twenty men, but there was nothing in the town when they returned; even its dwellers, a scant hundred of them, had fled. Thirteen of the garrison had gone off when Walker was barely out of sight, to what safety for themselves they could find. The other seven had remained. On the thirtieth of March, Melendrez, so long absent, had appeared with his brigands. The seven faithful had scattered through the town, fighting from behind adobe walls. When the ammunition was gone, they had retired into the willows at the river bottom, only to be hunted out, tied and dragged back into the town. Melendrez had slaughtered them all.

The thirty-four survivors looked to Walker. He was at the absolute end; he had no further object now but to lengthen his life by as many days as he could. The arrival at San Vicente on April seventeenth was followed immediately by an assault of taunts from Melendrez's men, who had been lurking near by. Mounted on sleek horses, well-fed and clothed, the Mexicans rode about on the outskirts of the town, dragging the red-starred flag in the dust behind them and shrilling obscenities at the filibusters.

A note came into the town under a flag of truce: it offered safe conduct to the border if Walker's men laid down their arms. Walker looked at it, called it a "Mexican promise," and drove the messenger from his quarters. He led the unopposed retreat from the town in the early morning, making for San Diego, on as direct a course as he could reckon. The men carried nothing but their arms and chunks of the mouldy beef, at which they gnawed hopelessly. The Republic of Sonora, "which is hereby divided into two States . . . which comprises all the territory . . . which is hereby declared Free, Sovereign and Independent . . ." was no more than a mistake, written in blood and torment, not to be explained by William Walker even to himself.

X

SAN FRANCISCO received him with honor. Why, is a question difficult to answer; San Francisco was not, in the Fifties, friendly to its failures. Walker faced the same penalty Watkins and Emory had paid in the courts: the former had been convicted of violating the neutrality laws, and the latter had pleaded guilty; each had been fined one thousand five hundred dollars.

For nearly a month after his return, Walker's case was in process of formation. In that month he had time to sum up, for himself, what he had gained by the expedition. He had not lost prestige among Californians, who possibly felt that his unsurpassed courage was enough to qualify him as a hero. He had learned, in the hardest way, a little about tactics. He had handled an irresponsible and at times explosive body of men with discipline if not competence. And for seven months he had lived too close to death without bowing to it to feel that he had altogether failed. Sometime, somehow, he would take more men to Mexico and, with the lessons he had learned to guide him, revive his government. He did not feel that the titles he had given Mexico's two States were mere words on paper; he considered them as living, albeit sleeping, truth and he believed himself fitted to give them standing in the eyes of the world.

In June he went on trial for the first time, accused of the crime of filibustering.

He defended himself, assisted by Edmund Randolph, who had traveled from New Orleans to California in 1849. The little man stood up boldly in the courtroom and spoke in his own behalf:

"In defense of the charges against me, gentlemen of the jury, I shall introduce evidence to show that at the time of leaving this port, my intention was to proceed to Guaymas, and thence by land to the frontiers, and I shall also prove that it was only after we had got to sea and beyond the territory of the United States that this intention was changed, so as to land at La Paz; and previously to this, it was not my intention to proceed and land there in a hostile manner."

The jurymen knew that what he said was a brazen lie. They could not have failed to see, some of them at least, such evidences as the bonds of the "Independence Loan" which were issued on May 1, 1853—five and one-half months before the expedition sailed. They were in denominations of five hundred dollars, pledged the "Republic of Sonora" to grant one square league of land to the holders and were signed: "William Walker, Colonel of the Independence Regiment."

But the jury was not in sympathy with any idiotic law which said that a free-born American, with the prowess of all Americans, could not go and civilize the "Greasers." They took their cue from the court's charge to the jury in the Watkins case: "From my heart I sympathize with the accused, but I am sworn to the execution of the law, and I must discharge my duty, whatever my sympathies may be. To the law and to the evidence, then, we must turn our exclusive attention. I may admire the spirited men who have gone forth upon these expeditions to upbuild, as they claim, the broken down altars and rekindle the extinguished fires of liberty in Mexico, or Lower California. It may be that they are not adventurers gone forth to build for themselves a cheap fortune in another land. But even were such my opinion of their purposes ... still ..." They murmured to one another that it was as plain as the nose on your face. The Judge couldn't say, "Acquit this man," because he was a judge—but they didn't have to convict him, did they? He hadn't done anything but what was right, had he? Well, then....

William Walker went forth from the courtroom a free and unencumbered man, a hero of the hour. Watkins had been convicted of helping him move upon Mexico; Emory had pleaded guilty to the same charge. But Walker himself, under whose orders they had acted, was acquitted. It is today a strange commentary on the justice of the period, but in San Francisco in 1854 it was no more than the will of the majority, speaking through twelve men.

Walker now interested himself in politics. In view of the accusations already being heard—that his entire purpose in leading the Sonora expedition was to gain fresh territory, ultimately to be added to the Union as slave states—the side he chose has deep significance. David Broderick's anti-slavery faction in the Democratic party was opposed to that headed by a Senator Gwin, who had come to California from Mississippi and whose followers were largely from the Southern States. Logically, William Walker, himself a Southerner, should have allied himself with Gwin's group. Instead he sanctioned the cause of Broderick, the abolitionist.

He engaged actively in the subsequent convention of the State Democratic party, held at Sacramento in July of 1854. The schism caused a confused session, at which both factions proceeded without heed to each other, electing their own officers and attempting to conduct business simultaneously in the same hall. No serious disorder occurred, however: it is true that a pistol was discharged with a resulting panic, but California regarded the business, on the whole, as an unamiable but hardly dangerous political gathering.

Particular attention must be paid to the slavery beliefs of William Walker, for when he had gone further in his chosen profession of filibuster the doomed institution figured often in his plans. For the time it is enough to know that he was by no means an ardent slavery man in California, any more than he had been in New Orleans. As a journalist in Louisiana, he had been the object of attacks by fellow editors because his policies were too conservative and too nearly the policies of the North. In California, there was no change; he remained on the fence. His expedition into Sonora, darkly construed as an involved and devilish plot, was what it was and no more: an amateurish and outlawed adventure directed by a superb egotist and conducted for the large part by Gold Rush undesirables soon to be eliminated by the Vigilantes.

With politics behind him, the restlessness of his past returned. He went back to the editorial desk, first in Sacramento and later in San Francisco. The *Commercial Advertiser* in the latter city employed him and there he met Byron Cole.

Whereas Edmund Randolph was his great and only friend, Byron Cole was the almost-stranger who took him by the hand and led him to what fate had bred and trained him to be. Cole had come from New England to found his newspaper. He had not crossed the plains to reach the gold country, as so many others had, but instead had come via Nicaragua, on the Vanderbilt Steamship line. When Walker joined the staff of his paper, it was beginning to belie its name and its end was a matter of weeks. The proprietor was the antithesis of the proverbial New Englander, a voluble and enthusiastic and free-handed young man who spent much time in the dirty little cubby-hole inhabited by Editor Walker. He talked constantly and he talked of only one thing: Nicaragua. He prattled on for hours about its natural resources, its minerals, the luxuriance of its vegetation, its ideal climate, its splendid physical situation, its perfection as the route for the canal that was to link the oceans. And always he brought the talk around to the one big point: filibustering. He described convincingly to a man who needed no convincing that in Nicaragua there was the greatest of opportunities for reclaiming a lost land.

His editor listened, his thin quiet face unmoved but his startling gray eyes deeper in color with the excitement that lurked behind them. He knew no more of Nicaragua than any newspaper editor knows of a backward and half-forgotten country. But he made it his affair to learn. He probably read Squier's admirable description of the country,* and other books on its history. Slowly there fell away from him (if it ever existed) any dread arising from the memory of Sonora. When the *Commercial Advertiser* suspended publication and Cole went off to Nicaragua with what money he had been able to salvage from the wreck, the men had a distinct and significant understanding. Cole was to see what immediate opportunities Nicaragua offered: Walker, rich with his reputation for daring, was to develop them.

The one thing that remains as an unquestioned monument to William Walker is the boldness of his aims. It has been shown that he drifted toward the Sonora fiasco, but although its beginnings were the formless motions of a man bored with his state, once it began

* *Nicaragua.*

there was, as far as the commander-in-chief was concerned, no slight-est hesitancy. When he became ready to enter Nicaragua, which was to be his major arena, there was to a degree the same casualness of plan. But in his own mind he knew where he was going, and why, basing what conclusions he reached on the conversations with Cole. For the better part of a year he thought of little but the possibilities of an invasion of Nicaragua. He worked harder on the preliminaries of this expedition than he had ever worked before; yet, although California professed to believe in him, his progress was slow and dis-couraging.

Not until June, 1855, did he arrive in the country from which accounts of his exploits were to go forth and alarm far governments.

BOOK TWO

The Immortals

BOOK TWO:

The Immortals ...

From the day the Americans landed at Realejo ... it was impossible for the worn-out society of those countries to evade or escape the changes the new elements were to work in their domestic as well as their political organization. ...

I

THE REPUBLIC OF NICARAGUA, thirty-four years free when William Walker first entered it, hardly seemed at first glance a country likely to attract a talented freebooter. It was one of the world's doomed nations: distraught, troubled, tormented, poor. It was the butt of other countries' jests and the victim of strong men's frauds; behind it lay three centuries of wretchedness and treachery. It lacked a single railroad, in a time when the United States was mad with a passion for giving the iron horse new paths on which to run; it had no telegraph; its roads were mires throughout the rainy season and impassable to anything but horses and donkeys; because of a ceaseless internal strife, which had given it revolution for twenty-five uninterrupted years, it had no postal service as such, no standing army, no judiciary. In brief, Nicaragua in the year of 1855 had nothing but location ... but that location was a prize worthy of the mightiest king's utmost strivings.

To bridge Nicaragua was to marry the oceans. And to marry the oceans was to control the seas, and to control the seas was to be Britain herself, or as great as Britain. The obvious and logical canal route would cross Nicaragua, using her great lake and the San Juan River as links. For reasons which will become apparent as the saga

53

of William Walker progresses, it was this route which complicated his efforts, lent him his greatest successes and turned against him forces too powerful to be defeated.

Columbus sailed along the coast of Nicaragua in 1502, still seeking the route to the East. He failed to find it, but his voyage blazed the path which, in 1521, a Spaniard named Gil Gonzales de Avila found easy to follow.

Avila left Panama, crossed the Gulf of Nicaya, and visited the leading chief of the land, one Nicaya. He found a form of civilization better than Spain's, for all its primitive simplicity: Nicaya's Indians had tribal council, the religion of the Aztecs, and science. They engaged in little wars, but more in a spirit of competition than in anger. There were large cities in the jungle, maintaining contact with one another over well-defined routes.

Chief Nicaya, witlessly hospitable to the Spaniard, presented him with the freedom of the village and gold to the value of twenty-five thousand pieces-of-eight. He lent him guides for the journey farther north to the eagle's eyrie later known as the city of Masaya. There Avila was received less heartily; so sinister were his unwilling hosts that he turned and marched at once for Panama, where the tale of richness he told awakened, in the breasts of his superiors, a most highly developed cupidity.

The country of Nicaya, Avila reported, was rich in all things: food springing from the ground, gold in the mountains, fish in the two great lakes, some vines which gave fresh water and others perfectly designed for hammock-weaving, mud that dried into hard bricks in the sun. He had seen most of the Pacific slope, with a climate better than that of the Caribbean side and less helpful to the spread of miasmic diseases. He described the grandeur of the volcanic peaks which stand at measured distances along the horizon from the Gulf of Fonseca in the north to the present border of Costa Rica in the south. The people, he said, were happy, well-fed, comfortably housed.

Don Hernandez de Cordova was sent with soldiers to retrace Avila's route, to war upon and subdue whatever opposition he met, and to seize and settle the new country in the name of His Most Catholic Majesty. How well Don Hernandez succeeded in implanting Spanish methods in Nicaragua is attested by the fact that, three centuries later, a faction of Nicaraguans imported William Walker's foreigners to subdue their brothers. Spain, following the evilly blazing torch of Cortez, made rotten what she seized.

The country into which Cordova marched was thickly peopled; he depopulated it, butchering as many as he conveniently could and shipping as many more to Mexico and Panama and Peru to be slaves. He bought fear with a terrible price: thousands of youths slaughtered and fed to the dogs, thousands of maidens given up to the pleasure of the Spanish for the nominal price of a bit of salted meat. For centuries Nicaragua's people were in bondage.

And then, inspired by Bolivar,* Nicaragua cast off its chains; in 1821. It was a part of the short-lived empire of Iturbide;** for another time it was represented in the inefficient and sickly Federation of Central American States. In 1852 it stood forth in full sovereignty, but the thirty-one years since the revolt against Spain had not been enough to overcome the habits of three hundred. Slavery continued, known by another name. The breaking of the Spanish chains removed only the idea of servitude and the aristocracy founded under the King continued to exploit the mass of the people, the politicos ruling and feeding well; the peons drudging and starving.

Nicaragua was thus made the scene of constant revolution, because all the politicians could not rule at the same time. In the six years immediately preceding William Walker's arrival, no fewer than fifteen persons occupied the uneasy presidency. Some were deposed by vote, more by assassination, a few fled into exile.

But for Nicaragua's one asset, therefore, the nations of the world would have left her to work out her own destiny, in whatever misery she chose to create for herself. This little tropical country, however

---

* Simon Bolivar, known as the "Liberator" for his ceaseless campaigns against the Spanish in the fifteen years following 1810, was the leading figure in the revolutions which resulted in the creation of South America much as it is constituted today. Venezuela, Peru, Bolivia and Columbia were Bolivar's theatres of operation and have come to regard him as a founder comparable to George Washington in the United States.

** Augustin de Iturbide, after a march on Mexico City in 1820, overthrew the Spanish crown and was proclaimed emperor on May 18, 1822. On May eleventh of the following year his government collapsed, because of financial and military practices unacceptable to the people, and he was exiled to Italy. Precisely one year later he sailed from England to regain his throne; at Soto la Marina in Mexico his disguise was penetrated and he was executed, on July 19, 1824, by officials of the Republic established by Antonio Lopez de Santa Ana.

rich in her soil and mountains, would have been only a small prize for England or the United States. But she had something that then appeared to be unique: a natural chain of river, lake and trail, which could reduce the passage between the oceans to ease and fundamentals.

Unhappy, insignificant, torn by internal discord, prey of villains from all the world—Nicaragua yet controlled, in the Fifties, the commerce of two seas and the cohesion, or lack of it, of the United States itself.

There are two great lakes in Nicaragua—the larger, named for the country, and the smaller, called Managua. Lake Nicaragua is a body of water more than one hundred miles long, and, at its center, about forty miles wide. It stores the waters of the mountains, releasing them to the Caribbean through one principal artery, the San Juan River. Between the two coasts, it was possible in the Fifties to move passengers and freight entirely by boat, except for a narrow strip of thirteen miles on the Pacific side.

Scarcely fifty years after Columbus visited the eastern coast, a Portuguese, Antonia Galvao, proposed that the river and lake be used as an interoceanic waterway; and from that day on, all classes of men interested themselves in the project. King Philip of Spain saw the danger of connecting two oceans through the very center of his colonies, with a nautical Great Britain as his arch-enemy, and he prohibited any efforts to build a canal. DeWitt Clinton and several associates obtained a canal contract in 1826, but failed to raise the necessary money and abandoned the scheme. Louis Napoleon wrote a pamphlet declaring the route to be the best possible between the Atlantic and the Pacific. The United States intermittently interested itself in Nicaragua and conducted several surveys of the route.

The one man finally to put the waterway to use was an uncouth, profane, boisterous genius named Cornelius Vanderbilt and called the Commodore. In 1849 he contracted with the government of Nicaragua to construct a passage, using the San Juan River, Lake Nicaragua and a thirteen-mile canal for the purpose. It is doubtful that the Commodore had any intention of building his canal; he did no more than to order surveys, which found the engineering difficulties too great. But with his contract, he received the right to transport passengers across the Isthmus. For this privilege he was to pay to Nicaragua ten thousand dollars annually and ten per cent of his profits. (His accountants saw to it that there were no profits.)

He traveled to Nicaragua himself, violently impatient with his agents, who maintained that the passage upriver in steamboats was impossible because of rapids scattered along its length. He personally navigated the first of his boats to use the system. From the moment of its establishment, his line, known as the Accessory Transit Company, did a rich business. Passengers from the east boarded steamers at New York or New Orleans, and were carried to Greytown,* port on the southern limit of Nicaragua's Atlantic coast. Thence they were transshipped to river vessels, which carried them up the San Juan to San Carlos, on the shores of Lake Nicaragua, one hundred miles away. Lake boats in turn bore them to Virgin Bay, on the Western shore, and the last stage of the Transit—over the thirteen-mile strip—was accomplished on Nicaragua's only macadamized road, in a fleet of sky-blue and white carriages decorated with the Nicaraguan seal. Pacific liners waited at the harbor of San Juan del Sur for the final leg of the voyage to San Francisco.

William Walker believed himself to be an instrument of destiny, and what awaited him in the tropics indicates that he might have been. Perhaps the entire course of the historical period would have been altered, had his expedition into Sonora succeeded. But he failed in Sonora and went on to Nicaragua. He became a small but alarming figure, dancing about in the middle of a country coveted by the United States (because it offered speedy contact with the distant West Coast), by Great Britain (for trade and the dual strength to be gained by controlling two oceans and weakening the United States), and by Spain (as a possibly reclaimable colony).

Destiny? Walker tries to be a doctor, tries to be a lawyer, tries to be a journalist; temperament makes him abandon all three. Walker tries to love and marry; yellow fever kills his bride. Walker tries to be president of Sonora; he is driven out. Walker returns to San Francisco with military knowledge learned the hardest way; and lo! Nicaragua, the troubled and coveted, appeals for his aid.

* Originally San Juan del Norte and renamed Greytown by the British. So designated throughout to avoid confusion with its west-coast sister, San Juan del Sur.

II

BYRON COLE, arriving in Nicaragua to negotiate a grant for the man
he called in all conferences "the renowned Walker," could not have
chosen a better time to drive his bargain. A president had died in
1853 and, in the following election, Don Fruto Chamorro was declared the winner. Don Francisco Castellon, of the opposition, challenged the election and in accordance with custom was exiled by
Chamorro as a foe to good government.

The division of Central America into five Republics was, at the
time, merely a geographical fact. Politically the Isthmus was divided
only in two: the Legitimist and the Democratic factions. The Legitimists represented the *calzados* (those who wore shoes), whereas the
Democrats claimed to be a people's party. Because this division of
political opinion was identical in all Republics, it followed that when
a Democrat—Castellon, for example—was exiled, he traveled to a
country then governed by Democrats and from there fomented a
revolution. The armies of all the Republics, in Walker's period, were
often on the march across international frontiers without a declaration of war from their governments. Castellon's case demonstrates
perfectly the free interchange of hostiles across frontiers. He fled to
friendly Honduras, where General Trinidad Cabañas was president,
and presently Cabañas ordered part of his Democratic army to assist
in Castellon's revolution.

Castellon, on his return to Nicaragua, made his headquarters at
Leon,* and laid siege to Granada. For six months his army under
Maximo Jerez fought a useless battle against an enemy strongly barricaded behind adobe walls. Casualties at last forced Castellon's men
to abandon the siege and retire to Leon. At that point, shortly before
Cole's arrival, the complex wheels-within-wheels turned again, and
the support of Honduras had to be withdrawn. North of Honduras
lay Guatemala, governed for the moment by the Legitimists, who,
when Cabañas sent part of his army to Nicaragua, sent part of theirs

---

* Between Leon, northernmost large city, and Granada, there had always existed a bitter
rivalry. Leon was the seat of the liberals, Granada of the aristocrats. In many of the revolutions, each party sought to seize the other's capital, for the tremendous weakening of
morale such a victory would create in the ranks of the enemy. Managua, present-day capital
of Nicaragua, is midway between Leon and Granada and was chosen as a compromise, to
minimize the ill feeling between Leonese and Granadinos.

into Honduras. It was a chain of attack in which Honduras fought Nicaraguan Legitimists and Guatemala attacked Honduran Democrats. And the ultimate threat—that incident which made Cole's proposition so welcome to Castellon—was the invasion of northern Nicaragua by the Legitimists of Honduras, until then inactive. Encouraged by Guatemala's hostile move, General Santos Guardiola (his name was powerful in proportion to his really talented bloodthirst—all Central America spoke fearfully of him as the Butcher) began to move down the Isthmus. However involved in its details, this philosophy of government and warfare was one satisfactory to the participants in the revolutions, for no matter where the war occurred, each side could be sure of a certain support from political adherents in neighboring countries.

Castellon knew but one piece of good fortune in this conflict. Shortly before he enlisted aid from the United States, Chamorro, the strong man of the Nicaraguan Legitimists, died, and his successor, José Maria Estrada, appeared too weak to hold the party together; there was hope, therefore, that if Castellon could find some help he could win.

The agreement reached between Castellon and Cole called for the employment of three hundred armed Americans to fight for the Democratic cause. They were to be paid salaries in gold and were to receive twenty-one thousand acres of land at the end of the campaign. Cole hurried to Sacramento, where Walker was serving as editor of the *Democratic State Journal,* and offered him the document, but Walker rejected it on the first reading. It was as clear a violation of the Neutrality Act of 1818 as it would be possible to draft, and Walker instructed Cole to tear it up, return to Nicaragua and obtain a "contract of colonization." He thought "something might be done" with such a document.

In a few weeks, Walker received the new grant, signed by Francisco Castellon, empowering him to enlist three hundred colonists to become citizens of Nicaragua, to till its fields and to be guaranteed "forever the privilege of bearing arms." Before signing the contract, he took it to the office of S. W. Inge, United States Attorney for the Northern District of California, who had been the chief prosecutor in the trials arising from the Sonora expedition. Inge, a man with neither love nor respect for William Walker, examined the contract with every hope of finding it illegal. But he handed it back at last and said regretfully that no law would be violated if Colonel Walker acted under it.

Walker went thence to find Major General Wool, nemesis of the recruiting for Sonora. Wool's headquarters were at Benecia, but from Inge, Walker learned that he had been in San Francisco that morning. He looked for the officer to whom he later referred, with contemptuous tolerance, as "the old gentleman" and found him waiting for a boat to return him to his headquarters. The General listened to the terms of the Castellon grant. When Walker had finished talking, he held out his hand. "I agree with Inge entirely, sir. Not only will I not place any hindrance in your way—but I wish you the greatest success."

The Filibuster needed no more; he was safe this time. There would be no army now to stop the shipments of arms and the reinforcements he would need. He cast off whatever uneasiness he had had and entered earnestly into his preparations. For the first time in months—it was now February, and he had been droning along at an editorial desk since the preceding June—life regained zest for the man who would be conqueror.

Wherever he went, he found citizens interested in his project. Lawyers and journalists gave him heartily of their congratulations, but not of money in the quantities he needed. He picked up a dollar here and a dollar there, but before he had been in San Francisco a week he knew that his expedition would have to be the most economical he could contrive.

He met one day a schoolmate from Nashville, Henry Crabbe, who revealed that he had recently made the Transit crossing and had entered into an agreement with three soldiers-of-fortune—Thomas Fisher, C. C. Hornsby and Julius de Brissot—to attempt to fight for Nicaragua. They had remained on the Isthmus to seek promises from the government. Walker parted from Crabbe without having considered a combination of forces, but such a union was suggested a week later, when Fisher arrived in San Francisco with a contract and a report.

Waiting in Nicaragua to see General Jerez, Democratic com-

CORNELIUS VANDERBILT

mander, the three had become acquainted with John H. Wheeler, then United States Minister to Nicaragua, and perhaps one of the most undiplomatic diplomats ever to embarrass the State Department. Wheeler, uncertain as to which faction would win and which, therefore, he should recognize, visited the camp of Jerez as well as the palace of the Legitimist president, Estrada. The three adventurers attached themselves to his suite, and under the protection of the United States flag saw both camps. Fisher remained in the Jalteva, a suburb of Granada, the utmost point Jerez had reached in his siege of the capital, and obtained from that officer a straight military contract calling for the services of five hundred men, to be given substantially the same emoluments as those specified in the first contract negotiated by Cole. The other two, meanwhile, entered into what Walker called a "quixotic agreement" to seize Castillo Viejo [the old castle], a storied fortress on the San Juan River, and so gain for the Democrats control of the avenue connecting the oceans. This venture never proceeded beyond San Juan del Sur, the Pacific seaport, whence De Brissot and Hornsby sailed for California.

Crabbe's interest was lagging; he now saw possibilities in California politics. He decided to give up the contract Fisher had signed, but Walker was too wary to accept it: first, because it appeared illegal, and second, because it had been signed by General Jerez, an authority of whose competence he knew nothing. Hornsby and De Brissot, however, decided to abandon the agreement they had helped negotiate and join Walker. They became two of his most faithful assistants.

Cole obtained the second agreement in December, 1854, but it was not until June of the following year that Walker was able to follow him with the first of the three hundred men promised in the grant. Laboring twenty hours a day, seeking funds and support, Walker's aloofness gave way to enthusiasm. His taciturnity fell away from him when he spoke of Nicaragua and he painted brilliantly a picture of opportunity and assured achievement. Between February and June his trim little figure could be seen at all hours on the streets of San Francisco, and it is safe to say he visited, at one or another time, the office of every financial leader the city then knew.

When he had finished his work, he was forced again to sail as he had to Sonora, surreptitiously and with too few men. There were fifty-eight aboard his ship when at long last it sailed through the Golden Gate. They soon earned the name by which they were ever afterward known: William Walker's Immortals.

NO MORE NO LESS, IMMORTALS, AS SUCH PIRATE, AS DRAKE AND BARBAROUS.

III

A THIRTY-YEAR-OLD brig, leaky, almost unseaworthy, and symbolically named the *Vesta*, was chartered for the price Walker could afford to pay. A variety of difficulties followed. The captain quarreled with the owner of the brig and refused to sail her. A creditor of the ship attached her, and when the sheriff's deputy came to serve the papers there was a ludicrous struggle on the deck, in the course of which the new captain fled, taking with him the ship's papers. Provisions for the voyage and for the period immediately following the arrival of the expedition in Nicaragua had been bought on credit; the ship was attached for their price, and a revenue cutter warped in against her stern to see that she did not evade the libel.

Walker, doing the work of three men, tried without funds to satisfy the implacable law. The sheriff seized the sails of the brig and stored them ashore. The few recruits who had signed up for quick and profitable adventure in a romantic country took to loafing on the wharf, discontented and dangerous. But soon the producer of this inept drama found a captain who, although he had never sailed the Central American coast, would run the brig out of the harbor, cutters and the sheriff be damned. Walker went to the owner of the ship and persuaded him to use his influence to have the libel for the provisions lifted. His technique was simple: he emphasized the obvious truth—that it would not be safe for any person to cause so dynamic a company as the Immortals to remain idle and thwarted on a San Francisco pier.

The libel was lifted, and was replaced with a new perplexity. The sheriff demanded costs of three hundred dollars for his part in delaying the *Vesta*. His charge was not only exorbitant but quite beyond the limits of the expedition's resources; the entire collections, of which the largest was a donation of one thousand dollars, had gone for food and ammunition and Walker was almost without a penny. He was not without cunning, however. He promised the sheriff his three hundred dollars, and that trusting official, unaware that the Federal libel was no longer in effect, agreed to return the *Vesta's* sails. The sheriff reasoned that there was no chance of the brig leaving port while a revenue cutter stood near by to guard her. And by speeding the tempo of his maneuvers, Walker maintained this deceit and opened the way for departure.

On the night of May 3, 1855, Deputy Sheriff Purdy, a former member of the State Legislature, stood guard aboard the *Vesta,* charged with the responsibility of seeing that the ship did not move. Walker limped aboard; seven weeks before he had taken time out from his labors to fight a duel with a W. H. Carter, of Sacramento, over some disagreement. The story told of the affair is that at the first fire Carter's shot struck Walker in the foot. Walker attempted to conceal his wound by scraping sand against the side of his boot, but the seconds saw the stain of blood and declared honor satisfied—the California code did not allow a second shot. This incident is mentioned casually, for so Walker regarded it; in his career he had dueled with an editor named Kennedy in New Orleans and with Graham Hicks in San Francisco. In his memoirs mention appears only of the third duel, with Carter: "While engaged in these preliminary preparations, Walker received an injury in the foot, which kept him in his chamber until the middle of April; and, in fact, the sore was not wholly healed when he sailed from San Francisco."

Deputy Purdy was invited into the cabin for a glass of wine and a cigar. Walker excused himself and went aboard the Revenue Cutter *Marcy,* where he obtained the aid of its crew in bending on the *Vesta's* sails. Walker shared his time between the deck, where he tried to hurry the government's sailors in their silent work, and the cabin, where sat Deputy Purdy. Whether Purdy was too stupid to know the ship was being readied for sea, or whether he was forcibly detained is not made altogether clear in the records; but when he heard the cutter moving off, a steam tug coming alongside and the thump of lines being passed, he started for the door. It was then one o'clock in the morning. Walker barred the deputy's way, saying, in the quiet tone which was invariably more effective than a shout:

"The *Vesta* is going to sail, Mr. Purdy." Like an actor he paused, before turning to the table. "There are wine and cigars and"—flinging them on the table with a dramatic thump—"here are handcuffs. Pray, Mr. Purdy, take your choice."*

The Deputy shrugged; no choice was offered. He sat down again and drank the good champagne provided for him until the *Vesta* was near the open sea and the work of the tug *Resolute* was finished. Then he went on deck, escorted by Colonel William Walker of the Nicaraguan army. Leaving the *Vesta* for the returning tug, he was neither dismayed nor angered by his experience: he was a Californian and so inclined to respect a shrewd trick.

There were all kinds of men on the *Vesta*, as there had been aboard the *Caroline* when she sailed for Guaymas. But this expedition profited by a greater percentage of experienced soldiers. Colonel Hornsby had fought through the Mexican War. Achilles Kewen, a Mississippian, had been with Narciso Lopez in an expedition to Cuba. Timothy Crocker, the youth who had led the charge of the nine volunteers at the Mexican border, was still not done with his fighting. Frank Anderson, another Mexican War veteran, had joined Walker, as had a surgeon, Doctor Alex Jones, newly returned from the Cocos Islands, where he had gone with a party to seek—vainly—the buried treasure indicated in a map given him by a dying and grateful patient. The private soldiers, who for lack of a crew had to work the *Vesta* (and did so bad a job that she required five weeks for the voyage from San Francisco to Realejo) were luckless miners, professional killers, grocerymen tired of groceries and cobblers weary of the last. They cheered lustily as the *Resolute* dropped astern; and on the first night they slept little, crowding the decks and stirring up a great commotion about the time they would have.

IV

THE Island of Cardon lies squarely across the mouth of the harbor of Realejo, blocking the waters of the bay except for channels north and south. It is a simple port to make: following winds and the tides permit a vessel to enter at almost any hour. The *Vesta*, arriving

---

* Harper's Weekly.

shortly before noon on June 1, 1855, sailed easily into the north channel and anchored full in the center of the bay.

It had been a hard voyage. The Immortals lining the rails remembered unhappily the storm in the Gulf of Tehuantepec, when there had been every reason to suppose that the rotten timbers would collapse and leave the brig bottomless and themselves bobbing corpses. They revived a little at sight of the country they had come to seize, and exchanged the first boasts they had had the heart to utter for five long weeks.

They could, in truth, see very little of the country. The shore was lined, except for a semi-circle of beach, with the rank growths of the jungle. On the north side of the harbor a little stream wound and disappeared into a tunnel of trees. A wharf and warehouses were to be seen, but no life, except that of the boatmen, who swarmed out in fleets of *bongos,* the native dugout canoe, to plead for the custom of the newcomers.

Walker, below in his cabin, busy with his plans and the study he had been making of Nicaragua since Byron Cole returned with the first contract, sent up instructions for the men to be mustered on the beach. They went over the side in surging impatience to be free of the tortured ship, and they demanded of the boatmen, in their harsh tongue, speed and information about the town and its saloons. In answer they received a flood of Spanish, with the broken explanation from the few who pretended to a knowledge of English that Realejo lay five miles up the creek.

On the shore, the officers assembled the Americans into the approximation of a line. The men were restless and impatient as they waited for Walker to come ashore, for there was not one among them who did not need a drink, as a tonic after the weeks at sea. They stirred in their ranks and talked in deep voices of what they expected to find in the new country. Walker always thought of his soldiers as noble regenerators—as an army with banners—but he led little better than a gang. The men knew no discipline. They had come here to fight and seduce and kill. They would plunder, given any chance. They spoke so insolently to the officers that Hornsby and Anderson, veterans of the United States Army, must have despaired at their lack of obedience and respect.

But when the ship's gig began to walk toward them on its long oars, carrying Walker and Ramirez, the Nicaraguan colonel who had been sent by Castellon to welcome the Immortals, the ranks subsided into unwilling silence. The little man, sitting stiffly in the stern-sheets of the boat and then limping mincingly across the beach, was the only person within reach who could control them. He passed along the line, with the air of an inspecting general, and their bold eyes fell before the distant gray of his. When he had finished his inspection he stepped back and issued curt orders:

The band was to go to Realejo, where quarters had been assigned to it. Until formally mustered into the army of Nicaragua, the men were given liberty. And for anyone who interfered with a lady, or in any manner outraged the church, a firing squad would be the penalty.

They went quietly to the *bongos* and re-embarked. The native boatmen pulled them away from the beach and as the first boat entered the stream, Walker in a fast single canoe vanished around the bend. When the boats moved into the waterway under the trees, the gloom and silence of the jungle fell upon and oppressed the passengers. The boatmen and the macaws chattered; but every other living thing lurked silently in the bush, watching the little procession. For a time the men of Walker's command were awed and hushed by the immensity of the growth through which they passed; then they began to talk again, asking an endless chain of questions. *Si, Senores,* said the boatmen, this is the way to Realejo. No, it has not always been so far from its harbor—once, long ago, it was on the shore. But the pirates came and plundered—regard, *Senores,* the smooth boulders in the river. These Morgan brought as ballast in his great ship, and threw overboard to make room for the booty he took back. He visited Realejo more than once—oh, indeed. So many times that the whole city had to move, to where it would be safe.

The delay on the beach and the slow paddling of the boatmen wore away the greater part of the afternoon; it was past four when the last *bongo* arrived at the wharf in Realejo. As the men·disembarked they lined up near the town's guardhouse. A Nicaraguan officer, slim and youthful, with a scarlet short-cloak flung beautifully over his shoulder, turned out his guard in honor of the newcomers.

The two bodies of men stood in striking contrast, on the street leading to the water. The native soldiers were distinguished only by the red ribbon they wore, with the inscription *Ejercito Democratico*. They moved to the uncertain beat of a drum, stepping awkwardly in the dust. They wore rough white cotton trousers, which ended a little below the knees, and shirts that hung saggingly from their shoulders. They were armed with the ancient, cast-off muskets of the armies of distant countries. Watching them, and commenting rudely upon their utter lack of military precision, were the Immortals, dressed and looking almost alike. They were tall, the soldiers of Walker—not a man of them failed to top his commander by a full three inches. They were either mustached or bearded; their faces were bronzed; their slouched carriage conveyed the impression of great latent power. They wore what they had worn in California, a utilitarian costume of heavy cotton breeches, miners' boots, blue, gray or red flannel shirts and felt hats. Fully half of the fifty-eight were twice or thrice armed, with revolvers or bowie knives or both, in addition to their long rifles. It could not be said that the Americans were altogether at ease in Realejo, but they seemed more so than the natives themselves. There was an apologetic air about the Nicaraguan soldiers: a tone and feeling in their movements like the characteristics of children trying to impress unsympathetic elders. The filibusters, on the other hand, were gruffly assertive. Within an hour of their arrival they had overrun the town, traveling in groups or in pairs. They found the *pulperias* with the instinctive directness of all undomesticated men; and until late in the night they crowded up to the crude, tin-covered bars, drinking and liking a liquor strange to them: *aguardiente,* the colorless, powerful and cheap rum of the sugar-cane.

The natives made them welcome; how wisely remained for subsequent events to show. Realejo was a shabby place, as were all cities of the country: its people were for the most part peasants, living in thatched huts crudely walled with a sort of wicker-work plastered with mud. Women of all ages stood in the doorways of these poor houses, wearing their holiday best and smiling at the tall bearded ones from the north; inside the curious Americans caught glimpses of bare rooms and of hammocks swung in the corridors to catch the breeze. In the *pulperias* the owners sold drink to the men whose tongue they could not comprehend, until the money was gone; and then they gave freely of whatever the house held. Extending itself beyond the limits of an instinctive hospitality, the town of Realejo lived, for this one night at least, in an atmosphere of relief: as though its oppression had already been lifted and it stood upon the threshold of peace and happiness; as though Guardiola the Butcher already had been sent flying back to his Honduras.

Walker was not seen on the streets that night. He went to the house assigned to his use and remained there with his officers, for he had plans to make. This was no mad assault upon a desert, as Sonora had been. This was what he had been building toward; this was a country soon to be his.

V

WILLIAM WALKER lived in a manner which leaves him open to infinite criticism. But two things he did better, perhaps, than any contemporary: he worked for his interests with an intense concentration, oblivious to every irrelevant thing, and once his feet were upon a path he followed it with a stoicism magnificent despite the falseness of his objects.

Before going to Nicaragua he had learned everything he could of its condition. From travelers on the Transit route he had heard of a beautiful country gone to waste—fields that could grow anything lying dead in the sun, churches and houses deep-pocked with the scars of old wars, towns half-peopled, with seven women to every adult man. He read books on Nicaragua, books on military tactics. He provided himself with maps and before he ever set foot in the country at the head of his foolhardy Immortals he knew its terrain as well as a native. When at last he sailed from San Francisco, he had learned much of what a military commander should know—and few of the dictator's lessons. The curriculum he prepared and followed lacked the essential course: he failed to study the people he expected to govern.

There were native warmth and hospitality, but there was also an instinct for treachery. Every man with whom Walker came in contact, aside from those he took with him from the United States, was a creature of taut nerves, mercurial and knowing no halfway emotion: he loved and he hated, but both completely. The friend who kissed another on Sunday might by Monday night be plunging a knife into his back. In the entire national psychology there was but one force: impulse. This vital truth Walker should have known; but he did not learn it until blood had run.

Nevertheless, he blocked out a rough course to follow, and throughout his time in Central America he was never far from it. It was well enough to profess, as he did at first, that he was merely a hired sword, but the most casual examination of his deeds shows that he was determined to dominate, and not to serve, Don Francisco Castellon. He had seen that a strong man could hardly fail to govern Nicaragua. With enough disciplined men at his back he could replace disorder with law, revolution with an iron-handed administration.

He rode out of Realejo on the morning after his arrival accompanied by Timothy Crocker, Colonel Ramirez and a Captain Charles Doubleday. There was a conflict of emotions in the small party of horsemen. Crocker was Walker's devoted aide; the loyalty he had given in the Sonora campaign was, if anything, intensified. Ramirez was sullen and aloof, a condition Walker was to remember. Doubleday, an Englishman who had been to California and while returning to the East over the Transit route had become sufficiently interested in Nicaragua to remain and command a company of riflemen, had little to say. He seemed to reserve his opinion until it could be given upon an action of Walker's, rather than upon the man himself.

Once on the road, they saw much to remind them of the troubled state of the country. A squad of native soldiers rested in the shade of a ceiba tree, and even Walker, new to the country, could see that they had the tenseness of prisoners seeking an escape and that their officers were little better than guards. At Chinandega the bells of churches deep-scarred with bullets were set to ringing, in honor of the *Yanqui*, and the townsfolk (only the women and the young and the old men remained) stood on the narrow sidewalks to see them ride through.

They arrived in Leon a little after noon. The Democratic capital was a city of some twenty thousand population, situated on the great plain between the two lakes and the Pacific Ocean. Cactus fences surrounded a few of the huts on the outskirts; but within the city proper the horsemen rode between rows of tile-roofed adobe houses. Once Leon had been on the shores of the lake, but legend had it that a Don, angered because his manners toward slaves had been criticized, had knifed the Bishop on the very altar of the great Cathedral. A Papal curse was supposed to have been put upon Leon and for years calamity visited it; the young girls were dragged away into enslavement by conquerors, plagues came in an endless succession, famine and earthquake destroyed life and the people's heart, until at last the entire population, led by its priests, marched from the city, abandoning it to the jungle between the rising of the sun and dusk, and built the capital Walker reached. The jungle overran the old city, reclaiming with startling growth what had been the streets, but leaving untouched, the legend said, the altar of the Cathedral, where the stain of blood remained as bright and accusing as it had been when the Don shed it.

At the grand plaza, one entire side of which was occupied by the gigantic Cathedral of Saint Peter, the horsemen halted and entered the government palace, where they were admitted at once to the office of the Provisional Director, or claimant to the Presidency.

Walker was unimpressed with Don Francisco Castellon, whom he found "not the man to control a revolutionary movement, or to conduct it to a successful issue." There was a definite air of indecision about Castellon: he spoke, walked, gestured hesitantly. When he had finished with the florid welcome his nationality demanded, he proposed to Walker that the Americans be enrolled as a separate unit, to be called the American Phalanx. Beyond this suggestion, however, he was unwilling to go without the presence of his new general-in-chief, Muñoz. Walker soon saw that Castellon was afraid not only of the results of the war, but of the men within his own party. Too, he guessed correctly that Muñoz was more interested in a truce than in victory. From Castellon he learned that the Democratic army had been placed under the command of Muñoz when Jerez's siege of Granada failed, and since had acted wholly on the defensive, executing no more formidable maneuver than a daily drill.

In the evening Muñoz was brought to see him. The two men were opposites in appearance, intellect and taste, and they clashed, politely but none the less violently. Muñoz, who had been handsome but was now inclined to be fat, wore a glittering uniform of red and blue, heavy with braid. Against Walker, who looked like a Methodist circuit rider in straits, he was flamboyant and noisy. The Filibuster found his conversation generally offensive: Muñoz talked glibly and without knowledge of the relative merits of Generals Scott and Taylor, whom Walker had studied assiduously, and later mentioned the trivial help he thought he might expect from the American Phalanx. He made it clear that he looked for nothing from Walker and was displeased that he had come to the country at all; and before the click of his boot-heels on the paving of the patio had died out, Walker had told Castellon bluntly that he would not serve under the general. A measure of his weakness was Castellon's acceptance, however half-hearted, of this ultimatum. He tentatively sanctioned Walker's first plan of action: to move on the city of Rivas, held by the Legitimists, and seize it and the Meridional Department, of which it was the seat.

Walker returned to Chinandega, where the Phalanx had marched in his absence. Under the Nicaraguan constitution, a mere declaration served to make a foreigner a citizen and Walker's men, all fifty-eight, so declared themselves and automatically were enlisted in the army. On June twentieth, the commissions for the officers arrived: Walker was colonel, Kewen lieutenant-colonel, Crocker major, and Hornsby captain. With the commissions came an order from the Provisional Director, instructing the American Phalanx to move at once against the enemy in the Meridional Department, and promising a support of two hundred native soldiers under the command of Colonel Ramirez.

Although they had been in the country less than a week, the wild spirits Walker had brought with him were already spoiling for a fight. They, who had been glad to quit the *Vesta* on the sixteenth, went back aboard her gratefully on the twenty-third, willing to withstand her tossing if at the end of the journey they could kill some "Greasers."

Muñoz's displeasure at the part to be played in the country's politics by Walker reflected itself in the actions of Ramirez, his aide. The two hundred natives promised proved to be one hundred. Supplies were slow in coming and totaled only a part of what Walker had announced would be necessary.

VI

THE company that left Realejo was bizarre, almost comical. Walker strutted about the deck, forever upon his dignity and insistent that every action, however minor, be conducted with full military etiquette. Ramirez sulked in a corner, his handsome face sullen. Mariano Mendez, a pure Indian who had been fighting in revolutions since boyhood, came aboard voluntarily, said Ramirez was a dog whose orders he would not take, declared Walker to be his own brother, and started a game of *monte* on a blanket. For the full four days of the voyage the game of *monte* went on and Mendez, who gloriously called himself a Colonel of Lancers, cheated the witless native privates grievously. Civil officers were aboard, instructed to form a departmental government if Walker should be successful: there were Don Maximo Espinosa, whom Walker described as of a quixotic cast of feature, to be Minister of Relations, and Don Francisco Baca, to be Prefect of the Department and collector of revenue.

The hundred-mile voyage required four days. It was a sickening journey. When time came to disembark at a point called El Gigante, added misfortune fell upon the party when the first crew off piled up the whale boat on a rock.

Bright moonlight made the landing easy and uneventful, except for the whaleboat mishap, but it was midnight before the fifty-five Americans and one hundred and ten natives were at last mustered on the beach. As they milled about, preparing for the march, heavy black clouds covered the moon. It was the midst of the rainy season, which extended from May until November, and the Nicaraguans murmured unhappily among themselves of the coming discomfort, the mired roads and the darkness of the night. Rain fell lightly as the first of the men moved away from the beach.

A native soldier who knew the country found the trail which he said led due east to Rivas, and the command, by twos, started over it.

The Americans marched in front, with Walker at the head of the column. Behind them a detail carried litters covered with hides, containing the rations and reserve ammunition. Ramirez's company brought up the rear.

For a short while the army moved at fair pace through the jungle. The men under Walker carried nothing but their arms and blankets and the natives had only muskets. They had gone a mile or so when the scattering drops turned into a torrent. The canopy of leaves overhead could not protect them against the great gush of the rain; in ten seconds every man in the line was drenched and frantic with his efforts to keep his rifle dry. The ground underfoot became slimy and the Americans cursed brilliantly as they moved forward two feet and slid back one. The precious guide lost the trail and old Espinosa complained that he had colic and could not go on. Walker ordered a halt and sent a runner back to ask Mendez to put out a party to look for the trail. The Americans stood in the rain, discouraged because there could be no improvement in their situation, while the Nicaraguans threshed about in the brush, calling to one another with idiot cheerfulness.

In a few minutes the downpour stopped and the trail was found. The army moved on. Clothing partly dried on the men and by dawn they were slogging along briskly, again happy at the prospect of a fight. They followed a route intended to avoid all settlements, and until nine o'clock did not pass a house; then they came upon a deserted adobe hut, at which they halted, building fires with the woodwork, and attempted to repair some of the damage done by the rain. In Realejo they had looked like giants against the small Nicaraguans, but here in the woods they were merely men who had been out in a downpour. The brims of their limp felt hats drooped over their eyes. Their beards were soggy and bedraggled, their boots squished when they walked. They looked at one another in the light of day and their guffaws silenced the parrots. The two commands breakfasted separately: the Americans on cold meat and hardtack, washed down with *aguardiente* prudently flasked and brought along, and the natives on cheese and *tortillas* and *tiste,* a drink compounded of chocolate, sugar-water and cornmeal, which they carried in fantastically carved gourds.

It was Walker's plan to hit Rivas sometime after nightfall. He passed the order to be ready to march again at one o'clock in the afternoon. The men, when they had finished eating, lay down where they were and slept heavily until that hour.

Throughout the afternoon they moved through the magnificent forest, the Americans talking constantly of the rich growths about them. The trail was lined with huge ceiba trees, and the flowering coeress, which adorns itself with golden blooms. As they advanced, all life except the macaws and the insects fled before them, and there was no sound but the shrilling of a million cicadas. Huge butterflies, with blue or red or multi-colored wings, fluttered about their heads. Marching columns of ants carried burdens of leaves to mysterious destinations. The men who had been in the tropics before pointed out the alligator ant, a black inch of poison, and warned against its bite.

It was a pleasant tramp. The air was soft and warm and perfumed thickly by the flowers.

And then, just before nightfall, it rained again. This time it was no torrential shower, but a steady downpour. The column again slowed down. The natives who were carrying the ammunition complained that they could not hold their footing and still move; the Phalanx began to grumble. They were approaching Tola, a village near the outskirts of Rivas and scouts came back with the news that there was a picket of Legitimists at that place, apparently unaware of the Democrats' approach.

They came into the road to Tola. The rain had half filled it with water, and the column which had been smoothly undulating suddenly began to writhe like a wounded snake. Walker held up his hand and the floundering stopped. He saw that it would be impossible to reach Rivas in any kind of order in the rain; half of his own command had not been able to keep the ammunition dry, and he was sure Ramirez's men had been even less careful than his own. He therefore elected to wait on the outskirts of the village while Hornsby and twenty of the Phalanx went ahead to capture the Legitimist picket.

Again the conquerors stood in the rain, bedraggled and discouraged. There was no shelter; they took the heavy drops on their heads and shoulders and saw the pools widen at their feet. Ahead there was silence, except for the patter on the trees, until Hornsby reached the village; then could be heard the faint crackle of rifle fire, and the duller thud of the enemy's muskets.

Walker ordered the main body forward. They marched into a silent, barred town, where even the dogs had lost voice. Hornsby came up as Walker entered the main street, to report that he had surprised the picket at a card game, had wounded four, but had not been able to capture the rest. Walker impassively received this bad news, thinking of the hours the Legitimists would have to prepare for him, with the pickets already on their way to Rivas with warning.

He ordered Doctor Alex Jones to bind up the wounds of the prisoners, silencing with a curt word the protest of Mariano Mendez, who thought they should be bayoneted or, if mercy were to be exercised, shot. The Legitimist troopers had fled without their horses, and these were commandeered for the use of the ammunition bearers. The men, except for sentries, scattered to the houses of the village, and beat upon doors until they were admitted. They slept until long after daybreak.

Again the march began, at eight o'clock in the morning. The day was clear and bright and the vigor of *falanginos* and natives alike had been restored by a full eight-hours' sleep. The company advanced briskly along the road toward Rivas. Mendez, by some Indian legerdemain, had obtained a fine white horse and, in the house where the enemy sentries had been attacked, had picked up a discarded lance. He had found a long pennon of cloth in red, the Democratic color, and with this streaming from his lance he rode gaily up and down the column, cheerily predicting awful butchery for the Legitimists.

Occasionally a woman from the market, with her empty baskets on her head, would step aside to allow the command to pass. From one of these Walker learned that the Legitimists had known of his coming almost from the day of the *Vesta's* departure from Realejo. A German had brought the news, the woman said; and Walker recalled that General Muñoz had given a German a passport to leave Leon for the south. He wondered about this, without alarm and too briefly; although he believed himself to be wise, he was an infant when he opposed such men as Muñoz. He was to discover in the next few hours, however, that no Nicaraguan was to be trusted.

The Legitimist army at Granada was commanded by General Ponciano Corral, who, Walker learned as he marched toward Rivas, had sent a large force to fortify the city and barricade all the streets.

The road his men followed led up the side of a hill. They climbed, sweating and panting because of the change in grade. As they came to the top there burst upon their eyes a scene of grandeur so striking that every villain of them stopped short to look upon it. The lake of Nicaragua, cobalt blue in the sunlight, lay before them. Rising out of its depths were the twin volcanoes, mile-high Omotepe, the tall cone that looked like a pyramid, and its shorter brother, Madera. Both were clothed nearly to their summits with the thick green of jungle growth. Below the road lay the lake shore, and to the south, pastoral in the distance, the towers of the churches of Rivas.

Mendez, riding past the head of the column at a full gallop, with his pennon streaming behind him, looked briefly at the wonder which had captured the Californians and said one word, "Omotepe." He was a policeman on Nob Hill, or a watchman at the Louvre: all he could see was a body of water with mountains in the middle.

They marched on. On the Rivas-Granada road, the guide had said, were two great estates—the Haciendas Santa Ursula and Maleaño— one or both of which Walker had decided to occupy as a base from which to operate against the city. A half mile from the town the column halted for the last time, to hear the plan of battle.

The objective, the grand plaza of Rivas, was a mile or more from the outlying suburban communities, and to reach it an attack company must advance along streets lined with solid rows of adobe houses. If he had had the counsel of an experienced soldier familiar with Central American tactics, Walker's task would have been comparatively easy; but neither he nor his men had ever come upon the sort of defenses they now faced. Corral's men had blocked the streets over which the attackers must pass with barricades of stone and debris six feet or so high; they also had established themselves in many of the houses nearest the plaza. The only successful method of attack for a force the size of Walker's was one with which he was not familiar: a molelike burrowing from house to house, with sappers and miners breaking a passageway for riflemen to follow. There was another possibility: his vanguard might have fired the barricades, which consisted in large part of furniture and other wood, and so diverted the attention of the defenders.

But, ignorant of such tactics, the commander outlined the only maneuver he could conceive: a headlong charge through the open streets. The Phalanx was given the job of reaching the plaza, with companies under Timothy Crocker and Achilles Kewen to keep clear what streets were taken. Ramirez's natives were to hold the rear and be on instant call as a reserve. Walker went in command of the main American body, with Hornsby and De Brissot as aides.

Crocker and Kewen went ahead, with thirty men. As they advanced, at a trot, they met scattered firing from the first few houses, poor huts roofed with thatch. The *falanginos* fired two short and vicious volleys and continued toward the town; and as the white-clad Legitimist outposts fled before their advance, they dropped individually to their knees and tried to hit the running men, aiming at their middles. Walker, who had taken one of the pack-horses as a mount, rode past the Hacienda Santa Ursula as a detachment was smashing in the door and gate panels with the butts of rifles and when he had proceeded another hundred feet he turned in the saddle, to see that the men were inside and the long barrels were pointing out of the low windows toward the town.

He rode on. The firing ahead was more regular and concentrated than it had been in the first minutes of the assault, and as he came up the center of the street he saw Crocker, dancing about in a fine Irish fury and calling his men the names of all the cowards who had ever breathed. Walker cried out, "How far are the men, Major?" and Crocker answered in his high, boyish voice, "They falter, Colonel; I can't get them on."

He was a terrible sight. His chin had been grazed and he wore a thick goatee of blood, which had dripped to stain his shirt-front. One arm dangled at his side, broken at the shoulder by another bullet. In his good hand he held a revolver, big and sinister. He shook his head as Walker turned to look for the native reserves and began to run back and forth across the street, demanding, pleading and cursing. The men of the Phalanx remained in their doorways, looking uncomfortable at some of the things Crocker said but not willing even under the lash of his tongue to go out into the curtain of lead the Legitimists were hanging.

Something of Walker's hold over them was gained in that moment. The Filibuster sat quietly on his horse, as though he were on a country lane, and ignored the buzzing slugs that threw up dust plumes at his feet or splattered into the adobe walls. He was not hit; once a bullet made the tail of his frock coat jerk upward, but his very incongruity in the scene appeared to charm him.

The ammunition litters could be seen, moving at the pace of a dying sloth to the scene of action. To the right a few natives, led by Mendez's red pennon, slipped cautiously from doorway to doorway, firing from time to time at no targets. Walker rode ahead a little, to a point opposite the doorways held by his farthest advance, and tried by persuasion to get the men to follow him, but they remained where they were, avoiding his cold gray eyes.

As he sat there, trying to ascertain the strength of the enemy and his own weakness, firing broke out in a new quarter. Enemy reinforcements from San Juan had arrived on the left and were attacking with good effect. Walker, who had been holding a pistol in his hand, now pointed it skyward and fired three times. As the men looked toward him, he waved toward a house near the hill of Santa Ursula, and they ran for it. The happy accident of the natives' bad marksmanship made it a successful maneuver; when Walker dismounted at the door of the house he found no dead, and only a few superficially wounded.

From this position the Phalanx kept the streets clear. Sharpshooters from the Plains crouched at the windows and picked off what soldiers wearing Legitimacy's white ribbons they could see. Presently, though, a scout slipped in the doorway, to report that the Legitimists were marching through back streets to get between Walker and the native force under Ramirez. Walker, turning to Crocker to ask him about it, saw a little black spot appear in the youth's forehead and the slow gush of blood begin as he pitched forward on his face. The commander went to him swiftly and felt for his pulse with the quick precision of his surgeon's training; when he stood up again his face reflected, ever so slightly, something akin to remorse that it should have been Crocker.

Kewen was next. The man who brought the information that the enemy, believing the day won, had started to withdraw part of its force toward the south, said that Kewen lay in the street, with a great hole in his throat and the ground for a yard around black with his blood.

Walker had taken the house intending to occupy it only until Ramirez could move up and support him. But as the afternoon wore on he knew that Ramirez had deserted, and that the Phalanx was alone in Rivas. Of the fifty-five originally engaged, fifteen were dead or too gravely wounded to be of help. The remaining forty were hemmed in by the force holding the barricades near the plaza, by the reinforcements from San Juan, and by the men who had moved to cut off the rear.

He could have retreated then, but he was too stubborn to retreat. He clung to an insane hope that something would happen to help him overcome a force ten times his strength. From one o'clock, when he ordered his men into the houses on Santa Ursula Hill, until nearly four he directed a dogged resistance, leading a foray into the street once to silence a four-pounder being trained on his stronghold; causing his men to fire carefully, so that each bullet would buy the most blood; moving from beneath a blazing roof when the Legitimists fired it with well-flung brands.

At four o'clock he ordered a retreat. Five of the wounded could not be moved and were left to die under the bayonets of the Legitimists. The active company, reduced to thirty-seven, gathered in one house and at a word from Walker poured from its doors and windows, screaming fiercely. The Legitimist flankers who had taken up posts in the thickets alongside the road, broke and fled before the vigor of the charge. The main enemy body guarding the road over which the Phalanx had marched in the morning declined to advance, fearing an attack, and in thirty minutes the remnant of the Walker force, guided by two Rivas boys, was retreating over cacao plantations, in a search for the road to the Transit. Walker had ordered the *Vesta* to cruise offshore and he hoped to go aboard her at San Juan, undefended since the Legitimists there had moved up early in the battle.

VII

THE American Phalanx was thoroughly beaten and looked it. De Brissot and Anderson walked with crutches improvised from tree branches, each with a bullet in his thigh. Doubleday, the Englishman, wore around his head a handkerchief, stained with dirt and blood. The men had fought steadily for more than four hours and their faces were blackened, their beards singed by powder flame. Of the thirty-seven, only twelve still had hats. And as they skulked through the back country, they showed none of the pride they had exhibited when they had streamed ashore from the *Vesta* two days before.

But although Walker had failed to take Rivas, he had given an excellent account of himself. With an effective force of fifty-five men, he had entered a town held by more than five hundred, maintained a position for four hours, and retired when he wished. His losses were six killed in action, five prisoners executed after the Phalanx evacuated Rivas, and seven wounded; the Legitimists by conservative reckoning lost eighty killed and nearly one hundred wounded. He had not gained his objective, but he had thrown a mighty fear into the hearts of all Nicaraguans; although his men had declined to advance up a street between solid blocks of houses and into a devastating fire, they had exhibited a fighting prowess not seen on the Isthmus since Cortez's veterans overran it. To the Nicaraguans who had opposed them, they were demons.

They marched until long after dark. At dusk, as they made their way along a narrow road, they met an old man, who shyly opened his coat to show a red rose, symbol of Democracy. A white rose, to have been produced had the party been Legitimist, fell to the ground, and was instantly covered with a bare foot.

They struck the road from Rivas to San Jorge about midway between the two places. As they moved toward the Transit Road, they heard bells at Buenos Aires: ringing for the Legitimist victory, Doubleday said cynically, but Walker thought it must be for vespers. They went through San Jorge long after nightfall without molestation; the town was locked and barred and the dogs alone had the courage to challenge the intruders.

HALFWAY HOUSE

From *Frank Leslie's Illustrated Newspaper.*

They quitted the highroad for a trail leading through the back country to the Transit, and until midnight went doggedly on. The mud was thick and the ground almost swampy; occasionally a group of two or three men would sink to their knees and have to be helped out. They camped in a deserted hut on a hillside two miles from the Transit Road, and slept as though they had been bludgeoned.

There was a little food left and in the morning they ate a sort of breakfast. Then they went on again. They entered the Transit Road about three miles from Virgin Bay, its eastern end, and traveled over it throughout the morning, hiding once in the bushes when a treasure train went through from the west, escorted by Vanderbilt's armed guards.

At a place called Halfway House, where the blue carriages of the Transit line halted, a California gambler named Dewey, known to Walker by repute, came up. He reported that a detachment of the Democrats, led by an Indian with a red pennon flying from his lance, had passed through San Juan del Sur the night before, presumably heading for Costa Rica, and that there were no Legitimists anywhere in the region. Walker, who neither liked nor trusted the man, suffered his company for the information he gave. When the adventurers walked into San Juan, Dewey rode in their center.

They occupied barracks on the ocean shore while Walker displayed the signals agreed upon for the summoning of the *Vesta*. The brig was nowhere to be seen, however, and he concluded that it already had called at San Juan, had failed to find the Americans installed there, and had returned to Realejo. He ordered a detail to patrol the waterfront and hold all small boats in harbor, but this action immediately proved to be unnecessary, for a Costa Rican schooner, the *San José*, came into port an hour after Walker's men entered the barracks. The wounded and then the well were sent aboard the *San José*. When the last had gone Walker followed. He was curt to the master of the ship, remarking that it was known the *San José* had transported Santos Guardiola from Honduras to Nicaragua, to wage war against the Democrats, and therefore was legally liable to seizure by the government. When he had finished talking, a tacit understanding had been reached that no libel would be pressed against the ship in return for the transportation of the Phalanx to Realejo.

There were two occurrences in San Juan del Sur, which have significance in a consideration of the character of Walker. The soldiers he had led into the town were nearly as wretched as the ones he had led across the border from Mexico; and yet, attracted by the Filibuster's personality, two men abandoned their paid-up passage to New York and enlisted in the weird army which came so brokenly into San Juan. They gave up security and a reasonable chance of human success wherever they might have gone, for danger and probably quick death. The circumstance lends credence to the really astonishing loyalty most of his men gave so freely to William Walker.

The second occurrence, by which Walker introduced Nicaragua to his ruthless strength, was in the matter of the gambler, Dewey.

This man was a vulture. He trailed along with the American Phalanx only because he thought, as did so many Americans then, that Walker was a freebooter, and that plunder was to be had. When he had tried to talk to the commander a little, and to propose diffidently certain projects that might redound to their mutual profit, he saw that he was dealing with an unusual filibuster, one who did not expect to steal whatever was loose in the country. So, at San Juan, Dewey dropped from sight and went to find an associate, known only as Sam, who ran a desultory boat service to the villages of the coast, and with whom he attempted the looting of the city.

When the beginning of this plot became visible, Walker was on the deck of the *San José,* waiting for the tide to turn. He was looking away from the shore, toward the ocean, half expecting to see the lights of the *Vesta,* when a shout from the rail attracted and turned him. The sky was red with flame, as red as the sky had been over Rivas when the Legitimists burned the houses containing the bodies of the American wounded they had executed. The barracks the Phalanx had recently occupied, which were in plain sight, were ablaze. Walker went quickly to the rail and stood there, his thin hands gripping it tightly. He ordered the men nearest him to take a boat and investigate the fire, which, fanned by a firm breeze from the ocean, appeared to be sweeping toward the center of the town.

The boat was back quickly, with a succinct report that Dewey and Sam had set the fire, secure in the belief that the townspeople would credit the Phalanx with the deed. Thus, while San Juan combatted a peril ostensibly created by Walker, Dewey hoped to plunder under cover of the excitement.

Walker realized at once that Dewey must be caught and punished. The conviction that he was a just man, which never left him, was then demonstrated; he sent a party ashore under Hornsby to find and arrest both Dewey and Sam. Sam was captured, but Dewey, with misguided strategy, fled to Sam's launch, which was hitched astern of the *San José*.

The sailor was brought before Walker. He was drunk and could barely stand; he was boastful and said that he and Dewey had fired the barracks, as "no more than the God-damned Legitimists deserve." In his book, Walker said that Sam was ordered to be tried, and apparently the trial consisted of the agreement between Walker and Hornsby that the man ought to be executed and left with a note on his body stating his offense, so that the blame for terrorism would not fall upon the Phalanx. He was sent ashore in charge of Hornsby, but in some manner escaped; and when Walker learned of this, he became even more determined that Dewey, crouching in the shallow hold of the launch, should die.

The master of the *San José* was on the deck when Hornsby returned and reported that Sam had fled into the brush. The Costa Rican, to Walker, appeared cynically certain that the sailor had been allowed to escape by a force glad enough to see the barracks burn.

Walker went to the stern of the *San José*. He called three crack riflemen and stationed them behind the barrels and crates being carried as a deck load. He gave orders that when Dewey showed himself he was to be killed, and went below.

The wind was unfavorable and the tide insufficient to permit the sailing of the *San José* before morning. Throughout the night the riflemen waited for Dewey to appear on the launch's deck. Of the three rifles, at least one was always trained on the small boat astern; the men dozed occasionally, but they were awakened by Walker, who could not sleep and spent the hours moving between the deck and his cabin. At sunrise they were still there: the three crouching riflemen on the *San José*, the gambler huddled in the launch's hold and Walker in the background, personification of sleepless justice.

A breeze sprang up. The schooner began to move out of the
harbor. Walker ordered the captain to cruise four or five miles offshore and to maintain a watch for the *Vesta*. Sam's launch bobbed
along behind the larger vessel, still silent, as it had been since Dewey
had fled to its refuge.

As the boat moved out of the harbor, a woman came onto the deck
of the launch. The marksmen nearly killed her at once, suspecting
for a moment that Dewey had donned skirts for his escape; but a
conversation in Spanish explained her presence. One of the riflemen,
who spoke the language well, translated quickly for Walker. She
was Dewey's woman, and wished to handle the rudder.

They waited. For hours they watched the launch, until their eyes
ached from the effort. Occasionally they could hear Dewey cough
and once the tension of waiting cracked in him for an instant and he
screamed obscene threats against Walker and all his men. Hornsby
suggested, late in the morning, that they riddle the launch with
volleys, and Walker might have done this, had it not been for the
danger to the harmless woman.

Dewey bore the suspense until nearly noon, and very well, considering that he had been drunk the night before and must have had
ragged nerves during the morning. Then, holding two revolvers,
he emerged from the hold. He seized the waiting woman as a shield,
and the rifleman who spoke Spanish called to her, "Get away from
him! You'll get killed——," but his words were lost in the reports
of the rifles to either side.

Dewey stood very straight for a minute and one of the guns he
held discharged itself into the deck at his feet. He clutched at his
stomach and his faced lived in the memories of his executioners
until they died, so torn was it with his pain. He coughed and the
blood ran from his mouth; he fell forward and lay still. The woman
lay on the narrow deck; one of the two bullets that had killed Dewey
had gone through his body and wounded her in the thigh.

They brought her aboard and Doctor Jones bound her wound.
Dewey's body, in a canvas sack, was weighted with a few stones
left from the *San José's* last voyage under ballast and allowed to
splash into the Pacific. The launch was scuttled. And Walker went
to his cabin pleased; the Nicaraguans would conceive from this a

respectful idea of American justice, and the evil-doers of the land would dread what they might expect, through all the future.

The incident of Dewey was in itself of little moment, even to Walker. The man was a blight on society; he had fled from California, where he had cheated and stolen and killed, and he had been active dishonestly in Nicaragua for a period of months. To Walker he was a symbol and little more; the firing of the barracks, after the desertion of Ramirez and the other treacheries, large and small, which the Americans had encountered, had convinced him that he must act with severity or perish.

VIII

THE *Vesta* was overtaken late in the afternoon and the command transferred to it. Walker remained in his cabin for nearly the entire voyage to Realejo, preparing a detailed report of the action at Rivas. He bluntly charged General Muñoz with having sent the German to warn the Legitimists of the proposed attack and assigned a reason for this: disinclination to co-operate with the Americans, and a possible hope in the commander's mind that the war could be settled by a treaty and his place in the government made permanent. Walker further charged that Ramirez had been ordered by Muñoz not to support the Phalanx, but instead to withdraw at the first sign of action.

At this time, Walker had no intention of leaving Nicaragua. What he had found there was not exactly what he had expected to find, but already he saw a future in which he might come to great authority, and he had no thought of abandoning such an opportunity. Consequently, he was merely bluffing when, as a conclusion to his report, he threatened to remove with the American Phalanx to another "field for their faculty and enterprise," unless the conduct of Muñoz and Ramirez was made the subject of an investigation. The message in this threat was clear: another field might mean the Legitimists of Honduras or Guatemala, or of Nicaragua itself. Walker spoke touchingly of the deaths of his comrades and of the fate of the five he had been forced to leave in Rivas, but it is fairly safe to say that he more rejoiced in than regretted the casualties; the few lives sacrificed gave him an argument far out of proportion to the worthlessness of the men who had lost them.

He was already a hero to the Nicaraguan poor. Stragglers from the Ramirez command had spread reports of the fury with which the Americans fought. That they had gained no objective did not weaken the impact of their demonstration against the odds they had found. Walker knew that when the accounts of the Phalanx's activity reached San Francisco there would be a rush of recruits, and that in a few months he would have a force of three or four hundred which, judging from the poor defense the Legitimists had offered at Rivas, would be enough to sweep the country clean and keep it indefinitely under the domination of settlers from the States.

In the days immediately following his return, he practiced a diplomacy that altogether deserted him later in his career. He knew Castellon to have the soul of a rabbit and he played on this weakness by remaining adamant in the face of all entreaty. Castellon sent a stream of envoys to Realejo harbor, where the American Phalanx remained; two of the more important were Doctor Livingston, long resident of Nicaragua and one-time United States Minister there, and Don Mariano Salazar, Castellon's brother-in-law and a rich merchant. Walker received a letter a day from the Provisional Director; the first avoiding mention of Muñoz, the next pointing out that in the present state of the Democratic party the conduct of the commander-in-chief could not be safely questioned, another announcing the marshaling of an army of one thousand Legitimists under Ponciano Corral at Managua, and still another saying that conscription was being pushed in the country controlled by the Legitimists and the force of their arms swelled daily.

Walker read and listened; and refused to serve until Muñoz was disciplined. So he achieved his major object—his men recovered from their exhaustion and were made ready for war again. He bargained shrewdly with Mariano Salazar, who was fat, friendly and had the cunning of an Indian, and by his bargaining obtained supplies of cloth and much powder.

He waited for ten days aboard the *Vesta*. Then with his men rested and the wounded no longer needing the care so necessary at first, he moved upstream to the city, intending to march thence to Chinandega and establish a permanent base. On the day of disembarkation, Castellon himself, in company with Salazar, traveled to the port and, finding Walker gone, followed him to Realejo.

The Provisional Director, old and gray and afraid, added his personal entreaties to those he had sent by messengers. He could not talk long, he explained, because the condition of the country was such that if it became known he was absent from his capital, enemies within the party would revolt and give Nicaragua a three-sided war instead of a two. Neither could he take action against Muñoz; the man was too powerful to be brooked. Walker pressed his advantage until he knew he could obtain no more concessions; and only then did he relax from his distant and injured attitude and agree to move his corps to Leon.

In a day or two, the American Phalanx marched to Chinandega, where the officials and townspeople extended themselves to be hospitable. There was a short pause there, before Walker agreed to base his soldiers in Leon. Since the return from Rivas, Castellon had repeated, with the tiresome monotony of panic, the danger which the capital of the Democrats faced and the strength it would feel once the Americans were there to protect it.

The night before the Phalanx traveled to the capital, two horsemen rode into Chinandega. One was Byron Cole and the other Bruno von Natzmer.

IX

WHEN Cole had negotiated the second contract with Castellon, and sent it to Walker in San Francisco, he regarded his action as the first swift step in an ordered march. He waited, the guest of Don Francisco in Leon, for Walker to announce his coming with the three hundred men who would save Nicaragua. A month went by, and two. He heard nothing. Nicaragua lacked both telegraph and cable, and the Legitimists held the Transit, which was the only certain source of news from the States. No newspapers from San Francisco came to Leon; as far as Cole was concerned, the contract he had obtained with so much shrewdness and so many promises might never have been written.

On his voyage to Nicaragua, Cole had met prospectors traveling to Honduras to hunt gold. When three months had passed without any word from Walker, Cole abandoned hope that the contract would be acted upon, and went to Honduras himself, following the slim reports about gold he could recall from his conversations on shipboard.

He was in the hills of Olancho when natives repeated to him garbled stories of the action at Rivas. With him was Von Natzmer, a cavalryman from Prussia. The two, having found no gold, turned southward the day they heard of Walker's first battle.

Between the first battle of Rivas and Cole's coming, Walker functioned entirely alone. Not since his beginnings as a filibuster had he shared more than surface confidences with his subordinates, but he was still too new to his business to be able, as he was later, to give up altogether a form of communion with some officer. Crocker had been his shadow, as in a small way Kewen had been, and their deaths in Rivas had been a greater blow than he cared to admit. But with Cole as his aide, and the competent Von Natzmer to help command whatever recruits might be attracted to his banner, he was ready again for action. The coldness he had shown Castellon and his reluctance to negotiate were no longer needful. He marched to Leon, to discover what his next move might be.

The American Phalanx reached the capital after dark, passing through a ring of altogether inefficient pickets, easy targets as they huddled about blazing fires in their white cottons. Walker reflected, as they neared the city, that any assault force, instead of being betrayed by General Muñoz's attempts at watchfulness, would have found the fires of the sentries beacons for its guidance. His feeling for Muñoz remained one of bitterness, because of the treachery at Rivas and in addition the original doubt he had had of the commander's military knowledge was now increased. But of his distrusts he said nothing and, when Castellon asked him to confer with Muñoz, particularly entreating that he not mention his suspicions, he agreed.

They discussed the enemy at Managua. Ponciano Corral, grand

commander of the Legitimists, was well barricaded in that city and was reported to contemplate an attack upon Leon. But Muñoz said— and he seemed to know—that cholera had struck the encampment.

Walker, as a doctor, knew about cholera. As soon as Muñoz told him of its spread in Managua he tried to put himself in Corral's place. The Legitimist General had an army of one thousand, an indefinite portion of which would be violently ill. What morale his troops had would be waning before the awfulness of a plague that brought diarrhoea and vomiting, shrank the features, shriveled the skin and turned it a dead gray; caused thirst and then the melancholy of the damned and, finally, a tortured coma. Picturing the situation for himself, Walker gave the first evidences that he had the mind a general needs: he reasoned that Corral, if he were wise, would march on Leon with all his infantry and cavalry, and also with his most important unit— the disease in his ranks. If he were not wise, he would retire. But only if he were a fool would he remain still, because if he did so cholera would decimate him and make his defeat at the first enemy offensive a certainty.

He expressed all this to Muñoz, but the Democratic general was no man to accept even logic from one he considered an intruder. He declined to co-operate in any venture against Managua and insisted that the entire campaign remain stagnant, until circumstance suggested the next movement. His was the philosophy of the tropics—*mañana*. Irritated but strangely patient, Walker accepted this lack of co-operation. Although his time in Nicaragua had been short, he had learned well, and had progressed to where he could accept with resignation, if not with grace, a situation of plot and counter-plot wherein he was, for the moment, merely a name.

The term "soldier-of-fortune" implies swashbuckling, romantic danger, incredible achievement. It is the purpose of this book to show that William Walker was a drab little man who fitted his deeds no better than he did his clothing. He had come to Nicaragua inspired with a weird multiplicity of aims: he was greedy, but not for plunder, and he was shot through with an idealism which led him to force his reforms down reluctant throats. Had he wanted nothing but trouble in the country of his adoption, he would have ignored Muñoz and Castellon and the rest and led his brigands away to swashbuckle to their heart's content. But his lust for power, and the realization that he could gratify it only by a series of compromises, forced him to wait.

Information from Managua, to the effect that Corral was withdrawing to Granada, came a few days later and gave Walker the opportunity he believed he needed. Asking for a native force of two hundred, he proposed a march against either Rivas or Managua. Muñoz opposed him, demanding that the Phalanx be divided into squads of ten and scattered among his own forces "to strengthen their morale." The meeting ended in bitterness and confusion, with Muñoz insisting that he would march north with his entire army and Walker again threatening to abandon the Democratic cause.

Walker went from the conference without yielding an inch. He had, in all the negotiations with the leaders of the Democrats, a single objective: to seize and hold the Transit road. Until he could accomplish this he was cut off from the United States and without expectation of reinforcement, for, lacking money, he could hope for the transport of recruits only on established steamer lines. It had been made clear to him, in Muñoz's hostility and Castellon's apathy, that the Democrats already regretted allowing the Americans to enter the service of arms in their country and the Phalanx to survive must become self-sufficient. His entire strategy in dealing with the Democrats had been aimed at their fear; he had exaggerated, so quietly that it became believable, the tremendous power of his forty-odd survivors.

On the very day that Muñoz proposed the dissolution of the American Phalanx, Walker returned to the long, adobe house used for barracks and ordered immediate preparations for a march. He had left with Castellon a requisition for ox-carts and horses. Long before his men could get together their scanty baggage, they heard the pad of many bare feet on the cobbles outside. They flung open the shutters and looked upon a force of three hundred Nicaraguans, being marched into houses across the way. Walker, after one glance, walked swiftly to the table he had been using as a desk and wrote a blunt ultimatum to Don Francisco Castellon: The Democratic troops bivouacked opposite the quarters assigned to the American

Phalanx would be moved within the hour or he would regard them as a hostile force and act accordingly.

Forty minutes of the hour passed, in a suspense unlike any Walker's men had known before. Riflemen manned the doors and windows, praying for an opportunity to start firing at the house across the way. Here Muñoz the inept and Castellon the frightened lost their last opportunity to dispose of Walker; their three hundred natives could easily have overwhelmed the thirty-seven *falanginos,* and so averted an infinitude of trouble. But in this hour Castellon could not dismiss his terror, so much part of his character, and in less than the hour allowed him he ordered the Nicaraguans to retire. As they turned the corner at one end of the street, the ox-carts creaked in at the other. The Phalanx moved for Chinandega, in a march not without suspicion; in Walker's words they kept a "sharp lookout to the rear, and were all the time prepared for any movement which might be offensive."

X

COLE remained in Leon to continue the persuasion of Castellon. The New Englander had not joined the army, but held a position as civil aide; he was a skillful bargainer and had some Spanish, and Walker believed that without a military title he might achieve more. He did. The original colonization grant was torn up and a substitute written, which gave each of the *falanginos* one hundred dollars a month and five hundred acres of land at the end of the campaign, and which confirmed them as soldiers of Democratic Nicaragua. Deep hidden in the document was its joker: authorization of William Walker to settle all differences and outstanding accounts between the Accessory Transit Company and the government.

The contract was sufficient to impel Walker to act entirely on his own initiative. He resolved to disobey Castellon's orders (that his force be held in the vicinity of Leon) and prepared his little army for a lunge at the enemy. His grandiose aims now were revealed by his manner; when two *falanginos* resigned to return to the United States, he delivered a fulsome address to their fellows, urging them not to turn back once their hands were to the plough and assuring them that "small as was their number, they were the precursors of a movement destined to affect materially the civilization of a whole continent."

The long-distance wrangle between Castellon and Walker was resumed when the Filibuster's plans became known. Castellon, discovering that Walker was determined to attack the Legitimists on the Transit route with or without support and authority, lacked the courage to forbid such a movement and, if necessary, to send troops to see that it was not undertaken. Instead he attempted merely to delay it, promising Walker help from Muñoz when that doughty warrior had returned from his sally into the North. Guardiola, it was reported, had left Granada for the northernmost Nicaraguan Department, Segovia. The Democrats had little strength there, and Guardiola was supposed to be forging a chain of Legitimists from Tegucigalpa, in his native Honduras, to Granada. If his attempt proved successful, the Democratic government would be hemmed into the one Department it held—Leon—and probably placed under the disadvantage of siege; and so Muñoz, at the head of his entire army, was moving to intercept and thwart the Butcher.

Walker continued deaf to Castellon's pleas, as he had been from the first dispute. Later in his career he tried to justify what he did by saying he had come into the country at the request of a recognized government and had acted under its orders, but that was another of the strange falsehoods he uttered in the apparently honest belief he was speaking truth. While Guardiola and Muñoz maneuvered in the North, Walker added whatever munitions he could buy in Realejo and Chinandega (paying in requisitions on the government) to the supply of powder Mariano Salazar had given him for agreeing to negotiate upon the return from Rivas. He commandeered, with what authority may be imagined from his other actions, all the supplies he needed except lead, of which there was serious scarcity. The natives did not use bullets, but instead sawed into slugs the thin iron bars of window gratings and, although these missiles served in their ancient muskets, Walker's rifles demanded honest bullets.

Walker's conduct in the matter of the lead adds to the total of his acts of warped justice. Someone within his ranks found that an English merchant named Manning, who had served as British consul at Chinandega, owned a large quantity of ingot lead. Manning was only one of the many English merchants who also served in consulates and his conduct was more or less typical of a foreign policy which sought to enjoy the benefits of trade without the responsibilities of colonial ownership. Great Britain, jealous because Spain had dominated the Isthmus for so many years, capitalized the financial weakness of the Central American countries by her merchant-consul staff; Manning, for example, lent money to Nicaragua at two or three per cent a month, depending upon the British warships forever hovering off the coast to guarantee payment. Should Nicaragua have refused to pay her debt to Manning the merchant, Manning the British diplomat would have called for help from his navy, and the ports of the country would have been blockaded.

Manning had temporarily ceased functioning as a consular official, but when the Filibuster sent for his lead the Englishman rejected the requisition the squad brought, sending Walker a warning that he was prepared to run up the British flag and under its protection defy every American in Nicaragua to molest him. Walker listened to the report of his speech, his gray eyes opaque and his clergyman's face impassive, and, when his soldiers had done, calmly ordered them to enter the house and take the lead. And if Manning should run up the flag of England, he added, they were to tear it down and trample it, thus repaying the insult offered to the Republic of Nicaragua. Finally, Manning was to be told that until he was given authority to fly the flag of his country he was no better than any citizen possessing military supplies.

Red-faced, Manning listened to this decision, delivered to him with a reasonable addition of insult and profanity, and meekly surrendered his lead.

XI

WALKER still needed more men and, inasmuch as no reinforcements had arrived from the United States, they had to be found in Nicaragua. He looked about for a reliable native officer, and found him in Don José Maria Vallé, part Indian, veteran of uncounted revolutions, magnificent in stature and in anger, and a talented picker of the guitar. Vallé had fought throughout the Democratic campaign under Maximo Jerez, but had retired from the service because of the appointment of Muñoz, whom he hated, and a bullet in his knee. Since the failure of the siege of Granada, he had ridden about the countryside on a great white horse, his guitar over one shoulder and his rifle over the other, haranguing the peons to rise up in their wrath and tear the Legitimist dogs to shreds, and soothing the women for the loss of their men with his soft music. He admired the Americans who had come to help and sang of his admiration whenever he could gather a crowd.

Walker went to him. He explained the difficulties he had met and his desire to strike a smashing blow at the enemy on the Transit Road. Vallé listened interestedly, said he would help, leaped on his horse and sped to Leon. He spoke with love and firmness to Castellon, who reluctantly gave him permission to march with the Phalanx, and when he returned to Realejo he had at his back one hundred and fifty men. He was an enthusiastic soldier, now impelled by two desires: to avenge the death of a brother slain by the Legitimists at Granada, and to overthrow Castellon and establish a new government. Walker was somewhat surprised at the second suggestion and asked how Vallé could plot against his friend; and the Nicaraguan said, with the philosophy of a lifetime as a revolutionary, that while he loved Don Francisco like a brother, in politics love could have no place.

The stream of letters from Castellon had not diminished. He wrote to Walker pleadingly and to Vallé demandingly. He caused to be circulated in the streets of Chinandega a report that Guardiola was at the gates of the town, and Walker thought cynically of this that apparently the only excuse Castellon could devise to keep the Phalanx from seeking a fight was to imagine one on their very doorstep. But the preliminaries, and the vexation of constant bickering, were behind the Filibuster. He embarked his men, totaling nearly two hundred with Vallé's natives, and stood upon the threshold of his greatest success. Even he, in that moment, could not foresee the forces he was to unleash against other men and against himself. Until the embarkation, he had maintained the appearance of being a servant of the Democratic party, but now he cast this pretense off.

His sailing was against the express orders of Castellon and had his surface objects not been the same as those of the Democrats the movement would have been regarded as counter-revolutionary. For the first time since his arrival in Nicaragua, he began to display openly what he was and at what he grasped. The ministerial Walker, having grown fangs, now wanted to act the lion.

The soldiers crowded the decks of the *Vesta,* the Americans eager for the start to be made. They had come back from the disaster at Rivas on July sixth, and it was now August twenty-third; for six weeks they had licked their wounds and chafed because they could not avenge them. And once they had moved aboard the ship and saw the prospect of action, they clamored for the process to be speeded up.

The ship was ready for sea and the anchor was being hauled up when a boat came alongside from the shore, a voice called in Spanish, "Dispatches for Colonel Walker," and a slim packet hit the deck. It was nearly dusk and Walker took his letters, undoubtedly with amused annoyance at the inevitability of them, to the binnacle light. Castellon wrote (even his pen quavered) that Muñoz had routed Guardiola in a great battle at Saucé, forty miles from Leon and near the borders of Segovia, but had given up his life for his victory. If Colonel Walker would come back and protect Leon, all would be well—with Muñoz gone a new commander would be needed. There was good reason to believe that Guardiola still meant to march on Leon. . . .

Walker folded the letter and put it with all the others. He ordered the brig to sea, but before she left the harbor, the *San José* came in, and Mariano Mendez and Colonel Ramirez were recognized among her company. Walker tried to arrest Ramirez to shoot him for his desertion at Rivas, but the pawn of Muñoz left the *San José* in a swift canoe and fled up the river almost before a boat could be put over from the *Vesta.* Mendez, the Indian leader, rejoined the Phalanx, hailing with delight the native troops, who immediately became the victims of his eternal game of *monte;* truly the maxim that the Latin American "would gamble away the sun before sunrise," applied to Mendez. His unabashed explanation of his own retreat at Rivas did not satisfy the Filibuster, but it did confirm his suspicion that Muñoz had ordered the Phalanx to be abandoned to butchery.

The *Vesta* sailed southward along the coast for six days. On the twenty-ninth she arrived off San Juan and Walker learned from two Americans who came out in a canoe that the Legitimists had fled at his approach. The *Vesta*, which arrived in the early evening, lay at anchor in the harbor throughout the night. While her people slept a prisoner was brought aboard.

Perhaps in these times we develop characters like Parker H. French, but there is something in the speed of transport and communication which removes from them much of their power to make villainy fantastic. French was a man with nothing to recommend him to the continued mercy of a normal society and it would have been a kindness to all with whom he associated had he been shot early in his life. But he was not shot, and he was a forceful figure for more years than he should have been, and because he was a man constantly on the watch for whatever skullduggery would benefit by his talents he entered the scene William Walker was now beginning to dominate.

When Walker was busy with his plans for the sailing of the Immortals from San Francisco, one of the hundreds of persons he told of his new venture was French. Walker knew him by reputation and did not trust him, but in his extremity he was forced to listen to anyone who might be of the barest service to his venture. Both Walker and French were megalomaniacs, but where the first had vision and luck enough nearly to wrest an empire from the jungle, the other was merely a crooked promoter. It was natural that French, meeting Walker in San Francisco, should tell of his great friendship for C. K. Garrison, shipping magnate and then associate of Cornelius Vanderbilt in the Accessory Transit Company, and to make offers of aid which Walker did not take too seriously.

French is supposed to have been a Bostonian. He arrived in Los Angeles in May of 1853, his clothing in tatters, his beard frightful and with a flapping sleeve where his right arm should have been. Within two days he was redolent of hair tonic and wore a costume of color and opulence. He spoke of big things he had done in the past, and big things just beyond the horizon, and merchants lost their cunning before the power of his tongue, extending to him limitless credit. Gradually, however, something of his unsavory past began to be whispered about. It was said that he had turned up in San Antonio de Bexar in 1849, with his impressive manner and a seven-hundred-and-fifty-thousand-dollar letter of credit on Howland & Aspinwall, New York bankers. Whether the amount is exaggerated one cannot say, but the letter of credit worked and in a short time French was in command of a magnificent train of one hundred wagons. He offered passage to the gold fields for two hundred and fifty dollars per person and Texans flocked to patronize him. His train was composed of the best Howland & Aspinwall's money could buy: fine coaches, each to carry six passengers and each drawn by six good mules.

The train started for California, but had proceeded only as far as El Paso when a troop of cavalry overtook it and demanded the surrender of French for the forging of the letter of credit and the defrauding of the army post, which had sold him some of his supplies. French and a few of his employees fought their way through the troops, abandoned the train and fled into Mexico. Here the record becomes confused; the gang seems to have arrived in Chihuahua with a few men but without money and to have attempted to rob its way to Mazatlan, whence, presumably, it hoped to proceed to California by boat. When the band reached Durango, the Mexican officials captured its chieftain.

Somehow French escaped from jail, losing an arm in the process. He arrived in Los Angeles in stinking rags, and when he had re-outfitted himself with his promoter's genius went on to San Francisco. In 1855, when Walker met him, he was a member of the California senate and asserted that he was interested in Nicaragua only for the glory of the Stars and Stripes. But even then he was engaged in another enterprise soon to send him flying from the outraged law; using forged powers of attorney, he had mortgaged much land belonging to an assortment of his colleagues and when his thefts became known he was off again—to San Juan del Sur.

Since the day in San Francisco when French had voiced promises of ultimate support from Garrison, Walker had forgotten him. But French had not forgotten Walker. As did everyone else in the era, he considered Nicaragua fair game for anyone who could exploit it and he was a sufficient judge of men and men's deeds to know that Walker was in the ascendancy.

He reached San Juan some weeks before Walker, accompanied by a mulatto servant named Tom, who seems to have had some Spanish. French remained in the background upon his arrival in Nicaragua, sending Tom to the *pulperias* and other gathering places of men, to describe the amazing achievements of his master, so talented an artillerist he could hit a man with a twenty-four pounder at a mile, ten times out of ten. As far away as Leon, a distance greater than its miles because of the war and the primitive communications, Walker had heard stories of the *Yanqui* whose one arm was yet enough to make him the greatest cannoneer of his time and who had come to win the war for the Legitimists. It goes without saying that French would have served whoever lined his pockets, but for some reason the Legitimists listened coldly to his proposals and he was forced to remain in San Juan. There he watched Walker's ship arrive and when a scouting party came ashore he purposely behaved suspiciously, so that he would be arrested and taken aboard.

He greeted Walker with confidence and enthusiasm, offering information of the enemy's strength and position which added nothing to what was already known. The hollowness of Walker's protestations that his intention was liberation and justice for the people to whom he had attached himself was indicated in the interview with French and in French's later association with the government of Nicaragua. Instead of sending the man away, Walker "did not care to examine the real motives of French" because such motives "are generally so tangled that he who attempts to unravel them is poorly paid for his trouble." He commissioned French to return to San Francisco, to see Garrison and learn what help the shipping man stood ready to offer, and to gather seventy-five recruits.

XII

WALKER concentrated for more than a week upon learning the detailed actions of the Legitimists and in preparing his troops for an engagement. Spies in Granada told him that Ponciano Corral

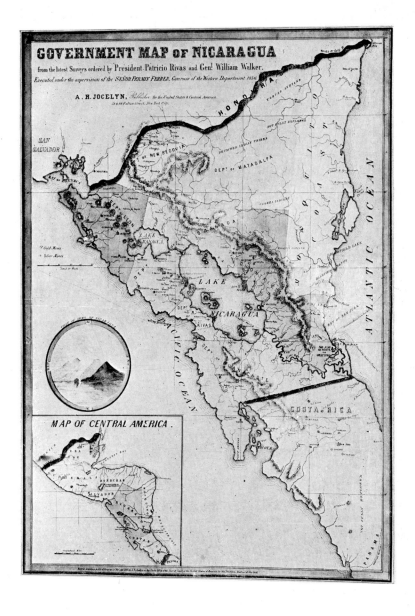

GOVERNMENT MAP OF NICARAGUA

from the latest Surveys ordered by President Patricio Rivas and Gen! William Walker.

Executed under the supervision of the *SEÑOR FERMIN FERRER, Governor of the Western Department 1856.*

A. H. JOCELYN, *Publisher for the United States & Central America.*
54 & 56 Fulton Street, New York City.

MAP OF CENTRAL AMERICA.

had about a thousand men, five or six hundred at Rivas and the balance at Granada. Guardiola, after his defeat at the hands of Muñoz in the North, had rushed to Granada in a state of great humiliation and anger, announcing when he was still miles from the capital that he would fall upon the filibuster dogs and drive them into the sea. He reached Granada a day or so after Walker landed in San Juan, and immediately took charge of two hundred soldiers for a march toward Rivas and the Transit Road.

With two wagon trains and twenty animals, Walker started for Virgin Bay, on the lake side of the Transit Road, a little after midnight on the third of September. His army marched over the fine paved highway, through a thick forest. The moon was bright overhead and the column, with the Phalanx ahead and Vallé's natives in the center and rear, moved cheerfully and swiftly. By three o'clock in the morning it had covered seven miles to a tavern run by an American and called the Halfway House, where Walker permitted a short halt for water and rest. The tavern-keeper, made skillful in diplomacy by the revolutions he had seen, offered the commander drinks on the house for his army, but Walker's innate puritanism was stiffened by the prospect of immediate action and the time when the *falanginos* could drink their fill was past. Thereafter, throughout his career in the Spanish American countries, the men who served with William Walker drank surreptitiously and with care lest they be discovered. If they had obeyed the Filibuster's orders implicitly they would have formed the most moral army in all history.

Virgin Bay was reached at nine in the morning. Gunfire had been heard in the night from the direction of Rivas, which lay to the North, and there was a report among the fearful natives of the little lake town that Guardiola the Butcher was on his way with a great body of men. The Americans set out pickets and prepared breakfast, willing after a thirteen-mile march in the night to discount the possibility of an attack.

They had barely finished eating, and some were spreading blankets in the shade of adobe walls, when musket-fire brought them up standing. They stood motionless, a hundred and more men, watching the Transit road. The outpost came into sight, firing and falling back with the precision of veterans; and so well did the pickets delay the enemy that Walker and his officers had ample time to estimate the emergency and place their men for defense.

North of Virgin Bay the ground rose slightly, giving an approaching force an advantage. The town itself was ringed with heavy picket fences and deep drainage ditches, offering defenders reasonable cover. Near the lake the bank fell steeply, furnishing a good breastwork, but leaving the riflemen behind it no alternative except to swim, if pushed to the point of retreat. At the edge of the village was a large warehouse of the Accessory Transit Company, surrounded by a palisade.

Walker moved swiftly to cover the rising ground on the North, sending twenty riflemen from his own Phalanx into the brush and native huts on the hillside. Vallé was to hold the Transit Road and hit at the enemy's center. On the lake side fifteen Americans overlooked the beach from a position in the Transit warehouse and behind its fence.

In a war as military men know it, the battle of Virgin Bay was no more than a skirmish. But to its participants, especially to those under Guardiola, it was a bitter and significant battle. The Legitimists came on, as quickly as the pickets would permit in the first minutes of the action and then more slowly, as the long rifles of the Phalanx began to pick off white-clad figures in their ranks. The Americans could not resist adding noise to the gunfire and throughout the engagement they kept up a shrill and terrible yelling.

The Legitimists came to within forty feet of the main position of the Democrats, where Walker stood, and then seemed to be appalled by the damage the rifles were doing. They hesitated and would have broken but their officers, distinguished by black coats and by the fact that they were mounted, rode through the ranks beating recalcitrants and zealots alike with dog whips and the flats of swords.

The rifles on the hillside kept it clear and prevented an advance toward the village from that quarter. Walker, after watching the general engagement for a moment, walked slowly across to where Vallé was holding off Guardiola's center. In this moment the commander of the American Phalanx was utterly quiet. He did not shout, he did not run and he did not fire the revolver he held in his hands except when there was a definite target before him. The gray of his eyes was brighter for the fire that burned behind them . . . and that was all.

Vallé was harder pressed than the men in the town itself. The enemy had taken a portion of the Transit Road by a flank movement and was attempting to advance along it. Walker moved among the natives redistributing groups of men and solidifying the resistance and, when he had seen that nothing but a miracle would let Guardiola in by way of the road, he returned to the village. As he moved toward the Transit warehouse, the Legitimists tried two charges; the first was repelled with bayonets and the second was broken up before it could be fairly launched by half a dozen screaming youths, who scaled the palisade and ran with savage enjoyment full into the ranks of the enemy, firing revolvers promiscuously but with splendid effect.

The battle ended there. Guardiola tried to get his men into order, but they were too scattered and too badly punished to be rallied. Stragglers from the Transit sector began to move through the forest in the general direction of Rivas and away from Virgin Bay and the ones who had tried to take the village now fired only feebly. A final attempt or two to take the natural breastworks on the lake front failed and Guardiola retreated.

The losses to the Democrats were trifling. Two natives died and perhaps a dozen all told were wounded. Walker, on one of his journeys between strongholds, was hit in the throat with a spent ball which caused him to talk in a whisper for days. Another slug hit him in the breast, but it was nearly spent and penetrated only to the center of the packet of Castellon's letters he carried there. Discarding the nest of letters in which the little leaden egg rested, he must have known a fleeting gratitude that Castellon had written so voluminously.

The enemy suffered sixty killed and more than one hundred wounded. The prisoners who were taken were ordered by Walker to be treated for their injuries along with the casualties of his own force, a procedure that struck dismay to the hearts of the native Nicaraguans. This was not war—in war the prisoners were shot as soon as they could be lined up!

But by observing the laws of what is called, with naïve irony, civilized warfare, Walker learned a valuable lesson. His grateful prisoners told him of Guardiola's tactics: how the Butcher had marched first for San Juan and then, having learned that the Americans had changed base, for the Transit Road; how, then, confident of victory, he had ordered bayonets greased for the swift dispatch of the prisoners and torches prepared for the burning of Virgin Bay; how his single cannon, a six-pounder, having failed him at the moment of contact, he had issued rations of *aguardiente* to nerve his frightened peons for a charge. Of this Walker later wrote, with one of his rare flashes of dry wit: "The empty demijohns which were picked up on the road after the action looked like huge cannonballs that had missed their mark."

The battle did more than strengthen the men's morale. It gave Walker a sharp view into the methods of combat in Latin America and undoubtedly suggested to him that he might well emulate such strategists as Guardiola. Although he never permitted enemy wounded or captured to be mistreated, he did follow Guardiola; in his mind he greased bayonets and prepared torches against the day when he would need them. The suspicion of a psychological flaw in the Walker character here intrudes itself again and subsequent events were to show that he took unto himself the cruelty of the Spaniard with rather more alacrity than would seem possible in an educated American. A study of the man finds the beginnings of his big moments in two dates: that on which Helen Martin died and that on which General Don Santos Guardiola, the Butcher of Honduras, greased his bayonets.

When the smoke from the rifles had blown over the lake and the excitement within Walker's ranks died down, the inhabitants of Virgin Bay emerged from their houses. Many of the poorer ones had taken shelter in the building of the Transit Company, where trunks and goods boxes had been piled against the doors and windows during the hostilities. The people were picturesque and frightened. The women wore full skirts and waists of cotton cloth, the latter draped over the shoulders and ending above the skirt to reveal the navel. Their hair was in twin braids down their backs and on the feet of some were soiled satin slippers. Their young sons were naked except for straw hats and cigars; the ones over fourteen were garbed in the cotton tunics and trousers of the peasant male. The little girls were miniatures of their mothers. As far as the inhabitants of Virgin Bay were concerned, what had happened was as much a part of life as the rainy season or the feast days of the church; but their fear remained, because the Americans were a new enemy possibly armed with advanced notions of cruelty. It was not until hours later that the men of Walker's command were absolved of the suspicion that they would rape and plunder and burn.

Although flushed with his victory, Walker could see that nothing was to be gained by pursuing Guardiola's tatters into Rivas. His advance to Virgin Bay had been undertaken mainly to convince the Democrats of the area, and his own men, that the Legitimists by no means controlled the country and that an opposing army could move through it at will. Guardiola's coming to Virgin Bay and the result of the encounter were happy accidents suggesting a profitable sequel only when Walker possessed the men and arms necessary for a further invasion into Legitimist preserves. As it was, he retreated to San Juan, leaving pickets where they might see the most and patrolling the countryside to the north with the few mounted men he had.

He reached the seaport on the fifth, quartered his men and sent a courier to Leon with the news of the victory. The courier reached the Democratic capital to find the house of the Provisional Director muted and dimly lighted. He entered the long room in which Castellon lay, to watch him die of cholera. Something of Walker's conviction that he was an object of destiny was here emphasized, because Castellon, spineless though he was, was the only man to whom the Filibuster owed allegiance. With the Provisional Director dead and the memory of what agreements they had reached in conversation in the possession only of himself, Walker need be even less responsible to authority and could dismiss his late patron as a man whose purpose in life had been accomplished: "He had fulfilled his task of introducing a new element into Central American society." The new element, assured by Don Nasario Escoto, successor to Castellon, of the fullest co-operation from the Democratic government, prepared to take what it could.

The picture was a changed one. In the beginning, Francisco Castellon was pitted against Fruto Chamorro. Chamorro died, Castel-

lon enlisted Walker, and new motives began to actuate the parties.
Walker owed obedience to Castellon and by his death was made
freer; but, too, his position became one he must maintain himself.
The present leaders of the two parties lacked the fire of their prede-
cessors for two reasons: the long duration of the war, now become
exhausting and monotonous, and the presence of the Americans.
Castellon, who had received Walker so warmly in June, had almost
immediately appeared to regret his act. But now even Castellon's
half-hearted support was gone, leaving the determination of the
future a matter more of might than of contracts or principles.

Walker spent a month in San Juan, uncertain as to his next move
and eager before he made it that his army be prepared. Until October
third, when reinforcements came from the United States, the men
drilled often, officers of the Immortals being detailed to school (in
anger and profanity) the Nicaraguans. The irresponsibles who had
arrived on the *Vesta* were now thoroughly part of the country; they
possessed Nicaragua as they had possessed San Francisco. Walker,
the pure of speech, must have winced at the inevitable God-damns
that preceded all their nouns. Off duty they frequented the Dime
Saloon, a place established by the French consul for the refreshment
of Transit passengers and taken, all but the deed, by Walker's privates. Shaded by a large ceiba tree, the saloon was a frame building,
its barroom overlooking the Pacific. Although they were supposed
to be earning one hundred dollars a month for their services, none
of the Immortals had been paid, except in worthless military script,
and they drank on credit. Long afterward, when Walker was in
complete control of the government, he received and examined a
staggering bill from the French host-consul and returned it with the
polite regret that the Republic of Nicaragua was not honoring such
obligations at the moment.

Food was furnished for the Americans by the peons of the region.
Walker had been opposed to conscription from the first and the con-
tinuance of this policy convinced the farmers that they could truck
their produce to market without being seized and flung into an army.
They came willingly enough then and accepted gratefully the requisitions they received in payment.

There was no money at all for the army, however, and to pursue the war the Filibuster needed funds. For some reason, Edmund Randolph and his associates in San Francisco were sending neither men nor supplies. For any major assault ammunition in quantities would be needed and, because the long war had all but exhausted the supply, it must be bought from agencies outside the country. Help in this emergency came from an unexpected source. Don Maximo Espinosa, who had been sent with the Immortals in June to form a civil government in whatever territory they might take, turned up in San Juan. He had fled from Rivas at the first sound of battle and had been in hiding for the following three months; but with other Democrats he was heartened by the victory at Virgin Bay and sufficiently emboldened to pay Walker a visit. The commander, although insisting he was a "hired soldier" and under the orders of the government, called upon his lawyer's wit and installed Don Maximo as Minister of Relations for the Department; and at once there was ordered a levy against the merchants of San Juan, to pay the costs of the army. Walker not only dictated this levy but directed its collection, in this instance again revealing the beginnings of the dictator's technique.

The levy was unpopular and productive of little money. Walker appointed one collector who was caught taking bribes from a merchant-smuggler. Mariano Mendez, the Indian, ranged the countryside with a little band of barbarians, killing what cattle he could find and selling the beef in defiance of revenue provisions. It was Walker's first attempt to exercise the prerogatives of government and from it he learned lessons in corruption he had not believed possible. Nicaraguans of the time said of their own civil servants: "The calf within the cow is not safe from them."

But circumstances and the man were creating in Walker a state of mind comprised queerly of determination, false motives, the vision of destiny and incomprehension of truths. The matter of graft merely appeared an obstruction to him, whereas in fact it was the philosophy of a people. He called it another item of proof that whatever the American element did would be right. But not even the knowledge that the Legitimist government was no more successful than his in raising money could make him realize the impossibility of changing the system. His attitude toward Nicaragua, from the first day he heard of the place in San Francisco, was smug; every time his policies were opposed he turned reformer without inquiring fully into the causes behind the opposition.

While he was deep in his concerns as the ruler of San Juan, the California steamship *Cortes* came into harbor, on October third. She carried the usual bullion for the East, private passengers and a company of thirty-five men, led by Colonel Charles Gilman and Captain George R. Davidson, veterans of the Mexico fiasco. The leg Gilman had sacrificed for the "Republic of Sonora" was replaced with a moderately comfortable peg and his black beard was two inches longer; aside from those externals the man was the same. He stumped down from the ship to become one of the Filibuster's officers. He had gathered men and some money in San Francisco, and in the traditional manner had caused to be shipped to the scene of revolution guns in cases marked "machinery," and powder in sugar sacks.

Gilman was badly needed, and could not have arrived at a better time. Walker, originally assisted by nearly a dozen officers, had been reduced in San Juan to a staff consisting of Captain Doubleday, Julius de Brissot and the ubiquitous, profane and fearless Hornsby. Gilman was a better thinker than any of the others; as an example, he introduced to Walker a fellow passenger whose acquaintance he had made on the *Cortes*. This was Charles McDonald, a Scot and an agent of C. K. Garrison. McDonald listened to the story of the Americans and, when Walker had done, indicated that Garrison might offer the Pacific vessels of the Transit line for the movement of recruits. McDonald did not commit himself in the first meeting, but he remained in Nicaragua as an observer, sending detailed reports to his principal in San Francisco and paving the way for the Accessory Transit Company conspiracy.

Walker chafed at delaying further, but he could not be sure of what region he should strike. Between October third and eleventh, however, he learned from Legitimist deserters who trickled into San Juan del Sur sufficient details of the enemy's situation to plan the next step in the campaign. Guardiola had returned to Honduras, a chastened butcher, and the full command of the Legitimist army was now in the hands of Ponciano Corral. The deserters reported that Corral contemplated an attack, and Walker allowed himself to be persuaded that the Legitimist actually was moving against him. The rainy season was not to end for another month and the roads were morasses, the streams torrents. Still Walker did not feel that he could trust the weather to be his best ally and keep the enemy at a distance, so he marched out one midnight to ambush Corral. The Phalanx and all Vallé's force huddled under trees in as dismal a time as they had yet known. The rain fell without pause, sometimes lightly in a shower and again in a downpour of drops as big as bullets. When morning came Walker had nothing to show for his maneuver but a sopping wet army and the glimmer of an idea that was to lead him to a victory greater than Virgin Bay. If Corral did not come against him, he reasoned, he was afraid. Therefore, the Americans must go against Corral.

Because his entire army was mobile, he did not turn back to San Juan at once, as he had intended, but went on to Virgin Bay, this time allowing the men a ration of liquor as they passed the Halfway House. And at Virgin Bay, the veritable gush of intelligence which greeted him made his next step an obvious one.

From spies he heard that Corral actually had left Rivas with the intention of seizing the Transit Road, but in some manner had learned of the Democratic army's march and preferred to fall back to the undefended Rivas. His army, the spies said, was in a panic. When Walker reached Virgin Bay the entire Legitimist strength, except for a corporal's guard at Granada, was behind the Rivas barricades.

Walker was encouraged by this, because it suggested to his agile mind the value of the feint in moving against Corral. But the vital intelligence he received did more; it propelled him toward a great feat of generalship. A courier was captured in Virgin Bay. His dispatches—from the adjutant general in Granada to Corral—described a state of utter destitution in the capital, with the government unable to help its commander-in-chief by so much as a single man or a single dollar, the people in despair, the city all but unprotected, and the spectre of Walker's Democratic army growing daily more terrifying.

He read, the ghost of a smile playing about the corners of the mouth that never smiled, and when he had finished he wrote a courteous note to Corral, informing him that he had examined the dispatches and intimating that they suggested an immediate attempt to end the war. This message went forward under a flag of truce to Rivas. Corral's formal reply merely acknowledged the receipt of the dispatches, but as Walker's little hands opened the note there fell to the floor a slip of paper, containing what seemed to be cabalistic signs. He could make nothing of them, but he had heard that Corral was a Mason and that there were such things as Masonic signs; he sent for Hornsby and De Brissot and asked them to interpret for him. Hornsby, having lived as far from books as he could get, could not decipher them, but De Brissot, after a glance, said that Corral would like to communicate confidentially with his enemy.

But Walker permitted the correspondence to die, returning to San Juan to organize his coup.

XIII

THE eleventh of October, 1855, saw the American Phalanx prepared and eager to be at its greatest work. The complete army of William Walker, swelled by recruits from among the passengers of the Accessory Transit Company and Gilman's thirty-five, numbered about three hundred and fifty. The natives under Vallé had been built up with Legitimist deserters and what reinforcements Leon had sent to the proportions of a rocklike reserve, against the background of which the *falanginos* could do their level worst. Discipline had been improved during the wait in San Juan; also the Walker army was, for the first time, reasonably well officered. Vallé continued in command of the natives, with Von Natzmer as his aide. Mariano Mendez, because of his brutalities to prisoners and his own men and his lusty activities as a grafter, was shipped to Leon and out of the service. As he left to board his ship he murmured wise advice to Walker: "You will learn that the Nicaraguans can be governed only with silver and the whip."

Artillery, in the shape of a brass two-pounder forwarded from Leon and an iron six-pounder presented to the American Phalanx by the skipper of the Transit ship *Queen of the Pacific,* was prepared for action. The few men familiar with big arms were assigned as artillerists. Food was gathered in quantity, along with every available bit of ammunition. On the morning of the eleventh, keeping his plans strictly to himself, the Filibuster marched eastward over the Transit Road, presumably to consolidate the position at Virgin Bay which he had won five weeks before.

The march consumed a full day. It was after dark before the men were in quarters. Walker was observed to be unusually restless and watchful of the waters of the lake. Presently a ship's lights appeared and the Transit boat *La Virgen* anchored off the embarcadero. Walker sent Hornsby and a squad aboard to hold her for orders. The captain protested against the seizure, maintaining without effect that *La Virgen* was a ship of the United States and as such beyond the sovereignty of the Nicaraguan government. Walker's high-handedness in this matter and the sincerity with which the captain sought to keep the Phalanx off his vessel put the lie to reports even then circulated in the United States that Walker was the creature of the Transit Company, acting with its sponsorship and financial backing.

The troops were kept in ignorance of the seizure of the steamer. At four-thirty on the following afternoon the command was ordered aboard *La Virgen* and the captain directed to sail her to Granada. Vallé's natives, first to sense their objective, were so overcome with enthusiasm that it was necessary for Walker to detail *falanginos* to keep them quiet by force of fist.

The little boat moved up the shores of the lake, showing no running lights and with canvas curtains hanging against the sides from the roof of the upper deck to the waterline. The moon was bright enough for her to be seen from the shore, but with the exception of the island of Omotepe, where the twin volcanoes loomed darkly over the moonlit water, there were no settlements of consequence, and the noise of the boat's passing and the showers of sparks her funnel sent up alarmed no one.

She skirted the fort at Granada, held to bare steerage-way in an effort to silence the throb of her engines. Three miles north a landing was made, the boat halting within a quarter-mile of the beach. A stout cable was put ashore and attached to a tree for the crews to pull their launches shoreward with it. In the cause of silence five hours were used up in landing the men and a few horses brought along for Walker and officers unable to march because of old wounds. At three o'clock in the morning, the horses were hoisted overside in slings and ferried ashore, making loud protest with hoof and whinny. The men set out at once, guided by one of the Legitimist deserters in a march "perplexed and difficult while it was dark." But when day dawned the guide quickly found the road from Los Cocos to Granada and the men, in the customary order—Phalanx, ammunition and supply trains, Nicaraguans—swung steadily along it toward the Legitimist capital. Again they encountered people from the markets, returning to their huts with empty baskets, and from these they learned that the Legitimists still slept after a night of drinking and dancing in the streets.

It was a quiet road, winding a little, and carpeted with heavy dust which the rains of the season had packed nicely. They passed the huts on the outskirts of the city and moved purposefully toward the first barricades, which could be seen blocking the streets leading to the grand plaza. When the towers of the churches were in sight the bells within them began to ring furiously and the column, without orders, hesitated a moment. Walker swung his horse quickly to the side of the road, where a barefooted grandfather waited with his baskets for the pathway to be cleared of these fierce foreigners. He leaned down from the saddle and asked in almost inaudible Spanish why the bells were ringing.

The peon looked toward the city, at the column of men moving past slowly, at the ammunition and the two small cannon, back at Walker. He spoke hurriedly, fearful and yet somehow gay. The *fiesta, Señor,* for the great victory of Pueblo Nuevo. General Martinez—with his own eyes he had seen him, *Señor,* riding into the city only yesterday—had beaten the Democrats in a terrible battle. Every Granadino celebrated the victory. *Aguardiente* was as free as water. All of this came in a voluble outpouring of Spanish, a good part understandable to Walker, who stopped the flow with a murmured *"Gracias,"* and a salute to the old man. He rode at a canter for the head of the column and as he passed his officers he imparted to them what he had learned.

At Rivas he had blocked out a complete plan of battle, only to be defeated. At Granada it was necessary for him only to march into the city and take it in the name of the Democratic government. Something of the unprepared condition of the Legitimist capital had been learned from the market people and more could be guessed from the alarm the suburbs displayed at the sight of so powerful a body moving upon the grand plaza. Walker left the head of the column and sat his horse on one side as the Americans entered the first paved street. The bearded Hornsby waved his arm and the first of the *falanginos* surged over an undefended barricade, made of furniture and logs and sandbags. The bells still rang in the church steeples, to celebrate a victory which would be no victory at all when this day was over, and not until the American Phalanx, traveling at the double through the town and meeting no interference, had come within sight of the convent of San Francisco did the peals break off in startled interruption. There were scattered shots up ahead and Walker spurred his horse, jumping him over the low barricades without a break in pace. Before he could enter the square the battle, if it could be called such, was over; the last weak enemy fusillade sounded from the second floor gallery of Government House as his horse cantered into the plaza's north end.

By ten o'clock in the morning the streets had been searched and every Legitimist disarmed or arrested. Shots from the tower of the San Francisco convent called attention to the place and a quick charge cleaned out a sharpshooter's nest. In the basement Gilman found a huddle of misery: nearly one hundred political prisoners, of all ages, tied hatefully to the walls with chains. Many suffered release dumbly and blinked in blind pain at the glare of unaccustomed sunlight, for they had been enchained for months.

Granada was taken at the cost of one casualty to the forces of William Walker. A native drummer boy exposed himself carelessly and was killed by a ricocheting bullet.

In the streets in the center of the city, the doors and windows remained closed until late afternoon. The American Ministry, however, admitted Walker and some of his men as soon as the firing had died down. John H. Wheeler, the minister, extended himself to pompous and undiplomatic lengths to make the Filibuster welcome. In his house and courtyard were the city's aristocrats, shaking and uncertain as to their fate at the hands of the barbarian from the

North. They shrank from him when he came in, but the slight figure he made and the quietness which seemed to have fallen upon the scene of his victory reassured them, and presently the old dons and the frightened women moved haltingly to the patio gate and out into the street.

There was no immediate enjoyment of his prize for the leader of the Democratic Army. His first hours should have been spent in visiting the defenses of the town and preparing for a permanent occupation, but the army he led was too potent a mixture to be allowed utter freedom at once. Riding across the plaza he saw several of Vallé's natives, distinguished by the red ribbon tied to their tunics, moving along the sidewalk laden with plunder. He rode quickly to where they had halted at his command and held a sword against the breast of the leader, until a guard could be called to take them off to the military prison, first establishment of the conquerors of Granada. Ethically Walker was right, but in this instance his action ran counter to his philosophy of expediency. He had endeared himself to Vallé and all his men by freeing the political prisoners in the Convent of San Francisco; he had weakened this feeling somewhat by refusing to permit summary executions of the few prisoners of war his assault had taken; now he all but destroyed it. Traditionally, the captured Nicaraguan city was ravaged and the conqueror departed with everything that could be moved. Every man in Vallé's force had suffered loss of property in one of the innumerable defeats of the revolutions and to be denied at this stage the right to retaliate blackened the fond looks they had cast upon the little American.

Nor was looting the only excess to be prevented. Vallé himself had to be disciplined when he drove in before his prancing horse two leaders of the Legitimists—one a Chamorro, kinsman of the dead President who had called down upon his country this very war. Vallé found them walking unfettered toward their homes. They had given their parole to Walker himself, but Vallé did not know this, and he captured them with all manner of threat and invective. His curses could be heard long before he came into sight of headquarters and when the men stood before Walker their captor was in a frenzy composed equally of grief and murderous lust. He spoke of the brother who had been killed at Granada, of his many true friends assassinated by the Legitimist dogs, of the cruelties of the enemy and its unworthiness to be admitted to the company of the human race, of the base treachery of those who would show mercy to aristocrats. Walker heard him out and talked quietly for a time of the manners of civilized warriors; until at last, losing patience with the old man and coming perilously close to making a deathless and dangerous enemy, he showed teeth. If Vallé molested another prisoner of war, he said curtly, Vallé would answer to William Walker. And his punishment would be summary.

By nightfall a form of order had been achieved. José Maria Estrada, the Legitimist president, had fled at the first shots, but about sixty leaders of the Legitimist party were listed as prisoners and released in the parole of various neutrals.

There was in Granada a merchant, Don Carlos Thomas, whose passion for the Democratic cause had not been so overwhelming as to cause him to abandon his business in the Legitimist capital. This gentleman came forward as soon as the rule of the city changed and offered his counsel to Walker. He was a man who "spoke and wrote English, French and Spanish with equal facility, and probably equal elegance, his English being, however, more Johnsonian than idiomatic. . . . The swell of his sentences was perfectly Ciceronian when, with a glass or two of brandy in his head, he began to dilate on the grandeur of the present crisis in Nicaragua." Exuberant over the victory Walker had won, Don Carlos wrote and issued, over the Filibuster's name, a proclamation "teeming with the rhetoric which characterizes Spanish-American productions [which] however, though offensive to taste, did some good. . . ."

At the hour of six o'clock this morning, [the proclamation read] I took possession of this city, after a slight resistance offered to the troops under my command by those of the supposed Legitimist Government. During the same little skirmish, three or four soldiers of the enemy had the misfortune to be killed; but after the triumph, which I was bound to obtain, no personal molestation has been offered to anyone; all those families who were expecting incendiarisms, robberies, assassinations, shooting and unutterable immoralities, as the lying Legitimists had repeatedly foretold, have seen and witnessed quite the contrary. My duty, as Chief of the expeditionary forces of a government liberal in principles, whose views are to maintain the vital interests of the State—protection to the laboring man, security to the citizen, encouragement of the arts, science and agriculture, etc., etc.—was to preserve and cause to be preserved, order. Thus it is that although I caused the arrest of Messrs. Don Dionicio Chamorro, Don Torbio Jerez, and other personages of high consideration, who were the principal agents of Legitimacy, I did nothing to them, except to deliver them to persons of responsibility, to be kept in custody. I shall then continue to occupy the other towns of the State, and death to him that opposes the imperious march of my forces, into which will be admitted, without distinction of color, all who may desire to join them.

The people of Nicaragua must not allow themselves to be deceived, for thus is the truth demonstrated by acts; and with that understanding, their happiness is in their own hands. Here it is—a Democratic government in its true sense, guaranties, progress and Liberty.

Having taken the city with a master stroke of strategy, Walker tried in every way he knew not to abuse what luck and skill had given him. There was some muttering against the law and order which he dictated for the capital, but it was among the native troops and nothing but praise can be accorded him for refusing to allow the city to be pillaged or its inhabitants to be molested. In other things he proved himself to be shrewd and far-seeing. One of the first men he sought out was Padre Augustin Vijil, a man of splendid figure, mind and memory, with a rich voice and an orator's cunning. Padre Vijil, as an attorney of Granada, had been involved in politics, on the Democratic side; and when he discovered himself fleeing into exile the thought occurred to him that the Mother Church would protect her own. He then became a priest and returned to Granada, where it was said of him that he showed an equal fealty to "fees and fervor, briefs and bead, courts and confession, cross examination and the cross." Walker learned that there had been a contest for the Episcopal chair of Granada and that Don Fruto Chamorro before his death had seen to it that Vijil was denied the honor; he knew, therefore, that the priest could hardly be sympathetic to Legitimacy.

Walker conferred with Vijil and, although he was as yet no Catholic, attended Mass at eight o'clock on the day after the capture of the city. The priest delivered a sermon which reflected the influences of Walker's interviews with him: "I have preached peace, liberty and progression to you, and you have cried more blood. Look at this man, General Walker, sent by Providence to bring peace, prosperity and happiness to the blood-stained country. We all owe him and his brave men many thanks. I charge you to keep this peace which promises so much."

With the leading Legitimists being watched by reliable custodians and Padre Vijil enlisting new support for him through the channels of the Church, Walker completed his mastery of Granada in a single, envisioned move. The power behind the throne of the Legitimist party seems to have been a woman called generally Niña Yrena, the descendant of one of the Irish giants who came to middle America with the Spanish conquerors. Not too much is known of Yrena, except that her house had been the gathering place of the most influential aristocrats for many years. Walker moved his baggage to this house and announced, with courteous finality, that Yrena must be his hostess for as long as he chose to stay. She was too wise a woman to deny him or to attempt to leave and for a matter of days the inevitable plotting that would have gone forward under her roof was prevented. Yrena was of middle age, with the gravity and apparent indifference of the Nicaraguan, and the quick, politician's mind of the Irish. In Walker's mention of his brief association with her, he unchivalrously emphasized her personal relationship with one Narciso Espinosa, confidant and aide of Fruto Chamorro, and indicated that it was in her bed that many of the strategies of the government were discussed and made ready. Later, when he was sure that she would do no harm, he moved to Government House, the executive mansion of Granada.

On Sunday afternoon Walker received a delegation which wished to declare him President of Nicaragua. He rejected this offer with calm thanks, suggesting that Ponciano Corral, sulking at Managua with his impotent army, be given the honor. Such a coalition, he felt, would heal all the wounds of the long war. As for himself, he said with disingenuous modesty that he would accept the position of commander-in-chief of the army and see that order was maintained throughout the Republic. The lesson he had learned best was that left with him by Mariano Mendez: "The Nicaraguan is ruled with the whip." Walker did not have the whip, but his hands had touched its butt and he was anticipating the moment when he would be able to swish its length through the air and hear the crack of its far end.

Minister Wheeler hovered at the edge of Walker's conferences from the first, as friendly as a hungry dog. A study of this envoy's correspondence with William M. Marcy, Secretary of State in Washington, shows clearly that he did not know enough to fill a diplomatic pouch with anything but drivel. Wheeler, accredited Minister to a recognized government, was among the first to make an invading revolutionary welcome. He had spent more than half of his fifty years in politics and he had gone off to Nicaragua with very little to guide him beyond the same sort of jingo patriotism that gave Walker his principal support in the United States. He should have remained in the background, denying the recognition of his government to either side until it became known which was the responsible one. But Minister Wheeler believed too devoutly in "manifest destiny" to stand idly by while it was performing its miracles. When Walker asked him to visit Corral and propose a truce he objected superficially—and left almost at once.

Wheeler found Corral gone from Rivas and the camp under command of General Pedro Xatruch, a compatriot of Guardiola. The Minister was held prisoner for two days and obtained his release only by threatening to bring down the wrath of the United States Navy on his captors. He then returned to Granada, having achieved nothing but an exchange of letters with Corral in which each promised the other the full punishment of Washington for his conduct.

Walker wanted peace. Although his army had been increased by more than one hundred men since his arrival in Granada, he felt that while he was busy waging war he would have no time for the reforms now uppermost in his thoughts. With Corral refusing to recognize his agents, however, he had no choice but to continue regarding the force at Rivas as a hostile one. Yet he was sure that Corral would be brought to terms without further warfare and so made no move.

Granada's Spanish construction, with streets radiating from a grand plaza, made it easily defensible against any force that might be sent against it. The one- and two-story houses, built mainly of adobe brick, were natural fortresses, their narrow, iron-barred windows excellent loopholes for riflemen. The original Legitimist barricades still blocked every street leading to the grand plaza and Walker manned them with pickets as a first line for any possible attack. The men were quartered throughout the city, no central barracks being available for them. The dwellings they occupied were similar in plan: a U or hollow square enclosing the inevitable patio, thick with orange, lemon, palm and a variety of other trees, with rooms opening on an outdoor corridor. Entire companies could have slept in some of the chambers, which measured a hundred by thirty feet. Food was prepared for each unit in the kitchen of the house it occupied. And although the filibusters could not have been the cleanest men alive, much emphasis is placed in publications of the time upon the vast amount of laundry beaten vigorously by native washerwomen on the shores of the lake.

The entire city presented a changed appearance after the arrival of the Americans. Competent riflemen patrolled the streets, sauntering under balconies on which sat the señoritas and their duennas, exchanging broken Spanish for soft Castilian. Walker called the introduction of Americans into the country a reform and there is evidence, to be fair, that some of the centuries-old indolence vanished in the presence of the active foreigners. As far as they were able, the *falanginos* pursued an American mode of life. They refused to sleep in the hammocks, swung between doors to catch the breezes, but instead rolled in their blankets on the floor. They transformed any number of *pulperias* into the tropical equivalent of a San Francisco barroom. And on one occasion, when a new group of recruits arrived, they held a torchlight parade, with a nondescript band playing "Yankee Doodle" and "Hail Columbia." The Nicaraguans watched the spectacle in astonishment, listened as the band played lustily before the Government House, where Walker was quartered, and heard the little chief declaim from the balcony:

"Fellow citizens and soldiers: This is perhaps the first time such music has been heard on the plaza at Granada. Let us hope it may be heard through future ages."

There is no question but that Walker was already imbued with the dictator's mania. He was overcome in his own mind with the magnitude of his opportunities, which he had not realized fully before. Later he was to abuse the enormous power thrown into his lap more by accident than by his own skill, but in the first weeks he decreed and obtained order. The Granadinos, whose city for years had been regularly attacked, captured, sacked and bloodied, were relieved and grateful at the manner in which the *Yanqui* waged war; the streets were well policed, the women unmolested; the merchants treated as fairly as an army offering only requisitions could treat them.

In some respects the Filibuster had genius. He demonstrated it here. Waiting for Corral to capitulate, he made certain that nothing but capitulation would seem right to the inhabitants of Granada.

XIV

THE stalemate might have continued for months but for the "destiny" in which Walker so thoroughly believed.

The agent who indirectly caused negotiations to be resumed was Parker H. French. Sent from San Juan to San Francisco for recruits, French had gathered up sixty men, persuaded the Transit Company's western office to furnish transport and sailed for Nicaragua. Walker's orders had specified that the men remain unorganized and be brought to wherever the Phalanx might be, but French was too ardent an individualist to follow instructions. He organized the new recruits into two companies as soon as they landed at San Juan, with Birkett D. Fry, a Mexican war veteran, as colonel, appointed other officers and conducted himself generally as second in command to Walker. The Californians were supplied with rifles and French obtained (by what means is not clear, but probably dishonestly) a brass six-pounder from the Pacific ship. With his force he marched irregularly over the Transit Road to the lake shore.

The lake steamer was waiting to transfer the Pacific passengers to the boat at the head of San Juan River, for the continuation of their journey to Greytown and New York. French took his soldiers aboard the ship—*La Virgen,* which had transported Walker's men—and ordered the captain to sail against Fort San Carlos, which dominated the entrance to the San Juan River. He criminally ignored the women, children and other non-combatants who were aboard the

SCENE IN THE BATTLE OF RIVAS

vessel, and went up against the fort as though he were paying it a social visit.

Where Lake Nicaragua emptied into the San Juan River, two hills reared themselves, forming a gigantic terrace. On the lower of these hills, nearest the lake, stood Fort San Carlos, built by the Spanish, armed with medieval weapons and, in the hands of a competent defender, all but impregnable. The second hill rose behind the fort.

La Virgen steamed across the lake to within half a mile of the stronghold. The captain of the boat and two men were sent ashore to demand the surrender of the fort in the name of William Walker's army. The commandant took the three messengers prisoners, and the cannon which had been making mouths at *La Virgen* from the wall embrasures suddenly emitted flame and solid shot. The range was too great and the boat was untouched. French and Fry then decided upon an infantry attack and started a company for the shore, but the combination of a sudden rain which wet the ammunition and the unavailability of any landing place other than those under San Carlos' guns caused this venture to be abandoned. Something of the fine courage they had shown when safe at San Juan here deserted French and Fry, and they ordered *La Virgen* to turn about and steam for Granada. The captain and his two men were left in Fort San Carlos' musty dungeon, to be released later by the efforts of the Transit company.

The new recruits were received in the capital with "loud *vivas* and a salute of democratic thunder—the bells of the city pealed out their joyous notes of welcome." The two leaders reported their arrival to Walker without mentioning to him the abortive movement against the fort. French was accepted into the army as of possible future value and Fry was commissioned a colonel because French had promised him such rank.

The Filibuster had withdrawn his garrison from Virgin Bay. The passengers who had been on *La Virgen* in its feint against the fort were quartered in the warehouse which had withstood Guardiola's charges in the battle six weeks before. Corral, at Rivas, learned of the attempt to attack San Carlos and sent troops to Virgin Bay to discipline the Americans. They fired into the Transit warehouse, killing three unarmed and innocent men. For hours the two hundred and fifty who had paid passage to New York and wanted nothing but the opportunity to travel there in peace were in danger of being annihilated. The Legitimists howled through the town like Comanches, plundered the house of the Accessory Transit and took the manager to Rivas as a prisoner, where his release was effected only after his company had paid a ransom of two thousand dollars.

Meanwhile, across the lake, the steamer from the Caribbean side which connected with *La Virgen* came up the San Juan River. As she approached Fort San Carlos, unaware that her sister on the lake had threatened that stronghold, a cannon boomed. A twenty-four-pound shot went through the boat's deck house. A California widow going home with her two children was killed instantly and her small son died after the cannon ball had carried away his two legs. Her daughter, also very young, was badly injured.

The dual attack on the Transit Company line became known as the massacre of Virgin Bay. The full blame for it can be laid to French, a man so insanely determined to be a leader that he used as a war vessel a boat loaded to the gunwales with innocents. Walker, apprised of the deaths when *La Virgen* came into Granada for protection, had one honest course open to him—the court-martial of French. If ever there was justification for a military execution, this incident furnished it. But the Filibuster remained blind. Perhaps he thought he could do no wrong and, because he had accepted French, he must support whatever crime the adventurer perpetrated. He rose to a livid fury (which means that his lips were thinner and his voice softer) at the tactics of Ponciano Corral. The retaliation he chose was unjust, cruel and dishonorable: without giving him the benefit of a trial, he ordered Mateo Mayorga, former Minister of Relations in the Legitimist party, executed in the grand plaza.

He explained this, first to Corral and later to posterity, as simple justice. Because the commander of a hostile force, isolated from his superiors by the structure of battle lines, had sanctioned a barbarous attack on non-combatants, Walker maintained with sorry logic that the civil government should be punished with the same barbarism. Much of the evil in this decision may be gathered from the few facts known of Mayorga—he was a quiet, cultured gentleman, who, when Granada was taken and his government fell about his ears, was among the first to seek out the Filibuster and surrender. He was paroled in the custody of Minister Wheeler, and did not, as did some of his colleagues, violate his word. He was utterly without blame in the massacre, for the deeds of Ponciano Corral no longer were the deeds of the Legitimist government. But he died, nevertheless, with the courage of an aristocrat, under the guns of a squad of Leonese soldiers who hooted at him as they fired.

From William Walker's first day in this country he had talked endlessly to those with whom he came in contact of the necessity for a new element in Nicaraguan society. The half-savage conduct of governmental affairs was the single great cancer he had come to remove. He was consistent, it is true, in preaching his doctrine even after the execution of Mayorga, maintaining that what he had done had been dictated to him by the laws of men. But already, with the foretastes of success, he was reverting to a philosophy which must have been a deep, sub-conscious conviction from his childhood. The wanton execution of an innocent man for the crimes of another was certainly neither a humane nor a logical act. Heretofore it has been seen that Walker made use of whatever came to his hand, but until he reached Granada there was excuse for his expedient methods: he was weak and to win he had to wield every weapon. As ruler of Granada, however, he was no longer weak. The capture of the city had been more than the addition to the Democratic territory of so many square miles of houses; it was a moral victory of incalculable worth. To the Legitimists, Granada was a symbol which in the Democrats' hands made their ultimate victory inevitable. Walker could have won without the execution of Mayorga; he could have won with honor and by bending over backwards to observe the rules. But he allowed the first evidences of a greed for power to show themselves; French was guilty, but to have punished French would have discredited Walker; Mayorga was innocent, but Mayorga's execution would drive unholy terror into the breasts of every other opponent. So Mayorga died, and the "Gray-Eyed Man of Destiny" attained his final stature.

He was gaining strength with every day. He had a staff of efficient officers greater than any he had commanded before: in addition to Hornsby, De Brissot, Anderson and Doubleday there were several newcomers. One was E. J. C. Kewen, brother of Achilles, who had died in the battle of Rivas. There was Captain Adolphus Sutter, son of the discoverer of California gold; DeWitt Clinton, descendant of the distinguished New Yorker; and Colonel A. F. Rudler, then an unknown but ever afterward to be at William Walker's right hand.

While the Filibuster presided at the councils of these aides, Corral, after the Virgin Bay massacre and before the execution of Mayorga, moved his force to Masaya. To reach this old Indian town he had to skirt Granada and travel ten miles or so above it. Martinez, leader of an army farther north, had fallen back to Managua, on the shores of the lake after which it was named, and waited there behind his parapets. Walker therefore had an enemy only to the north; the road to the south and the Transit route was open and free. What had happened, in the four months since the arrival of the Immortals, had been a reversal of position: Walker now held what the Legitimists had held, but in gaining it he had not given up the city of Leon, fifty miles north of Managua. It was Martinez's blunder, after having defeated the Democrats at Pueblo Nuevo, not to have pushed on to Leon, which was as poorly defended as Granada; had he done so and captured the Democratic capital, morale would have been weakened equally on both sides.

Walker received scattered and unreliable advices from travelers and spies. He did not wish to move from Granada, believing that Corral soon or late would be starved into making the first move. He was wrong about the starvation, but right—as far as the effect was concerned—about the execution of Mayorga. Corral, busily constructing barricades in the streets of Masaya and preparing to withstand a siege, was shaken when Walker's messenger entered his camp with the news of the Secretary's death. The messenger also told of the sixty other hostages and informed Corral that they would be shot without trial if the Legitimist army again misbehaved.

Ponciano Corral was an intelligent man—no general, but with enough knowledge of war to recognize defeat. He accepted Walker's warning for what it was, a promise to execute virtually the entire Legitimist party if he did not come to terms, and on the evening of October 22, 1855, dispatched a courier to say that he would arrive on the following morning to treat for peace.

The efforts of the Immortals, and the ones who had followed them, had found their first great reward.

XV

COLONEL FRY and a picked company escorted the Legitimist commander from Masaya to the outskirts of Granada, where Walker waited. It was a bright day, with the sky and the lake matching each other's blue, with the peons in the doorways of their huts watching the grand general as he passed. Walker, up since six and with a full day's paper work already behind him, met his opponent formally; the two saluted and rode wordless through the streets to the center of the city.

The entire grand plaza was ringed with armed men. Even though he believed Corral to be beaten, Walker was too shrewd to minimize his advantage and in addition to the force under Democratic arms— now about five hundred—he had put muskets into the hands of a large body of California passengers, waiting to be carried across the lake and on to Greytown. He watched Corral as they rode and he could see the commander's courage wane as he became aware of the strength opposed to him.

The negotiations took place in Government House. Corral was empowered by President Estrada, then in Segovia, to treat for the Legitimist government in all respects; Walker negotiated only as a commanding officer, his acts subject to the approval of officials at Leon.

In all respects, Walker's conduct at Granada had been that of the soldier-of-fortune. The gross immorality of the execution of Mayorga could not rob it of its effect as a weapon. His insistence that the city be not plundered had made him more acceptable as a conqueror to the Legitimist sympathizers. Now, in a conference for peace, he displayed even greater skill than had been shown in the capture of the city. He retired into the background and let Corral dictate his terms. With the cold detachment of a gambler he paid out all the rope he felt Corral would need.

The treaty suspended the war as of October twenty-second, named Patricio Rivas, Legitimist and one-time port collector of San Juan,

President of the Republic for fourteen months, or until an election should be called, decreed that the cabinet ministers should be taken from all four Departments of the Republic, decreed "general oblivion" for all past conflict and political fault, consolidated the debts of both factions into an obligation of the coalition government. Corral agreed to reduce his forces at Managua and Masaya, Walker to reduce his at Granada and Leon. The white ribbon of the Legitimists and the red of the Democrats were abolished and a blue device, bearing the words *Nicaragua Independiente,* was substituted.

Nearly all clauses were of Corral's authorship. Walker sat across from him, head inclined a little to one side in the pose he always assumed while listening, a barely audible "yes" his only occasional comment. But late in the conference he remarked softly that he would, of course, be appointed commander-in-chief of the armies. Corral, wily bargainer, was caught off guard. He had gone too far to oppose this demand; Walker had trapped him neatly by encouraging him to take the lead in the proposal of all terms. He tried to evade the point, but Walker was quietly insistent: the Democratic chief, surely, had the right to be remembered? General Corral, for the sake of peace, could do no better than appoint a man whose conduct throughout had been that of an efficient and honest servant?

So Corral agreed, having no other choice. He returned to Masaya, to tear down his barricades and move his army to Granada. Before he left the last prop of the Legitimist cause crumpled, when the garrisons at Fort San Carlos and Castillo Viejo abandoned their posts and left the San Juan River open to free commerce.

Walker, in four months and starting with fifty-eight men, had taken a nation. He held Granada; he had defeated the Legitimist forces; the future operation of the Transit route was something he could protect and if necessary control. McDonald, Garrison's agent, who was in Granada when the treaty was signed, immediately turned over to the Filibuster twenty thousand dollars in gold, exhibiting a power-of-attorney from Garrison which convinced Walker that the money could be lawfully "borrowed." The debt was secured by the revenues due Nicaragua from the Accessory Transit Company. Charles Morgan, New York associate of Garrison, honored the draft when it reached him.

Parker French, the irrepressible, had much to do with this loan. He continued to take a leading part in the affairs of the government and was in fact subsequently appointed Minister of Hacienda in the Rivas government—but the reason for this cannot be discovered. Walker crushed any officer who tried to project himself beyond his rank and why he neglected to eliminate the dangerous French is to this day a mystery. The twenty thousand dollars cannot be the answer, for Walker himself did not care about the money he could get and McDonald would have bargained with or without the presence of French. But French stayed, the first of a series of small errors.

It was decided that the troops of the Legitimists should march into Granada on October twenty-ninth. The entire filibuster army was busy throughout that morning. Streets were patrolled, houses searched again for stands of arms or other harbingers of treachery. The men were drilled and instructed in their manners. When, at eleven o'clock, the Legitimists began to march in, Corral riding at their head, the Phalanx and its native auxiliary were drawn up in battle array on the plaza. One shot was needed that day to create an appalling slaughter, but neither the tense Americans nor the careless natives fired it. The beaten army shuffled through the streets and only its head, where rode the General, was given cheers. Walker and Corral met near the entrance of the Cathedral Cabildo, riding toward each other across the plaza. One was in his dusty black coat and flannel shirt, the other brave in braid; one rode a sorry black nag and the other a prancing white beauty. They saluted, dismounted and embraced each other. The plaza rang with sound, diffident *vivas* from the natives and wild whoops from the Americans. Then, attended by their two staffs, the commanders walked arm in arm into the Cathedral, where Padre Vijil awaited them.

There was a brief religious ceremony, a choir sang a *Te Deum,* and Corral and Walker emerged from the church. The Legitimist troops were broken up into companies and marched to the quarters assigned to them—quarters cunningly scattered among the houses occupied by the Democrats.

Don Patricio Rivas, the new President, reached Granada the next day. He was as helpless as Castellon had been, a petty politician similar to the occasional misfit a sovereign American state will elect to be its governor. To the natives he was known as *Patas Arribas* which, when spoken as Spanish, has a sound kindred to his name and which, freely translated, means "topsy-turvy." Corral had suggested this man as President, and Corral saw to it from the moment of his arrival that whatever he did would be dictated by the best Legitimist minds.

The inauguration took place in the Cathedral. The church was dark except for devotional candles and the lights on a small table placed immediately before the altar railing. A crucifix and a Book were at one end of the table and the state documents at the other. Padre Vijil stood behind it, facing the party walking slowly up the main aisle, which included Walker, Corral, Rivas and the minor officials of both parties. The President's oath was administered with all the richness of voice Padre Vijil could command. Walker, standing in the background, presented himself as only the agency which had caused the ceremony, until Corral, at his side, nudged him. No agreement had been made that the two commanders would take an oath, and it may be that Corral acted merely under the inspiration of the Cathedral's solemnity; it is more likely, though, that he hoped to force Walker, the non-Catholic, into a refusal which could be used later as a talking point against the Filibuster. But Walker did not hesitate; he swore, kneeling in the spot a moment before occupied by old Topsy-Turvy, to obey and uphold the treaty of peace. Corral did likewise.

When they left the Cathedral, Walker went alone to his quarters. The new President and General Corral left together. Walker's suspicions did not leave him after the taking of the oath and the apparent laying down of arms. For days he watched as Rivas and the defeated General walked together, and spies repeated to him some of the remarks of Corral, the most significant of which was the cryptic sentence spoken to Niña Yrena as he walked past her gateway: "We have beaten them with their own cock."

On October thirtieth, one week after the capitulation, the government commissioned General William Walker as commander-in-chief of the armies. For the second time Corral insisted upon an oath and for the second time the conqueror—who then belonged to no church—took it without hesitating.

Until the very last day of the month, Walker was without support from the Democratic leaders. He had his own officers and a few auxiliaries, such as Carlos Thomas, but he needed sorely the presence of the politicos from Leon. General Jerez arrived, however, on the thirty-first, and the matter of a cabinet was discussed with President Rivas. Walker's few backers in Granada itself had come to him to report the dominant part Corral was taking in all government actions and to urge upon him the necessity of packing the cabinet with as many Democrats as possible. On the minor offices, Corral did not protest too loudly, but when the name of Jerez was mentioned as a possible Minister of Relations he objected violently. There was too wide a gulf between the requirements of the office and its candidate, he said; Jerez held to principles disorganizing to and destructive of society. Walker left the subject of Jerez and the Ministry of Relations, and proposed Parker H. French as Minister of Hacienda; and for some reason Corral accepted this nomination without argument. Fermin Ferrer, a Democrat, was appointed to the Ministry of Public Credit, Corral to the Ministry of War and the opponents returned to the name of Jerez.

All of Walker's Scottish blood came out when he wanted something. He was quiet and tenacious; he would leave his subject for a time, but always return to it. Thus it was in the disagreement over Jerez. He argued and insisted, finally falling into a monotonous reiteration of the necessity of having Jerez among the cabinet officials, and at last he won his point. He had proved himself Corral's master in the unethical phases of the conduct of war, he had evaded the sly pitfalls of the oath, he had out-maneuvered the General for the command of the army, and now he proved himself to be a better politician. Had he accepted the surrender of Corral and taken no further part in the negotiations, it is doubtful if any more trouble with the Legitimists would have come his way immediately. Such behavior, in view of the position he now held, was unacceptable. He was the law; he was the dictator; what strings there were he must pull. Patricio Rivas was President, by edict of two commanders of armies, but he was a poor and uneasy puppet. Corral was a defeated General and nominally the power behind President Rivas; but when the government had been formed, Walker saw to it that the army of the

Legitimists was disbanded and its members scattered to their huts.
Walker had found type and an old press in Granada, and he gave
himself a voice—*El Nicaraguense,* a newspaper published half in
Spanish and half in English, of which many copies were sent to the
United States to tell of the beauty and future of Nicaragua, and of the
joy with which the population regarded William Walker, the "regenerator." John Tabor, one of the Immortals who had been a printer,
was editor of this newspaper. He printed what Walker wrote for
him, or what Walker suggested, and when fighting threatened he
abandoned his stick for a rifle.

On November first, Walker found it necessary to execute still another man, one of his own. Patrick Jordan, an Irish-American from
the New York slums, shot up a street while he was drunk, slightly
wounding two *falanginos* and killing a native. Walker heard the
evidence of the case, ordered a court-martial and told its members
to make an example of the man. Jordan was ordered to be shot
and all the pleas that were made for him—from the native's mother,
from Padre Vijil, from comrades in the Phalanx—had no effect what-
soever upon the Filibuster. For a matter of two days his heartless-
ness toward one of his own men reacted to his disadvantage even
among the Nicaraguans. But then the wheel turned for him, as it
almost always did, and Jordan's death became the peg upon which
to hang a more momentous condemnation.

The next to die was Corral. Smarting from his defeat, hating
William Walker and all his works with the dangerous, smouldering
passion of his race, he wrote—on the day Jordan was arrested—letters
which were to make him a corpse within a week.

XVI

WALKER was asleep in the inner chamber of Government House
when footsteps in the courtyard awakened him. He was as rigidly
puritanical in his sleeping as in his other habits; he had contempt
for the man who drowses on awakening and needs coffee and time
to recapture his faculties. When Vallé came in the door, hissing to
awaken him, he was already sitting on the side of his bed, alert and
waiting.

Vallé made a ludicrous figure. His guitar hung from one shoulder, his rifle from the other. He was breathless with his haste and smelled of the sweat he had larruped out of the body of his horse. Walker had to caution him about the noise he made, because he was swearing in a frenzied anger and in the smatterings of three languages.

The Filibuster lighted a candle. Vallé handed him a little packet, taken from a courier more friendly to Democrats than to his employers.

Walker read. Impassively he finished the last of the letters, and looked up. His gray eyes were bright in the flickering light. In that quiet voice he ordered the guard tripled and no one to enter or leave the city until morning.

He shaved and dressed in his immaculate fashion. He sent for Hornsby and ordered the entire government assembled in Government House at once, to hear the letters in the packet. When they came, he walked into the room, contained and sinister, a tiny figure even among the small Nicaraguans. He announced without preamble that they were gathered to consider charges of high treason against General Ponciano Corral and before their gasps could leave their throats he began to read. The first letter was to Santos Guardiola at Tegucigalpa:

> My Esteemed Friend: It is necessary that you write to friends to advise them of the danger we are in, and that they work actively. If they delay two months there will not then be time. Think of us and of your offers. I salute your lady; and commend your friend, who truly esteems you and kisses your hand.
>
> P. Corral.
>
> Nicaragua is lost; lost Honduras, San Salvador and Guatemala if they let this get body. Let them come quickly, if they would meet auxiliaries.

The second was to Don Pedro Xatruch, also at Tegucigalpa:

> Friend Don Pedro: We are badly off. Remember your friends. They have left me what I have on, and I hope for your aid.
>
> Your friend,
>
> P. Corral.

The third also was addressed to Guardiola:

My dear Sir and Friend: I enclose to you letters from the General, who does not write much on account of insecurity; but you already understand all he wants to tell you and it is enough if you consider the sufferings of a man who had been forced to the sacrifice to do what he has done, and to whom they already deny what was offered him. We all expect a fatality, and always with hopes which at the end always turn out illusory. We all confide in you, and only in you, to redeem this beautiful section of Central America. We hope that you and the real friends of Honduras will not be indifferent to our disgrace. Thousand probabilities, many elements, a good deal of disposition, and much repining!

If things here go on badly and cannot be remedied, I will with pleasure once more become a Hondureño.

I felicitate you and participate in your pleasure in returning again to your beloved country. Always remain there and may tyranny never again take root in that soil to be there forever buried.

I salute Lady Anita and you. With all frankness, command your friend, etc.

Tomas Martinez.

They sat stunned and silent when he had finished reading. Only Corral, his olive skin a little pale, seemed calm in the immensity of the moment. He said nothing for a time, but when the eyes turned toward him and he stood alone, believing himself a patriot, he spoke. He told those gathered to listen to the proofs of his treachery that he would do it again for Nicaragua. What he said has not been preserved in his words, but it could not have but followed the classic form: "I only regret that I have but one life to give for my country."

When the shock had worn off, there was a resurgence of the old Legitimist-Democratic party division. The supporters of Corral were appalled at what he had done and what its cost to them must be; the Democrats did not even try to hide their exultation. Jerez, poor Jerez, beaten at Granada, opposed by Corral first on the battleground and then in the council chamber, demanded that Martinez immediately be replaced at Managua with a trustworthy officer of the true feeling and punished with his commander. Neither Martinez nor Xatruch, however, was captured.

Corral spoke only once more before the meeting adjourned. He asked that his court-martial consist of Americans. He hated them and he had opposed them with his life as stake in a fool's gamble;

but he respected them. He saw in the faces of the Leonese nothing but hatred for him and glee over his forthcoming execution; but the Americans emulated their commander and were detached, as prosecutors should be.

He had expected it, he had looked for it with every move Corral made, but when the actual plot was revealed, Walker was shaken. He remembered a number of things: the Legitimists' insistence that Xatruch and Martinez be retained in command of the Masaya and the Managua garrisons, the oaths which had meant nothing to the one who proposed them, the completeness with which Corral had prepared his plot.

And Rivas, even more than Walker, was frightened. He had not been privy to Corral's plans, but he had known that Walker was not accepted as a permanent figure in Nicaragua. Rivas was placed under guard, along with the rest of the Legitimists, and waited trembling for a squad to come for him. His fear of being suspected made him a most willing instrument for whatever Walker required and when the court-martial was named—Colonel Hornsby, president; Colonel Fry, judge advocate; Parker French, counsel for the prisoner—he approved it with pitiful eagerness.

Corral was tried on November 6, 1855. He offered no more defence than he had offered at the time of his exposure, asking mercy only in the name of his daughters.

". . . forasmuch as he had invited General Guardiola and Xatruch to come and with armed violence disturb the peace of Nicaragua, and for conspiring with the enemies of the State to overthrow the government of Nicaragua; and forasmuch as he had held treasonable correspondence with Generals Guardiola and Xatruch . . ." he was condemned to death by the fusillade but commended to the mercy of the commander-in-chief.

The general-in-chief, however, considered that in this case mercy to one would be injustice to many. Walker had solemnly sworn, with bended knee and on the Holy Evangelists, to observe and have observed the treaty of the twenty-third of October; and he was responsible before the world, and especially to the Americans in Nicaragua—as well as before the throne of Heaven—for the faithful observations of his oath. How could the treaty continue to have the force of law if the first violation of it—and that, too, by the very man who had signed it—was permitted to pass unpunished? As an act of right and justice, none could reasonably impugn the sentence of the court, and Walker considered the question of policy as clear and unequivocal as the question of justice. Not only did duty to the Americans in Nicaragua demand the execution of the sentence, but it was politic and humane to make their enemies feel that there was a power in the State capable and resolved to punish any offenses against their interests. Mercy to Corral would have been an invitation to all the Legitimists to engage in like conspiracies, and would have involved them in further difficulties, which many of them managed to escape. It was after such reflections as these that Walker determined to approve the sentence of the court and Corral was, accordingly, ordered to be shot at mid-day on the eighth of November.*

All Granada, it seemed, was opposed to the execution. Again Padre Vijil, the firmest friend the Filibuster had in all the country, came to plead for the life of a condemned man. The city took on an air of mourning, waiting for a hero to die and dreading the instant. Corral had proved himself, in his dealings with the people, kinder and more understanding than many of his colleagues in the Legitimist party. He was devoted to his principles and in his way as good a leader as so backward a society could produce. His friends remembered now his good deeds; they descended upon Walker's headquarters in parties to plead for the mercy of the commander. But he refused mercy; even when the daughters of Corral, who would be impoverished by his death both emotionally and financially, came to him he "closed the painful interview as soon as kind feeling permitted." To the suppliants, he in all likelihood said what he later wrote: "He who looks only at present grief, nor sees in the distance the thousand-fold sorrow a misplaced mercy can create, is little suited for the duties of public office."

(Smug little man! Outlaw, egotist, executioner, plotter. Filled with the conviction of his own infallibility, sufficient master of the pen to make it almost plausible even to investigators into his thoughts and deeds three-quarters of a century afterward. Doing wrong, prating right. Ordering death like a god.)

The execution was set for noon in the grand plaza of Granada.

* *The War in Nicaragua.*

At nine o'clock they began gathering, the market people, peons from the surrounding farms, merchants, men of the professions. They formed along three sides of the square, close-packed. Up from them came a soft murmur, almost a sighing. Within the square, at intervals, stood the *falanginos,* booted and felt-hatted, armed with rifles and revolvers and bowie knives, chewing tobacco and discussing profanely the execution and the beauty of its day.

Noon came and no tramp of firing squad could be heard. The crowd whispered, "He has been saved! The Little One has given him back his life."

One o'clock. Rumors, any number of rumors. Corral had confessed to a fuller plot and implicated others, who were to be tried with him appearing as chief witness against them. Corral had escaped and was fleeing into exile. Corral had been given two more hours of life, to weep over his daughters and to feel their tears warm upon his cheeks.

The last rumor proved truth. At three minutes to two the bootheels could be heard coming from Government House. Fierce, bearded Gilman, stumping along on his peg, led his hollow square of twelve men. Inside the square walked the pale, self-possessed figure who was to be, in three minutes, a martyr. The crowd broke before the hollow square and it marched into the shadows cast by the Cabildo.

They shot him in the Latin-American fashion, kneeling, with his back to the guns. The ragged roar seemed to echo forever, and thousands of backs in the crowd winced with the impact of the slugs. General Ponciano Corral fell forward, his hands outstretched and clutching futilely at his country's earth; and the instruments of justice turned and clumped back through the lane they had made in the crowd.

Dozens of the spectators ran to where Corral lay, ignoring the men of the Phalanx for all their guns. They dipped white handkerchiefs in the bright blood and clipped locks of the General's hair. They went away, slowly, and with looks cast back, wondering what had been gained by bringing the callous little *Yanqui* to rule their country.

But the opposition to the execution altered not at all the steady march of William Walker. He had disposed of a great enemy and he could see no more—surely he could not see the thousands of doubters he had created, for if he had his justice might possibly have been compromised. His success now began to corrupt him, his strength to swell his ego, his ego to demand expression.

Although in the main his men continued to support him, Captain C. W. Doubleday, the English veteran who knew more of the Spanish American mind than Walker was ever to learn, at last rebelled against the Filibuster's tactics. Doubleday, thirty years later, wrote a book* in which Walker was given, for the first time, realistic treatment. The author described how he had been taken into the confidence of Walker and of their long walks together on the beach that lay below the series of terraces leading from the lakeside to Granada, and added:

I was at this time the recipient of much confidence from the man whose "strange, eventful history" came near marking an epoch in American history.

Whether the confidence implies honor, or the reverse, will be interpreted accordingly as men view political convulsions, which are rarely all wrong on one side and all right on the other, the usual partisan manner of describing them.

We took long walks on the beach, the rhythmic wavebeats seeming to emphasize the gigantic plans of empire he unfolded.

In his plan, the present popular movement was to obtain a temporary success in order to demonstrate to the hierarchical oligarchy their necessity for his aid, by which he would in the end wield the temporal power over Central America and Mexico in unison with the policy and influence of the Mother Church. Then faction and Church combined would conquer a unity of power over the Central American States, with himself, of course, as the central figure.

Once united, the old boundary question—were any necessary—would furnish pretexts for adding Mexico to the Central American Empire. The United States, under the domination of Southern ideas, which were supposed to be favorable to the measure, could be relied on to vindicate the "Monroe doctrine" in saying "hands off" to any possible European interference with his scheme.

For the rest the plan was simple. Conquest was the end, and by the simple method which is epitomized in the saying, "Nothing succeeds like success." This was to be the talisman to draw to his standard not only the bold spirits ever ready to follow without asking questions, but also the more timid who courted safety by an adhesion to power in any shape.

* Reminiscences of The "Filibuster" War in Nicaragua.

The impediments of constitutional law were, of course, considered as mere cobwebs to be brushed aside by the power which, like Louis the Fourteenth, could declare, "I am the State."

Such was the policy outlined by this bold and capable, but not sagacious man; not sagacious, inasmuch as he took no account of a factor in modern politics all powerful now, however insignificant it may have been anterior to the first French revolution—that of popular ideas.

As his scheme included the re-establishment of slavery in a population the majority of whom were of mixed African blood, and an affiliation of power with the Church in a time when freedom of thought had made progress, it came at too late a day in the world's history.

I listened to this conspiracy against the popular liberty, for which I had entertained a romantic attachment, and my heart was sad. He was ambitious of power, while I was merely philosophic.

" 'Tis in ourselves that we are thus, or thus."

I was young, which is my excuse for venturing to remonstrate against the course that such a man had determined upon. As well have bid Niagara to stay its torrents. He was offended—he could now afford to be, for there were plenty of able men willing to do his bidding. I tendered my resignation, well knowing that, as victory was assured, I could be spared. If the flattering offers he made me of advancement, and the regrets of friends I had made in the army, could have solaced me for the destruction of my idols, I might have been satisfied. Mere power, however, had no attraction for me. I yielded so far as to accept indefinite leave of absence instead of resigning.

XVII

AND now the little doctor-lawyer-editor was as mighty a soldier as he had hungered to be. Too frail to fight the smallest of his filibusters, he was yet the biggest and strongest man in Central America. Also, he was the blindest.

The dictator requires more than daring and luck to gather to himself the sort of dominion he wants. Walker had much of the ruthlessness of any other dictator, but he was cursed with two fatal weaknesses: he was stubborn and he was impatient. His stubbornness was in large part due to the conceit that he could recognize and proclaim justice, for with this philosophy he would accept no compromise with those he considered wrongdoers. And the dictator has not yet lived who has been able to remain utterly true to his principles; somewhere along his road there is an opportunity to betray himself for gain and he seizes it. Likewise, the successful dictator is not impatient; one may say he lacks patience, but the lack always falls short of an active characteristic, and if need be he will wait for his ends. Walker could not. He decided; he decreed. He wanted; he took. He tried; he failed.

To himself, when Corral had gone, he was the center of a stage limited by the borders of Central America. Possibly later he would go against Mexico, but for the moment he concentrated on the subjugation of Nicaragua and the plans of a military government for the five republics on the Isthmus.

Why he did not see to the outer limits of the arena one cannot say. He was no dolt; he was a product of a rapacious civilization and he should have known that rapacity was not by any means a prerogative reserved only for the United States and its agents. With a handful of men, virtually no backing and opposed by plotters a hundred times more treacherous than he could ever learn to be, he had become the ruler, in effect, of a sovereign country. He made full but unwise use of this power. Having beaten his way to his present pinnacle, he thought to crush all opposition, reckoning without the significant forces: the British Empire, the confused politics of the United States, the filibusters who waged their wars with check-books instead of fifty-eight Immortals.

One can see the situation from a distance and almost pity Walker that he looked upon it obliquely. Had he stood off and considered the picture as a whole, he might have stepped back into character and continued to play the hero. As it was, he became the villain of the piece.

Great Britain had rather more than a passing interest in Spanish America. At odd times she had taken over colonies on the Isthmus, and because of the Monroe Doctrine or other opposition had given up what she had seized. But she had not by any means abandoned hope that the Union Jack would fly in those countries. Her commanders cruised their warships along both coasts, prepared at any time to occupy whatever territory London ordered them to occupy. Her Foreign Office was privy to every political and financial secret of the five Central American Republics. Reports were received from consuls and also from such former servants as Manning, who told how Walker had taken his lead and defied his flag. There was a nice deliberation about Britain's policy toward Walker and his prize; but he should have sensed even the unobtrusive opposition being formed to thwart him.

A second actor on this stage was the United States, a blundering low comedian in baggy pants. After the capture of Granada the American public, almost to a man, believed in Walker and what he was doing. But it was 1855, there was a presidential election coming in another year and the Filibuster was too potent a force for either party to adopt him. Bleeding Kansas had not yet become a Free State and the Border Ruffians and John Brown fought the issue of slavery on its soil, with Sharp's rifles and Bibles. It was understood and freely circulated that William Walker had the support of the Southern States and that as soon as he absorbed enough of the Middle American territories they would be annexed to support slavery. The wavering policy of President Pierce and his inept Secretary of State, Marcy, was dictated by a factor no more controllable then than now—the vote. They wanted to support Walker for the sake of the South, they wanted to denounce him for the sake of the North. If they drove him out of Central America they committed a wrong and a treachery—the wrong against Nicaragua, which had hired him, and the treachery against their own people, who would feel that fear of England had dictated the move. Despite this venality, there remained a hint that although he now played the clown Uncle Sam might at any moment step out of character and read in the ringing voice of the hero the curtain line.

Next, and most important, was the figure in the background, an uncouth boatman, tobacco-chewing, ungrammatical, profane and the founder of a dynasty—Cornelius Vanderbilt. He had conceived and built the Accessory Transit Company. They were his ships that carried passengers to California at lower rates and by a route five hundred miles shorter than Panama's, thereby saving two days. He had actively controlled his company in 1853, when he went to Europe and convinced our British and French cousins that the Yankee was a vulgarian. But while he was gone, his two associates—Charles Morgan in New York and C. K. Garrison in San Francisco—put into practice what they learned from the master. They manipulated the stock of the Transit Company, made large profits for themselves and caused equally large losses to Vanderbilt. When Vanderbilt returned from Europe he is supposed to have written a letter to Morgan, accusing him of double-dealing and saying with characteristic forthrightness: "I won't sue you, for the law is too slow. I'll ruin you." Finally, as a sort of afterthought of the gods in the preparation of this confused comedy, there was the Kingdom of Mosquitia.

The west coast of Nicaragua is a pleasant country of plateaus and volcanic mountain ranges, well watered and productive. The east coast is the reverse and fits more nearly into the average conception of the tropics. Along the Caribbean, for more than two hundred miles from Cape Gracias á Dios on the Honduran border to Greytown, it is a low-lying land of swamp and jungle, inlet and cove. The inhabitants of Walker's time were little better than the country they occupied; some were full-blooded Mosquito Indians, others Indian-Negroes, called Samboes, others Spanish-Negroes. They were a depraved and shiftless people, infinitely more indolent than the epitome of laziness which occupied the western coast. Their dwellings were huts made of slanting poles upon which thatch was piled, constructable in a few minutes and in many instances so close to the water that canoes could be dragged up into the doorways. They lived in these open-sided hovels, insensitive to the screaming of the inevitable macaws and parrots roosting on the roofs. No more need be said of their worth and possibilities than this: In the seventeenth century missionaries visited the coast and abandoned it after a single survey.

At first only the Indians were there. Then the buccaneers found that the innumerable coves and inlets gave them shelter when men-o'-war pursued them, and a few of these brigands went ashore and reared families with whatever women came to hand. A slave ship was wrecked on the coast and its Africans saved themselves, to become free and the ancestors of the Samboes. Until late in the seventeenth century Esquemeling, the lieutenant of Morgan, and other pirates frequented the coast and, when it had served its purpose for them, they suggested to the Governor of Jamaica that he seize it for the Crown.

In 1687 the Governor sent a ship from Jamaica to bring from Mosquitia a chief selected at random. He dressed this chief in European garments and held an obscene coronation ceremony, in the midst of which the newly-discovered "King of the Mosquitoes" tore off his foreign clothes and climbed a tree. There, jabbering like an ape, he remained until the Governor lured him down with rum. He was given a cocked hat and a document assuring him that he was the King and specifying cannily that his domains were under the protection of Great Britain.

In 1740, the first King having died and no other having been appointed, England again worked in the country, treating with the various tribal chiefs for their suzerainty. Spain opposed the gesture, but it was not until nearly fifty years later that England again retired from Central America, to await a more favorable moment.

With the overthrow of Spanish dominion on the Isthmus, the Lion was back again. Another chief was selected and taken to Belize. He was given a cheap crown, a sword and a "sceptre of moderate value." His name was Robert Charles Frederick and from Henry Dunn, who wrote a book called *Guatimala, or the United Provinces of Central America,* in 1828, we have an eye-witness account of his coronation.

There was a procession to the Church at Belize, [now British Honduras] where Robert was to be crowned. He bobbed about on an unaccustomed horse, wearing the uniform of a British major; his subordinate chiefs had been dressed in the pantaloons of British seamen and wore cast-off scarlet uniform coats. His Majesty arrived at the church and:

> [He] was placed in a chair, near the altar, and the English coronation service was read by the chaplain of the colony who, on this occasion, performed the part of the Archbishop of Canterbury. When he arrived at this part: "And all the people said, let the King live forever, long live the King, God save the King!" the vessels of the port, according to a previous signal, fired a salute and the chiefs, rising, cried out, "Long Live King Robert!"
>
> His Majesty seemed chiefly occupied in admiring his finery, and after his anointing expressed his gratification by repeatedly thrusting his hands through his bushy hair and applying his finger to his nose, in this expressive manner indicating his delight at this part of the service.
>
> Before, however, his chiefs could swear allegiance to their monarch,

it was necessary that they profess Christianity, and accordingly, with shame be it recorded, they were baptized in "the name of the Father, Son and Holy Ghost." They displayed total ignorance of the meaning of this ceremony, and when asked to give their names took the titles of Lord Rodney, Lord Nelson, or some other celebrated officer, and seemed grievously disappointed when told that they could only be baptized by simple Christian names.

After this solemn mockery was concluded, the whole assembly adjourned to a large schoolroom to eat the coronation dinner, where these poor creatures got all intoxicated with rum; a suitable conclusion to a farce as blasphemous and wicked as ever disgraced a Christian country.

To "get all intoxicated with rum" was by no means a novelty to King Robert. He was a village drunkard of the finest stamp. For all the years of his reign he kept himself nicely plastered, and he found, as time went on, that to be a King helped him achieve this condition. Strangers came to him and offered vast quantities of rum for his mark on pieces of paper. He took the rum and signed away thousands of acres of his domain, to traders and other civilized opportunists. Some of his regal grants applied to lands in Honduras and once he gave away half of Costa Rica, but the traders did not seem to mind and it is a certainty that King Robert did not. The one important grant of his reign was that made to Samuel and Peter Shepherd, of the Island of Jamaica; in return for no one knows how much rum, the Shepherds received a document assigning to them twenty-two million, five hundred thousand acres of the Mosquito Coast.

King Robert died and George William Clarence, his son, succeeded. The British government, meanwhile, learned of the grants and appointed a regent who nullified them on the ground of King Robert's perpetual drunkenness.

The Kings of Mosquitia continued to rule until they no longer had value. Then England calmly appropriated the Mosquito Coast, on the grounds that it was hers as a protectorate. The chaotic condition of Central American politics made this simple enough: Nicaragua protested but weakly, and Englishmen ruled her eastern coast.

The nightmare kingdom leads inevitably to William Walker. During the Mexican War, Britain foresaw the addition of California to the United States and used her foothold in Central America to keep her power on the Pacific intact. In 1848, the port of Greytown was seized as lying within the limits of the Mosquito Kingdom. Ultimately, England believed, the San Juan River would be the first waterway between the oceans and by occupying the Eastern seaport she thought to control the key to Atlantic and Pacific commerce.

The history of Greytown was one of endless discord. In 1850 the Clayton-Bulwer Treaty was signed, binding the United States and Great Britain to a co-operative program on any canal between the oceans. Before the ink was dry on this document, Sir Henry Lytton Bulwer, Ambassador to the United States, informed Secretary of State John M. Clayton that the conditions did not apply to the present British holdings in Central America and, with poor diplomatic skill, Clayton accepted this interpretation. Greytown, therefore, remained in the hands of the British. Not until a year before William Walker's arrival was there a serious disorder; in 1854 a dispute of long standing between the native port officials (who were Britain's creatures) and the Accessory Transit Company caused a riot in which Solon Borland, United States Minister to Nicaragua, was injured. A month later the U. S. S. *Cyane* appeared in the harbor, demanded an apology and prepared to bombard the town when it was not forthcoming. The commander of H. M. S. *Bermuda* protested, but only by note because the force under his command was "so totally inadequate against the *Cyane.*" Commander George H. Hollins replied that he regretted the "force under your command is not doubly equal to that of the *Cyane,*" leveled his guns and from 9 A.M. to 4 P.M. on June 13, 1854, used up his government's powder and shot to level fifty or so miserable huts and to make homeless three hundred ignorant natives. When he had finished, Greytown was in ashes and British prestige there, upon which the natives had depended, appeared to be gone.

William Walker, strutting in Granada and being distantly dignified to his men, either knew nothing of all this history or he did not file his knowledge in an appropriate place. Contrary to his own beliefs, the reform of Nicaragua was not an occupation in which he could engage without regard for outside forces. History shows that what Great Britain gets she holds; in this case, while she had nominally retired from the Nicaraguan coast, there was no indication that she would not return as soon as a fresh opportunity for solidifying herself should appear.

XVIII

WALKER went ahead with full belief in his destiny. He had an army to give teeth to his decrees and a newspaper to explain them plausibly to the only country whose opinion of his acts he valued—the United States. The government he had created was recognized, forty-eight hours after the execution of Corral, by Minister Wheeler—prematurely, to be sure, but for the moment officially. While it did not exactly pour in, money was to be had; after McDonald had turned over the Transit Company's twenty thousand dollars, Parker French appeared with nearly a thousand ounces of silver bullion. From six o'clock in the morning until midnight the Filibuster was busy at the tasks that pleased him most: assembling and checking supplies, inspecting troops, requiring President Rivas to sign such orders as needed the sponsorship of a civil authority. None of his power changed him outwardly, whatever might have been done to his mind and soul. He remained quiet, soft-spoken, level-eyed. No boasts passed his lips; he lent the impression of extreme modesty. Never once did he smile, never once did his voice rise above the gentlest tone. Travelers on the Transit line came to Granada for a look at the Filibuster, expecting to find a roaring, magnificent soldier-of-fortune, and when they had seen him they went away doubting that the stories of his prowess could be in any degree true.

But the dreams that had driven Doubleday away from this country went on inside his queer mind. One of the first documents he gave President Rivas to sign was an appeal to the four other Republics of the Isthmus for a peaceful communion. They were urged to lay down arms so that all Central America might live in harmony. His hypocrisy in this appeal is so audacious as to be almost an achievement; while his couriers carried his message to four capitals, he was devising in his tidy little office the plans for bringing recruits into the country, and writing, for Editor John Tabor to print in *El Nicaraguense,* such glowing descriptions of the country that footloose Americans (who could handle rifles) could not but come to him.

His gestures toward the other republics appeared transparent even to them; San Salvador alone replied, merely because the Democratic party at that time happened to control San Salvador. Honduras (where Trinidad Cabañas had been overthrown), Guatemala and Costa Rica were all Legitimist and would have none of the Walker-Rivas combination.

Bishop José Hilario Herdocia, Vicar-General of the See of Nicaragua, only a few days after the capture of Granada, had written from Leon to congratulate Walker—not for his seizure of a city, but for the worth of his aims. In November, French went to the Bishop without Walker's knowledge and obtained the silver bullion—supposedly stripped from the frontal of the great Altar of Mercy and from the Hall of the Virgin of Mercy in the vicar's own church. Walker, although professing not to approve of French's avarice, took the silver. It was not until much later that he disposed of this dangerous criminal, by an action that might have been, had a humorous man made it, the most delicious irony: the day came when Parker was sent to the United States as Nicaragua's diplomatic representative to Washington.

There was no immediate need for such an envoy, however. For while Minister John Wheeler was delivering in the name of the United States a profound congratulation on Nicaragua's emergence from darkness, and President Rivas was as bombastically responding, a State Department dispatch was on its way nullifying such exchanges. Fearful of England, fearful of the effect of recognition on the vote of the North, Secretary Marcy ordered Wheeler to take no cognizance of any authority until it could be ascertained beyond doubt that it was the *de facto* government of the country. Wheeler's report and Marcy's instruction crossed; the recognition later was withdrawn and the Minister reprimanded.

As the days passed, and the conviction of his selection as an agent of fate grew upon him, Walker became more and more contemptuous of the help that might be given him by outsiders. From his own writings it is clear he believed at this time that the battle was won and already looked forward to an irresistible expansion beyond the borders of Nicaragua. Like all intolerants who by the weaving of circumstance find themselves on a crest, he damned and cast out all who opposed him, rebuked and dismissed supplicants who required his aid—and who, in return, might have aided him.

One such supplicant started emissaries for Granada on November ninth, a few days after Corral had been shot. His name was Henry L. Kinney, a Texan who had been a broker of one sort or another in the United States nearly all his life. (Walker called him "the Mule Trader.") At about the same time that the Immortals were forming in San Francisco, Kinney was preparing to sail for the Mosquito Coast with a shipload of colonists. He had purchased from the Shepherds their grant to twenty-two million, five hundred thousand acres and formed a million-dollar corporation called the Central American Company to take over the lands. Kinney has been called a filibuster of the same stamp as Walker, but the statement is open to argument; he seems to have been less deluded and a better business man.

The United States harassed him unmercifully. His ships were held up, he was indicted for violation of the neutrality laws, legal bear-traps caught him every time he stepped. It was only at the prodding of desperation that he sailed at all, with thirteen followers, aboard a small schooner called the *Emma*. Kinney and others claimed later that their enterprise was indorsed by President Pierce, Attorney General Caleb Cushing and Sidney Webster, private secretary to the President; it is known that Kinney and Pierce were friends, but what caused the government to withdraw any support it may have given the Central American Company is not known. In any case, Kinney arrived in Greytown, on September 6, 1855, after many hardships, including the wreck of his schooner.

His destination was found to be a cheerless place. It was described, after the Hollins bombardment, by Laurence Oliphant, the English journalist, in these words: "How extended soever the traveler's experience of dreary localities, Greytown must ever take a prominent place among his most doleful and gloomy reminiscences."* Its people were shabby in flesh and spirit. They were kept alive by plantains, the banana-like staple, and liquor; they ate, lounged in the sun and did no toil. Although not so warm as the western slope of Nicaragua, the town seemed unendurably hot because of the humid-

---

* *Patriots and Filibusters.*

ity rising from the nearby swamps and the utter absence of breeze. In the mornings the dew saturated the flimsy walls of the huts and depressed the early awakened. There were two lodging places, a lousy hotel operated by a German and a Negro's rooming house, by all odds the cleanest place in Greytown. Kinney went to neither, but occupied one of the better huts of the town.

To Kinney, with all his plans dust, his money gone, his health broken, and nothing to see but the physical wretchedness of Greytown, Walker must have appeared the luckiest man alive. Kinney's organization in New York had been careful, well-financed and apparently destined to success, whereas Walker, departing from San Francisco, had given the appearance of an impulsive daredevil, with no possible hope of success. And there was Walker, everybody's hero; and here was Kinney, an expatriated failure.

Kinney might have returned to New York and reorganized his company, or he might have resumed the occupations he had left to become a filibuster. But the filibuster does not give up—the great number of them who have died against adobe walls qualifies the breed to stand among the most inveterate gamblers of all time. Kinney sent two of his associates, with an escort, over the San Juan route to see Walker. They arrived in Granada early in November. They asked and obtained an audience with Walker. They irritated him slightly by not coming to the point, but when they had finished explaining their mission he gathered that Kinney sought an alliance between the Phalanx and the Central American Company. Walker's gray eyes gleamed and he said succinctly, "Tell Governor Kinney, or Mr. Kinney, or Colonel Kinney—or by whatever name he styles himself—that if I ever lay hands on him on Nicaraguan soil I shall most assuredly hang him."

The delegation exhibited its respect for General William Walker by deserting to him in a body. Kinney, using what for hope we shall never know, remained in Greytown. There was some disposition on the part of Walker's Nicaraguan allies to treat with Kinney; but Walker himself had little part in such gestures, instead dictating ridicule of "Farmer Kinney" for publication in *El Nicaraguense*. Some months after the visit of the delegation, Kinney's claims were outlawed by a Walker-dictated, Rivas-signed decree and the Texan, at the instigation of Carlos Thomas and others, came to Granada for a conference. Thomas pledged his own life as a guarantee of Kinney's safety.

The two, failure and success, talked throughout a long afternoon. At evening it appeared possible that some alliance might be formed. Kinney had offered his services in the enlistment of recruits, in the raising of money in the United States and in negotiations with the government at Washington. Unfortunately for Kinney, however, his was not a quiet tongue. He discussed his plans with Rivas and other Nicaraguans and was charged to have said that one colonist was worth five soldiers and that if Walker were not curbed his army would eat the country into destitution. When he returned to see the Filibuster the next morning he was threatened with execution; but when Walker learned the promises Carlos Thomas had made, he compromised by sending Kinney back to Greytown under escort.

Meanwhile, another petitioner had arrived in Granada. He expected encouragement and the help of arms; he believed truly in Walker's constantly reiterated idealism. The treatment he received was less than he deserved, for General Trinidad Cabañas, of the Republic of Honduras, was a patriot, a gentleman and a courageous leader of armies.

He knew much, this little Walker, but he knew nothing of tolerance or patience or that indefinable necessity in a ruler, human sympathy. Throughout his life there runs the strange thread of arrogance. Touched by a fragment of success, he immediately became the bully. To his credit be it said that he bullied not the weak, but those whom he considered approximating his own stature: the Legitimists, with the execution of Mayorga and Corral, the administration in Washington, with the rebuff of its one-time favorite, Kinney, and his own party, the Democrats, in the case of Cabañas.

At a time when it behooved Dictator Walker not to alienate the single friendly country he had in all Central America—San Salvador—he chose to offend the man it was sheltering. This little gamecock of a country had hailed Walker upon the fall of Granada as the fit successor to Francisco Morazon* and in its press predicted

* Honduran who became President and General-in-Chief of the Central American Federation in 1830. He was exiled in 1840, executed two years later and then revered as a great patriot.

a brighter day for Democracy throughout the Isthmus. Cabañas, hiding there from his arch-enemy, Guardiola, who had come into power in Honduras, also looked to Walker.

Cabañas was invited to visit the Filibuster in Granada and on December 3, 1855, was escorted into the capital by Colonel Hornsby. Cabañas came not as a beggar, but in the belief that he had earned a favor. In the early days of the war which Walker had terminated he had lent Nicaraguan Democracy many of his troops. He had sheltered Castellon and Jerez before that, when Don Fruto Chamorro exiled them, and his encouragement and money had made the revolution possible. Walker admitted Cabañas to be one of the few honest men in all Central America, and conceded that the aid he had given Castellon had weakened him so in his own country as to cause his overthrow. But Walker was a selfish man and he was not yet ready to war upon other countries. He overruled the plea of Jerez, the Minister of Relations, that Cabañas be given men and money. He made clear to President Rivas that an offensive movement from Nicaragua against Honduras would bring about a coalition of the other governments—Walker said that all four would ally themselves against Nicaragua, but from the evidence it is likely that it would have been Honduras-Guatemala-Costa Rica against Nicaragua-San Salvador. Clearly, in his own words, are shown his methods: "To have sent troops to Honduras, even with the design of re-establishing Cabañas, would have afforded a pretext for the declaration that the Americans of Nicaragua were aggressive in their nature. *It was only necessary for the Americans to wait in order to have their enemies move,** and it would have been unwise to hasten the struggle by seeking to restore a man, however worthy, who had just been driven from his own State."

Walker says, unkindly and probably unjustly, that Cabañas was a man of narrow mind, a Federalist dwindled by age to a Honduran official. He sought, by his quiet words, to persuade the patriot to wait. But Cabañas could not wait. Officially he was President of Honduras, and his term would not be up until January thirty-first of the following year; with only two months remaining he believed that Guardiola should be driven out at once. His view was a reasonable one:

* Italics mine.

Guardiola, once formally elected President, might be too powerful to be overthrown by an internal revolution. He, Cabañas, had been that strong; it had required the soldiers of Guatemala to win for Guardiola.

The old man remained in Granada for nearly three weeks, awaiting an answer. The appeal he had made to Walker was rather more than that of a politician seeking to regain something he had lost, for there was a certain idealism in it. Cabañas, watching the progress of the Americans in Nicaragua, saw the greatest possibility of worthy governmental reform since the dissolution of the Confederacy. It is safe to say that he accepted on face value Walker's own definition of his objects: the introduction of a new element into a worn-out society, from which would come true democracy. Cabañas, in these circumstances, becomes a somewhat pathetic figure; he talked with Walker and waited for promises to be fulfilled, but as the days passed disillusionment crept upon him, and then fear for the future of all the Central American countries. Recognizing at last the selfish motives of the Filibuster and foreseeing the inevitable result of his visit, he went from Granada to Leon, where he received the note informing him that Nicaragua could not engage in any Honduran disputes. Before leaving Granada, however, Cabañas conferred with Minister Wheeler, who forwarded to Washington this illuminating report, written on December 24, 1855:

> On Saturday, December 15, 1855, I called to return the visit of General Trinidad Cabañas, now on a visit by invitation and the guest of this government. He appears to be about 50 years old, and is esteemed one of the most liberal and honorable men in Central America. . . .
>
> He said, as I was about taking leave, that he would be happy to have some confidential conversation with the Minister of the United States, touching Central America, and asked me if my government approved of citizens of the United States coming to Central America; and if these persons attempted to destroy the nationality of Central America would the Government of the United States prevent it.
>
> I replied that the Government of the United States could not, nor would not approve of any attempt by any foreigners or our own citizens, to destroy the nationality of Central America—that our fixed policy, from the days of Washington, was non-interference with domestic difficulties of any Nation—and to avoid all entangling alliances. That our

Neutrality laws were strict, and that President Pierce would faithfully execute them.

That an expedition of Colonel Kinney, with professed peaceful objects to Central America had been stopped—that he was now indicted in the United States courts; that recently the officials of the British Government had been indicted and punished in the United States for enlisting men to serve in the Crimea. But that these proceedings were confined to acts done in the United States—that when our citizens were out of our territory and embarked in a foreign service—as they had the right to do, they voluntarily transferred their allegiance from their native country and placed themselves under the jurisdiction of another Government. That they were not responsible to the United States, nor the United States responsible to them—they were only responsible to the Authorities and Laws of the land where they had sought their new residence. So that, as our laws now stood, as far as General Walker and his associates were concerned, the United States could exercise no control over them—no more than over the citizens of Nicaragua; which they had become under their naturalization laws. He then asked me if Guatemala, joined by other governments, made war on Walker to drive him from the country, would the Government of the United States use any efforts to protect him.

I replied certainly not, for the reasons stated.

He then stated that he was dissatisfied with the condition of things now in Nicaragua. The belief was current that all the officers and emoluments of office would be absorbed by North Americans. To this I replied that there seemed to be no real ground for this opinion. The President of the Republic was a native of Nicaragua, so were all of his Cabinet. All the Governors and Prefects of the different Departments were also natives—that Walker had been tendered the presidency, but declined it—his efforts seemed not to tend to discourage or depress talent, but to elevate and improve it. Had he not acted thus, he could have been President instead of Don Patricio Rivas. General Cabañas then expressed a want of confidence in Don Patricio as opposed in his heart to Democratic principles—and believed the slanders from Costa Rica had origin in him.

I replied that the character of Don Patricio personally and politically had been that of an honest man—that he was too old to engage in intrigues and the fate of Corral was a warning. In return I asked him to say what in his opinion was to be the result of matters here. He replied that if General Walker did not receive soon strong reinforcements, that Guatemala, led on by Carrera, and Honduras, led on by Guardiola, both, he said, unscrupulous and unprincipled—desperate and bloody for he knew them both very well, and had fought them on many bloody fields—would make war on Walker and drive him from the country or kill him. To this I replied that if they did, they would be badly whipped. That every steamer brought more persons to Nicaragua, some to work the Lands, some to Merchandise, some to the Mines—but most to the Army. In this the Government of the United States had no hand—but the spirit of enterprise and adventure, points so prominent in the American character. That the Government of the United States had no desire to possess Central America; that if it did, and the States desired it, it could not well be accomplished, as the Clayton-Bulwer treaty read. General Cabañas then expressed great admiration for the Monroe Doctrine, and hoped that the United States would pursue and drive England out of Central America—that the course of the English towards his Republic had been oppressive, arrogant and insulting. The Island of Ruatan had been forcibly taken, which commanded their coast; and was constantly extending their power and possession in Central America. On a recent occasion, he stated, some of the citizens of Honduras went to Ruatan to recover some property and they were insultingly driven off by English officials. . . .

The rebuff of Cabañas ended the momentary quiet the Republic had enjoyed. Minister of Relations Jerez and Minister of War Selva, the latter a staunch Democrat, resigned. Selva went to San Juan del Sur where he embarked for San Salvador—to wait, he said, "until *hombres de bien* are restored to power in Nicaragua."

Walker forgot both Kinney and Cabañas as soon as they had been rebuffed. His consideration of them had centered upon one question: "How much good will an alliance with either do me, now?" He made a mistake there. He should have remembered, for it is the one thing all dictators must learn, that the profit in a friendship is as nothing to the loss in an enmity. Whereas his enemies had been legion and weak, now there were added to them a pair of men whose influence might in time become important. Kinney, for the time, did nothing; but Kinney was a good friend of President Pierce and the day was approaching when everything Walker had done would depend upon the attitude of the administration at Washington. Cabañas, returning disillusioned and bitter to San Salvador, had in his grasp an instrument he hastened to use: the manifesto. He spoke so violently against Walker that San Salvador, alone of all the Republics to hail the Filibuster, turned against him and began to rival in her publications the hostility of the irreconcilable to the south, Costa Rica.

But Walker, approaching the year which was to be his biggest, saw no danger in these responses to his coldness. His recruits were coming in from the States; every boat brought new men, as eager as the original Immortals for a fight to the finish with whatever "Greasers" came to hand. So great was his fame in the United States that all kinds flocked to his banner. One boat brought, early in December, his two brothers, James, the weak, and Norvell, the wicked. There is no evidence that William received either of them with warmth; to him they were of the same importance as any other two men who became citizens of what was fast becoming William Walker's Nicaragua.

Another arrival on the boat that brought James and Norvell was a Colonel Billy Wilson, a wealthy United States Army officer who had resigned to take a fling at the tropics. Colonel Wilson does not figure in the history of the Nicaraguan war beyond the moment of his arrival and then only because his luggage consisted of six Saratoga trunks filled to bursting with uniforms and linens of every sort. He was a bibulous Colonel and he gave generously of his clothing to those fellow officers who might need it; the wounded who later tore the finest of linen from their backs to make bandages did so because William Walker was of sufficient stature in America to lure into his army an officer, a gentleman and a dandy.

But Walker wore none of Billy Wilson's clothes. Walker clung to his black frock coat and his flannel shirt. Walker remained long hours at his desk, when Norvell and Billy Wilson were trying to drink each other under the table.

The Filibuster was now truly the man of destiny. And such men walk alone.

BOOK THREE

The Gray-Eyed Man

BOOK THREE
The Gray-Eyed Man . . .

To destroy an old political organization is a comparatively easy task, and little besides force is requisite for its accomplishment. . . .

I

IN DECEMBER, 1855, at the end of his first six months in Nicaragua, Walker began to approach a fullness of success. A good portion of his progress was the result of a natural aptitude for the sort of intrigue with which he had surrounded himself; but as much, if not more, was due to his uncanny luck. He engaged in the irregular politics of the time and place as a gambler, often taking the long odds and almost always winning. Muñoz died in battle at the exact moment when his death would permit Walker to dominate Castellon and so further his ends. Because of Muñoz's death the campaign resulting in the capture of Granada was undertaken; and with Granada in hand, Castellon died, giving the Filibuster a free hand. There were other instances where luck and little more carried the regenerator forward: Parker French's blunder at Virgin Bay, for example, and the massacre which followed, were turned from loss to profit. Executing the innocent Mayorga, instead of the criminally guilty French, cowed and defeated Corral.

Because he played constantly to the church, and so enjoyed the support of bishop and priest, Walker became the idol (momentarily) of every Catholic—which meant every Nicaraguan And very soon after he seized Granada, the unlettered Indians of the back country accepted him as savior, in a ceremony invaluable as publicity. They

155

did this not because he had won a battle or two, or because his *falanginos* were terrible fighters; he was their god because his eyes were steel gray, almost pupilless and had the depth of the sea and the steadiness of granite.

The Aztecs, when they had been tumbled from civilization to degrading bondage by the Spaniards, comforted themselves with a legend: that a fair-haired, white god would come from the north and set them free. All up and down the Isthmus this legend lived in one form or another. To the Indians of Nicaragua, it was told by their fathers in its original form, but with added prophecy: "The deliverer will be a gray-eyed man." At first glance, the description when applied to Walker is too pat, and the suspicion arises that it originated in his agile mind; but five years before he saw Nicaragua a missionary, Frederick Crowe, published a book called *The Gospel in Central America*. The legend in its Nicaraguan conception was reported in this book. But for Missionary Crowe, the hope of the Indians would become one more of the tricks Walker used to further his end; and even with this suspicion removed, there remains the possibility of its shrewd use by Walker to encourage deification—always a device of the dictator. However likely this, it is true that a delegation of Indians visited Walker at a coincidentally good time, bringing him gifts and acclaiming him as the savior for whom they had waited in suffering and faith. In *El Nicaraguense* for December 8, 1855, appeared this account of the visit:

> If we were disposed to believe that the race of prophets did not die with Isaiah and Jeremiah (and why should they?) we could say that this traditional prophecy has been fulfilled to the letter. "The Gray-Eyed Man" has come. He has come not as an Attila or as a Guardiola, but as a friend to the oppressed and a protector to the helpless and unoffending. The prophecy is deemed by the Indians as fulfilled; for last week we saw in Granada a delegation of them, who rarely visit this city, who desired to see General Walker.
>
> They were charmed by his gentle reception and offered to him their heartfelt thanks for their liberation from oppression and for the present state of quiet in this country. They laid at his feet the simple offering of their fruits and fields, and hailed him as the "Gray-Eyed Man" so long awaited by their fathers.

We cannot know positively what part Walker had in thus giving to the world the fact that he fulfilled prophecy. But it can be seen that the addition of the sobriquet lent impetus to his drive toward mastery. At no time in the remainder of his life was the phrase "Gray-Eyed Man of Destiny" out of his mind; in victory and defeat alike he foresaw always a shining goal at the end of the road he traveled, because he was the chosen. It is probable that with the sophistication he had learned in cities he was at first mildly contemptuous of the faith the simple Indians had in him, as a child of their strange gods; but for all his sophistication, he was as superstitious as they and grew to believe, more than the sincerest of them had believed, that the legend was true and great.

II

CHRISTMAS EVE, 1855.

In every house of Granada, down to the poorest, there was a corner set aside for the representation of the *Nacimiento*—the birth of the Christ Child. There was in each house a grotto, shaded by palm leaves and housing the miniature figures of the Virgin and her Baby. Some of the grottoes were lighted almost theatrically by arrangements of candles and mirrors, others belonged to the poor and in the darkened rooms could barely be seen. For that day all houses were opened to those who could worship at the spectacle of the Nativity and in this year the naked children, the Indians, the peasant women in their bare feet and the ladies in their shawls were supplemented by the tall, fair men from the North. In the Cathedrals the tableaux contained figures of almost life size, lighted from above by masses of candles; and all day, from the outlying villages, the peons and their families came to worship. Until midnight the streets were filled with the shuffling natives and the pace of their spirit drove from the Granadinos the tension they had known since the little *Yanqui* came. As the clocks reached twelve, the bells (Granada was a city of bells) chimed gently, and the people cried out: "Christ is born!" with a fervor eighteen centuries old.

And in the grand plaza, ordered there by William Walker, the Phalanx presented arms, uncovered, dropped to one knee to pay homage to the procession moving through the streets—a throne upon which were life-sized figures of the Christ and his Mother, covered with a canopy and carried by priests. The Filibuster knew how vital to these people was the religious observance of the Virgin Birth and saw to it that his men pretended to a reverence few of them had ever known.

Thus came Christmas to Granada. Although it came in gladness, there was little to be thankful for. It was true that William Walker had for a period suspended the war, but a new one appeared inevitable and meanwhile cholera ate at the lives of the people—and, too, at the American Phalanx. First, when they were new in the country, it seemed that the plague passed them by; but now they were dying, the good with the bad. By Christmas Walker had lost Gilman of the peg leg and Davidson and many anonymous privates, who lay buried beneath the sands of the beach.

But Walker paid no heed—to Christmas, to cholera, to dead Gilman, whose funeral he attended. In the week between Christmas and New Year's there were tasks to be performed, against the magnitude of which the lives of men could be of no moment.

III

FILIBUSTERISM, of course, was no new venture for men when William Walker engaged himself in it. It had been going on for many years before he was born; it continues to the present day, in one form or another. In the modern counterpart Mussolini's legions take Ethiopia, or a William Walker in a paneled New York office signs the checks for a distant revolution, so that his oil company will receive rich concessions from a new regime. Walker enjoyed a combination of circumstances calculated to give his expedition great stature in the eyes of the misfits and failures. His private soldiers, coming to him in droves on Cornelius Vanderbilt's Transit ships, were men who could not earn fortunes except possibly by staking their lives for them. His officers had seen the advantages in soldiery, wherein the officer has an authority beyond his power to acquire in civil life. And in the United States there were men of another stamp who looked upon Walker as their beau ideal and sought to emulate him.

It is a pity that the latter class could not have followed a more worthy example. They were in their way patriots, however misguided in their aims: merchants and politicians of the Southern States who believed firmly in the rights of slavery and who expected Walker's successes to give them the advantage in the approaching "irrepressible" conflict; the dogged ones who believed Cuba should be free; and the "manifest destiny" fanatics.

At the beginning of Walker's ascendancy, there was living in New York a Cuban named Domingo de Goicouria. He was a friend of Vanderbilt and an accepted member of New York society. He was fifty-five years of age, the son of a wealthy Cuban merchant; and in England, as his father's representative, he had learned in his youth something of liberalism. Efforts to emancipate his native island occupied his entire adulthood and brought him exile, first to Spain and later to America. In the United States he was an adviser of Narciso Lopez; he is said to have counseled Lopez against attempting his last, fated assault upon Spanish authority in Cuba. He was the personification of the educated Latin: fine featured, soft-spoken, given to considering every proposal carefully and then applying logic to its disposition. He wore a long gray beard, not for the patriarchial appearance it gave him, but to fulfill a boyhood oath that he would remain unshaved until Cuba was freed.

When the news of Walker's victories in Nicaragua came to him in New York, he communicated with the Filibuster. His emissary, Colonel Francisco Alejandro Lainé, arrived at Granada in December, to find Walker at his busiest; a new colonization decree had been drafted and forced upon President Rivas, and its inducements—two hundred and fifty acres for every American who settled in the country, with an extra hundred for families—were thought to assure the Filibuster of a constantly growing army. But although this decree gave Walker what he wanted, he listened to the offer Lainé made in the name of Goicouria. What Lainé had to suggest was altogether illegal: if General Walker would accept the assistance of Domingo de Goicouria now, then when all Nicaragua was definitely under control, Goicouria would expect its armed assistance for a revolution in Cuba. Here again we see the true William Walker, stripped of the romance and daring the imagination gives the soldier of fortune. Cabañas and Kinney had been rebuffed, the first because to have helped him "would have afforded a pretext for the declaration that the Americans were agressive in their nature"; the second because he had no right in territories he had bought for money. But Goicouria (at the sources of wealth, according to Lainé, and able to gather up and dispatch hundreds of recruits) was something else again. Seeing profit, Walker became, in the few moments he talked with Lainé, a Cuban patriot as well as the regenerator of Central America.

Throughout this phase of his career, Walker concentrated upon men; he wanted more and more Americans in his service, and to get them he ignored other and more important matters affecting his dictatorship. His gestures toward recognition in the United States were all more or less tentative; he appears to have believed that if his army grew to a sufficient size and he conquered more of Central America, recognition would follow as a matter of diplomatic routine. He must not be too harshly condemned for his narrow viewpoint, for his very nature and situation robbed him of the perspective he so urgently needed. His problems were manifold. President Rivas was his puppet, but only as long as he could continue to hold the strings. To the north Cabañas, the idol of a large share of the Honduran population, was issuing hostile manifestoes from San Salvador and inflaming Democrats and Legitimists alike against a common enemy. To the south Juan Rafael Mora, President of Costa Rica, was officially antagonistic and promising war at the first opportunity.* There was no money in Nicaragua and the arriving Americans had to be armed, clothed and fed, if they were to be of any value in the inevitable conflict. One boon he had; one tremendous problem had been solved for him before he came into the country—transportation. The Transit Company carried his recruits without question, in bodies of fifty or a hundred or more. From San Francisco on one line, and from New Orleans and New York on the two others, they traveled as passengers without the expenditure of a penny by the Filibuster. This was his lifeline; as long as the Transit ran, he was invincible.

---

* As early as November, President Mora had issued a manifesto, denouncing Walker and his men as "a band of adventurers" come to Central America to "seek in our wives and daughters, our houses and lands, satisfaction for their fierce passions, food for their unbridled appetites." Being unsure of his power at that time, however, Mora confined his lust for filibuster blood to flamboyant declarations.

So, having this assurance of life, he characteristically destroyed it.

His great friend, Edmund Randolph, who had followed his fortunes from New Orleans, who had defended him upon the collapse of the Sonora expedition and who had quietly furthered the cause from his San Francisco law office, appeared suddenly at San Juan del Sur on December 17, 1855. With him were C. K. Garrison's son and McDonald, the agent. As a telling argument for the message they bore, one hundred recruits marched off the San Francisco steamer at their heels and were part of the Nicaraguan army before nightfall.

McDonald and young Garrison informed Walker of the confusion which had arisen over the Accessory Transit Company's control. The original maneuvering of Garrison *père* and his associate in New York, Charles Morgan, had won stock control temporarily. But upon the return of Vanderbilt from Europe they had been outboxed on the stock exchange and control of the company had again passed into Vanderbilt's hands. It was now proposed that the Transit charter be voided and a new one prepared in favor of Morgan and Garrison. The matter of the twenty thousand dollars Walker had accepted from McDonald at the fall of Granada was mentioned, as were the hundreds of free passages extended to Walker's immigrants.

Randolph's part in the negotiation was purely that of an attorney, but it is not unlikely that Walker's great friendship for him helped greatly in what followed. Walker had spent much time in a study of the Transit Company's contract and the returns Nicaragua had received from the operations of the line, and he was convinced that the country had been cheated. Walker and Randolph were both lawyers, sufficiently skilled in the cunning of their profession to make a plausible case. They worked for all of January and part of February on a declaration, which, when completed, accused the Accessory Transit Company of failing to build a canal, as agreed in the grant of 1849, of failing to build a railroad and of depriving the State of its rightful share of the profits. Presented to President Rivas, the decree gave that harried gentleman his first joyful moment since the coming of Walker into power. He signed it eagerly, seeing beyond the sheets of foolscap a country no longer exploited by American financiers and no longer overrun by American adventurers.

But when Walker presented a second decree, President Rivas rebelled. He read provisions which granted to Edmund Randolph as attorney for the firm of Morgan & Garrison more than the Transit Company had enjoyed. Believing that he had disposed of an enemy in the Transit Company, he found that he was expected to "sell the country" to a stranger who had been in secret conference with Walker for weeks. He refused to sign.

But in the end, poor Topsy-Turvy had to sign. Some of the decree's more rapacious provisions were stricken out, but it still did what he did not want it to do—gave to an American combination the right to use Nicaragua as a highway.

This decree was signed in mid-February. The Transit properties were seized and a commision named to determine the amount due the Republic for the use of the route since 1849. And meanwhile, the United States talked of little but the Filibuster.

IV

Upon the fall of Granada and the flight of Estrada, the Legitimist president, the authority of Senor Marcoleta as Minister of Nicaragua to the United States should have ended. But Estrada, following the execution of Corral, set up a government in Segovia, and in a proclamation discountenanced all the acts of his luckless general, damned the provisional government of President Rivas as an engine set up by traitors, and continued—on paper—to conduct the affairs of the country. Washington, manned by unaccomplished diplomats, therefore found itself with two problems instead of one: the first whether to encourage or discourage Walker, in either choice forfeiting a certain bloc of national support; the second whether to recognize Estrada— manifestly almost an impossibility because facts belied his claims—or to recognize President Rivas and so lend the impression to the world that the filibusters were the creatures of the United States.

There was peace to be kept with England, and so the administration recognized neither party. On New Year's Day, 1856, Marcoleta was still in Washington. He attended the President's White House reception on New Year's Day, attempting by his presence to rebuke a government which would tolerate a William Walker, and received sympathy and courtesy from his former colleagues in the full measure due an accredited minister.

In December, Walker had sent Parker French to Washington as minister, in one of his few moments of weakness. Forcing President Rivas to appoint the man was worse than weak: it was stupid. Walker had erred in permitting a conscienceless adventurer to get a foothold in the country, but instead of admitting his error and sending a scoundrel into the exile which was his due, the Filibuster dispatched him to the capital of the one country whose support could be won only by the exercise of skilled diplomacy. And French, arriving in America, made farce comedy of his mission. He reached Washington in late December and was promptly rebuffed by Secretary Marcy, who held that the principals in Nicaragua were not citizens of that country and therefore not qualified to set up a government.

Opposed rather generally by the press, the Pierce administration was trying to maintain the neutrality laws and yet not alienate the powerful South and the equally important "manifest destiny" bloc. Thus it was that when French went to New York, the Federal officials could devise no satisfactory curb for his open recruiting of men. Pierce issued a proclamation warning all persons against encouraging or participating in filibuster activities, but the document was not worth the time taken to write it. The spirit of the times was against him. Advertisements appeared* and brought crowds of adventurers for every ship sailing to Nicaragua. The extent of the government's futility was summed up by an editor of the New York *Atlas:* "Like India rubber, North American filibusters jump higher every time they are stricken down."

Among works performed by French in New York was the organization of troops to sail aboard the *Northern Light* on December twenty-fourth. John McKeon, Federal District Attorney, attempted to prevent this sailing, but his raid on recruiting headquarters found it bare of leaders. He went thence to the rooms of French, in the St. Nicholas Hotel, where ensued a lively exchange. McKeon threatened to seize every boat on the Transit line and French re-

---

* "WANTED:—Ten or fifteen young men to go a short distance out of the city. Single men preferred. Apply at 347 Broadway, corner of Leonard Street, between the hours of ten and four. Passage paid."—*New York Herald.*

marked quietly that if this was done his country "which was poor, to be sure," would probably buy them in. To McKeon's demand that French reveal the number of recruits obtained and the plans for transporting them to Nicaragua, the latter requested that the questions be put in writing. McKeon refused, on the ground that French was no minister of Nicaragua; French conceded this statement, but as an individual demanded that all questions be written. The District Attorney, who saw himself coming off second best in an encounter with an oily rascal, charged French with a criminal past and asserted he could force him to answer questions. And French, still amused and mildly contemptuous, asked if he had brought a warrant, shrugged when McKeon said no and offered to submit to arrest without the formality. McKeon left in a red fury, and from his office ordered that no clearance be granted for the *Northern Light*. Somehow the red tape broke, however, and the ship had to be halted in the bay by a revenue cutter. A few whiskered misfits were brought ashore, after admitting that they were going to "jine up with Walker," and producing simple black pants buttons, given them as the secret sesame to Nicaraguan passage. The ship then proceeded.

Denied all real help by Washington, McKeon obtained a warrant for the arrest of French. But when the United States Commissioner had issued it there arose the question of French's status. Washington ruled that he was not a diplomat, but intimated that courtesies were being extended to him unofficially. McKeon then fashioned an ultimatum, directing French to leave the country within a specified time, as an exchange for the dropping of any charge against him. French ignored the warning, was arrested, released and, by demanding an immediate trial, forestalled any further effort to prosecute him; the charge was violation of the neutrality laws, but McKeon was more angry than prepared.

Seldom has the United States been so helplessly between the devil and the sea. The public was all for Walker; boys not out of their teens tried to get aboard the ships, and more than a few succeeded. Using New York as a typical point, we find the riffraff of the streets being gathered up in a wave of popular enthusiasm and sent wholeheartedly to spread the doctrine of "manifest destiny." Tickets were furnished them almost without question by the Transit Company, co-operating to the limits of its accommodations. Crowds gathered on the piers to cheer the *Star of the West* and the *Northern Light* as their paddles churned the river into foam, and the yelling of the hoodlums on their decks put the steam whistle to shame. Whatever the officials did to stop the great exodus to Nicaragua was hooted in the streets and on the town's steam cylinder-presses. And one cry was never silenced—England, England, England. In Washington, Secretary Marcy labored to keep peace among the Central American diplomats, to suppress French and yet not offend him, to appease England without bowing before her will, to ride a dozen horses at once, only to be called toady to England a hundred times a day.

And still the recruits went out. New Orleans sent its share, on the subsidiary Vanderbilt line running to Greytown. Vanderbilt, returning from his pilgrimage to Europe, had seen in the Walker movement a guarantee of huge revenues from the Isthmus for an indefinite period, and had gladly signed requisitions for unnumbered tickets to the arena of destiny.

The New Yorker who watched this bedlam could not but have agreed that the failure of William Walker was a possibility too remote to be considered. For a time there was no news but Walker; the slavery issue, for years a recurrent page-one favorite with the editors, was pushed inside to whatever space could be spared for it. The New York *Herald,* the New Orleans *Picayune* and the San Francisco *Alta California* were among the papers which sent correspondents to Nicaragua and these gentlemen dispatched long, prejudiced accounts of the events in that country. There had been nothing to compare with the magnitude of the Walker story since the discovery of gold; and it would be nearly five years before Civil War copy would surpass it.

Of the many dark rumors which sought to explain Washington's vacillating policy, several had some small basis in truth. It is reasonable to suppose, for instance, that the manner in which Walker had treated Colonel Kinney had alienated Pierce, whose private secretary, it will be remembered, had been interested in the Central American Company. There is no question but that pressure from

England had its effect: the United States knew well the lengths to which Britain's policy of empire would carry it, if its interests were jeopardized. Finally, it is not impossible that the supposed determination of Walker to resurrect slavery in the middle-American Republics conjured a certain governmental opposition.

But for a time, in New York and Washington, the Filibuster could do no wrong. French, this once in his career, was a popular hero. He strutted; he told again and again the romantic story of his lost right arm; he proclaimed on behalf of Nicaragua. He inflated himself to the proper size—and then the sharp pin of memory pricked him. Stories of his exploits in the past began to be printed and on January 23, 1856, attention was drawn to the Senate Military Affairs Committee report of 1855, wherein the full story of the wagon-train fraud was revealed, with particular stress laid upon the purchase of two thousand dollars' worth of supplies from the army at San Antonio with French's bogus letter of credit. Overnight he was reduced in the public mind to proper stature: a vagabond and a rogue. The newspapers, yesterday his earnest champions, called him "humbug" and worse. The New York *Mercury* said wryly, "In bitterness of spirit, let us exclaim with Sir Harcourt Courtly, 'Will nobody take this man away?'" A few editors, it is true, with sympathetic cynicism inquired why French's questionable past was considered to disqualify him for diplomatic service, but sympathy could not redeem him; any value he may have had as aide to Walker was irretrievably lost.

Chronology may here be set aside, for the good of continuity, to conclude the story of Parker French. Denied recognition several times by the Washington administration, his commission was revoked by William Walker when it became known that his unsavory past was causing a loss of public esteem for the entire filibuster movement. He returned to Nicaragua in April of 1856, tried to explain his failures to his chief, was coldly sent away and returned to New Orleans. For a time he attempted to capitalize on his experiences, lecturing, promising to write a book and seeking to connive with Cornelius Vanderbilt. His light finally flickered out when Walker, writing in *El Nicaraguense,* disowned him on behalf of Nicaragua and mentioned that "he at present is doing the [Nicaraguan] administration all the injury his genius is capable of."

He is reported to have been imprisoned in Boston late in the Civil War after a period of brilliant espionage work for the Confederacy; the merit of this report is doubtful.*

The exposure of French harmed Walker greatly in the United States. Thinking people, who had believed firmly in the Filibuster's military and administrative genius, began to wonder why so accomplished a leader should be assisted by so black a scoundrel. And this feeling had no more than reached the murmuring stage when news of the revocation of the Transit charter was received. Instantly, all New York knew Walker for a blunderer. To New York none but a madman would antagonize deliberately the ferryman-become-giant—Cornelius Vanderbilt.

The news of the charter revocation was a sensation in New York and cause for glee in Washington. Vanderbilt wrote twice to Secretary Marcy, demanding the protection of the United States in the unwarranted seizure of the company's property: but his defiance of the government (which a few weeks before had been told that the company was a creature of Nicaragua and as such in no wise connected with the United States) now redounded to his embarassment. The press, while it gaily referred Vanderbilt to Nicaragua for justice, began for the first time to break down the legend of Walker's greatness. The New York *Herald* bluntly called the Filibuster a fool and pointed out the obvious truth: that Vanderbilt could re-route his company, possibly through Costa Rica or Panama, and so choke off all replenishments for the American Phalanx.

Thus, the Filibuster, by his choice, was placed altogether on his own on March 1, 1856. He had an army of 660 Americans and a variable number of Nicaraguan allies. He had a little artillery and ample food. He had the friendship of two powerful shipping men, who for the moment could not furnish him with ships, and the enmity of a more powerful one who probably would tie all the steamers tightly to their piers. If ever the time would be ripe to declare a test of the strength of American occupation of Nicaragua, it had come.

It was Costa Rica, antagonistic toward the filibusters from the moment of their arrival, which took the lead, aided by Great Britain.

* *Reminiscences of a Ranger.*

V

THERE was one Central American who had resisted Walker from the day his Immortals landed. This was Juan Rafael Mora, President of Costa Rica, unswerving aristocrat, cruel adversary, skilled politician and violent nationalist. His reply to Walker's first circular, pleading for good-will from the other Republics, has been quoted heretofore. When Walker learned how bitterly Mora resented his presence, he tried in every way he knew, from November of 1855 to the following March, to conciliate him. He wrote a personal letter to President Mora, again asserting a "fervent desire for peace and good understanding." He directed President Rivas to send a commission to emphasize Nicaragua's good feeling. Headed by Leon Schlessinger, a German Jew whose only claim to fame in Walker's service seems to have been an understanding of Spanish, it included Manuel Argüello and Captain Sutter. Schlessinger and Sutter were driven from the country by Mora's orders: Argüello, whose appointment to the cabinet had alienated several Democratic leaders, proved where his loyalty lay by deserting to the Costa Rican army.

Throughout January, the *Boletin Official,* Mora's organ at San José, and the communications of his minister in Washington to the Secretary of State hammered at Walker and his followers. The Costa Rican Minister, in a protest against "a great crime . . . hatched and set on foot within the territory of the United States and [backed] with the moral force of the nation," demanded that the adventurers be disowned before they could gain a position where they would be received with open arms, "arrayed in holiday attire for annexation and to be exalted, their booty to be legitimatized."

In the face of so violent a feeling, Walker was impotent. He had seized a country and was controlling it, but he lacked the essential which would safeguard his prize: peace. Increasing his army constantly, he succeeded only in undermining what he had sought to build. The Transit Company revocation lost for him much of the ground he had gained in the United States and the sending of French to Washington served merely to bolster the charges of the Costa Rican legation. Increasing his armed forces transformed San Salvador, the only country originally eager to be his friend, into an open enemy.

Late in February, the Nicaraguan garrison at Hipp's Point, an isolated post where the Serapiqui River joins the San Juan and where boats to Costa Rica passed, sent him a pouch of mail, intercepted aboard a British steamer. It contained an exchange of letters sufficiently indicative of the British foreign policy of the day to be reprinted. The first was from the Foreign Office to the Costa Rican Consul General in London, Edward Wallerstein:

London, Feb. 9, 1856.

Sir: I am directed by the Earl of Clarendon (Foreign Minister) to acquaint you that having referred to the War Department your letter of the 12th Ultimo, requesting that a small supply of arms may be furnished to the Government of Costa Rica. His Lordship has been informed by the Department in reply that 2,000 smooth-bore muskets (Wittons) which are not so highly finished as the Line Pattern Musket of 1842, can be supplied to this service at £1.3.0 each, or if it should be preferred, 2,000 of the Line Pattern Musket of 1842 can be furnished at s55/8d each.

As soon as Lord Clarendon is informed by you of the species of arms which you decide upon, he will communicate further with the War Department, and request that the arms may be placed at your disposal.

The letter from Wallerstein to Mora was even more significant:

London, Feb. 16, 1856.

Much esteemed Sir and Friend: The mail which brings the correspondence from Costa Rica has not arrived and in consequence I have nothing to say to you in regard to mercantile business. As to public matters, you will please refer to my communications of today to the Minister. By this you will see that this Government is willing to put 2,000 muskets at my disposal for the service of the Republic of Costa Rica. Nothing is said in the note about the time of payment, and consequently the British Government agrees to my proposition. However, I have not made up my mind to take them previous to receiving instructions from you, or which of the two kinds of arms to take. In case I should take them previous to your being able to write upon the subject, I will send them in the month of March, if a vessel sails for Punta Arenas, without further orders from you. I have not yet replied officially to Lord Clarendon to offer him my most sincere thanks in my own name and that of the Republic for his manifestation of sympathy and friendship for Costa Rica. . . . All this is very good, but I don't like the intelligence from Nicaragua, where it seems Walker is establishing himself firmer and firmer every day. I cannot understand how the other States did not unite themselves from the beginning to expel him from Nicaragua. I have letters from Guatemala and San Salvador requiring me to request from this Government help and succor; but what can be done for Republics or people who do not make an exertion to help themselves? When I was telling Lord Clarendon that Costa Rica already had an army of 800 men on the frontier of Nicaragua he was much pleased and said "that was a right step," and I am persuaded that my having made that insinuation is one of the reasons for giving us the muskets. The questions pending between this country and the United States are very complicated, but there will be no war for this reason: that the gentlemen in the great Republic observe that although the British do not boast or say much on the subject, they are determined to punish the Yankees for the least insult to the national honor. To the eyes of the whole world—of this country in particular—a war between the two nations would be one of the worst of evils; but to Central America the case would be very different, as Walker and his associates would soon be kicked out of Nicaragua.

I send to the Government a copy of the *Times,* in which is found a letter from Mr. Marcy to the American Minister to Nicaragua. Though this letter appears to censure the Minister, and holds out a threat to Walker, the true sense is, that in a short time the government of the United States will recognize Walker's government. May God help us.

On February twenty-ninth, Mora mobilized nine thousand men and declared war on the Americans in Nicaragua. The most violent act of all the war that followed was the proclamation he issued to:

The President of the Republic of Costa Rica to all Its Inhabitants:
Fellow-Countrymen, to arms! The hour that I foretold to you has arrived. Let us march into Nicaragua to destroy that wicked phalanx which has reduced her to the most shameful slavery! Let us march to fight for the liberty of our brethren.

They call on you, they expect you to rise up against her oppressors. Her cause is our cause. Those who today rob, revile and assassinate them, audaciously defy us, and endeavor to bind upon us the same bloody chains. Let us fly to burst asunder those of our brethren and to exterminate their executioners to the last man.

We do not go to contend for a piece of land, or to acquire ephemeral power; not to achieve miserable conquest or much less for sacrilegious purposes. No! We go to struggle for the redemption of our brethren from the most iniquitous tyranny. We go to help them in the fruitful work of their regenerator. We go to tell them "Brethren of Nicaragua!

RETREAT OF THE COSTA RICANS

Arise! Annihilate your oppressors. We come here to fight by your side, for your liberty, for your country! Union, Nicaraguans, union! Bury your internal differences forever! No more party feuds, no more fratricidal discords! Peace, justice and liberty for all. War only on filibusters!"

To the conflict, then, Costa Ricans—I march at the head of the national army. I, who rejoice this day to see your noble enthusiasm, which makes me proud to call you my sons, wish always to share danger and glory with you.

Your mothers, wives, sisters and daughters animate you. Their patriotic virtues will make us invincible. In fighting for the safety of our brethren, we shall fight likewise for them, for their honor, for their existence, for our idolized country and Spanish-American independence.

All the loyal sons of Guatemala, San Salvador and Honduras are in march upon that horde of bandits. Our cause is holy; triumph is certain. God will give us victory and with it peace, concord, liberty and union in the great Central American family.

Mora marched at the head of three thousand men on March third. President Rivas declared war on the eleventh, a day after Walker had issued the least wise of all his proclamations: a declaration against all Legitimists in Central America. This said that because "our overtures of peace have been rejected, our propositions of friendship . . . treated with scorn and disdain . . . nothing is left for the Americans in Nicaragua but hostility to the Serviles [Legitimists] throughout Central America. A very large proportion of the so-called Legitimists of this State are either open or secret enemies to our presence on this soil. They owe us for the protection they have had for their lives and property; they have paid us with ingratitude and treachery.

"Against the Servile parties and Servile Governments of Central America, the Americans in Nicaragua are bound, by the common law of self-protection, to declare eternal enmity. Our proffered friendship has been rejected. We can only make them feel that our enmity may be as dangerous and destructive as our friendship is faithful and true.

"The troops of the Army of the Republic of Nicaragua will assume and wear the red ribbon."

Again Nicaragua was divided, red ribbon against white. Again the threat of American domination throughout the Isthmus had been voiced. And again William Walker lost something he could not regain; the faith he had instilled in the people dwindled further and made him still more the unwelcome stranger who had first intruded upon them and now sought to bully them.

VI

MORA's first move was against the garrison at Hipp's Point which had been intercepting his mail. Walker chose to ignore this feint and instead gathered a force for a march into Guanecaste, a Pacific slope city in disputed territory, thirty-odd miles from Rivas. Before this march was attempted, however, he received reinforcements of two hundred and fifty Americans from New York, headed by Domingo de Goicouria.

There was irony in the arrival of the reinforcements. They embarked on a Transit boat which left New York a few days before the one carrying the decree of revocation docked. Cornelius Vanderbilt learned too late that he had paid passage for two hundred and fifty soldiers who would support the man even then attempting to ruin his company. Walker, in Nicaragua, offered in this instance his usual self-justifying comment: "The price of these passages is so much secured by the State on the indebtedness due from the corporation."

When the Cuban arrived in Nicaragua he learned with the greatest dismay of the revocation of the Transit charter. He tried to impress upon Walker the foolhardiness of a course which would antagonize Vanderbilt, the greatest of all filibusters, a man who battled from behind the impregnable entrenchment of a limitless checkbook. Perhaps it was this that alienated Walker; perhaps it was the obvious integrity of Goicouria and his devotion to the cause of freedom; perhaps it was his beard. In any case, the little general did not like his new aide; he accepted the reinforcements he had brought, but he rudely rebuffed him when he sought to offer advice which, it was to be proved, was the product of wisdom.

The American Phalanx now approximated what Walker had had in mind in San Francisco. The force of some six hundred was organized in two battalions. In addition to Americans avowedly of the army, there were nearly as many engaged in business and labor in the country and these Walker formed into volunteer companies, with the thought that in an emergency he could double his force by the wave of an arm. In all, his resources, at the time of Mora's declaration of war, were in excess of one thousand men.

Walker summoned Leon Schlessinger to his headquarters. The officer had sulked since his ejection from Costa Rica and had intimated that nothing but the command of an invading force would redeem his lost honor. Walker therefore gave him four companies (two hundred and forty men) and ordered him to march toward Guanecaste, just across the Costa Rican border. It was an unwise move, because Schlessinger was no commander. Walker, unfortunately, knew nothing of the man's military background; as in the case of French he accepted him on face value alone. Schlessinger was the son of a German-Jewish tailor, had enlisted in the Austrian army, attained to a corporalcy and then, for some undisclosed infraction, been dishonorably discharged. He next enlisted in the Hungarian army and again became a corporal; but when he visited his home he was attired glitteringly in the uniform of a lieutenant. He appeared in the United States as a dashing major, with great tales of his adventures; served in one of the Lopez expeditions against Cuba, and was for a time confined in a Spanish prison.

The force he headed was as incompetent as its commander. He had two companies of Americans, one entirely French and one German. Explaining his selection of Schlessinger, Walker said that he understood French, German and Spanish and so could maintain communication with all his men; common sense should have told the Filibuster that the best disposition of the continentals would have been to scatter them throughout the army. The polyglot command marched out of Granada on March 12, 1856, pennons flying from lances and the native drummer beating loudly but without rhythm.

Walker wanted to hit Guanecaste to weaken the morale of the Costa Rican people; but more, he wanted to assure himself that the Transit would not fall to the enemy. Schlessinger's instructions were to occupy whatever he could capture and scatter spies throughout the southern part of Nicaragua, to watch and report Mora's movements.

Schlessinger's command was in absolute confusion even before it left San Juan del Sur on the sixteenth. The American companies tried to march with some sort of order, but their best efforts could not make the advance any better than floundering. At Salinas, on the border, Schlessinger sent his only surgeon back to Granada, where he could bind up no wounds.

Walker then fell ill and could do nothing to aid Schlessinger. Dengue, or "breakbone fever," struck him as he worked at his desk. His head ached constantly and he shivered in the heat of the tropical noon, gripped by racking chills. On Sunday morning, March twenty-third, he could not rise from his bed; his bones, to the smallest one, ached to the marrow, his eyeballs seemed to rest in sockets of fire, his back felt broken and his flesh scourged by the touch of the sheets. His many freckles were varied by mottled red spots. Far back in his mind he must have watched the progress of the ailment; he was a doctor, remember, and all interest in the ills of the body could not have left him.

As he lay, quite light-headed with his raging fever, the sentry at the door came in with a note. It was signed by Major Brewster, who had headed one of Schlessinger's American companies, and it told succinctly a story that drove all consciousness of sickness from Walker's mind and made him get up and take a boat immediately for Virgin Bay.

Schlessinger, the note said, had proceeded as far as Santa Rosa. There his troops had rested, lounging about on the ground with no evidence of discipline. An arms inspection was ordered but never held; sentries were not set out. As the men lay on the ground, a mounted scout came into the camp, crying, "Here they come!" "They" proved to be Manuel Arguëllo, the turncoat Legitimist, at the head of five hundred Costa Ricans, Mora's advance guard. Schlessinger could not be found to direct the battle and Brewster and the other Americans tried futilely to offer resistance. The French and German companies broke and fled into the jungle, thrashing about like a herd of startled boars. The Americans held a corral for a few minutes, and again an abandoned hut, but Arguëllo's greater numbers forced them back with the loss of an indefinite number of prisoners who were promptly executed. Brewster was returning to Virgin Bay, his note said. Where the rest of the men would turn up he had no idea.

At Virgin Bay, Walker first questioned the few stragglers who had reached there from Costa Rica, and then returned to Granada, to order the army into Rivas. The civil government was transferred from Granada to Leon. Rivas and Granada were placed under martial law, and Don Fermin Ferrer, one of Walker's staunchest supporters, was left in the capital to handle all civil affairs for the Democracy. Patricio Rivas and the balance of his cabinet went to Leon, again solidifying the support of the Democrats, but also widening the rift with the Legitimists. Moreover, Topsy-Turvy, once freed of Walker's constant presence, seemed to have gained courage and in an address retracted the declaration against all aristocratic governments. He declared, hinting at the treachery he even then contemplated, that he had removed to Leon only to promote a friendlier feeling with Guatemala, San Salvador and Honduras, of which San Salvador alone was Democratic.

The defeat of Schlessinger occurred on March twentieth and that gentleman appeared at Rivas five or six days later to report the causes of his failure. Blaming the inexperience of his men, the strength and equipment of the enemy and a number of other obvious factors, he had all but persuaded Walker that perhaps the defeat was no more than part of the Filibuster's destiny when the remainder of his officers and men reached headquarters. They told stories so identical and so honest that Walker ordered Schlessinger court-martialed for neglect, ignorance of the duties of a commanding officer and cowardice in the presence of the enemy. Schlessinger violated his parole and deserted to the Legitimists before the court-martial could find him guilty and sentence him to be shot; Walker affirmed the sentence *in absentia* and ordered his disgrace published to all the civilized world.

It is not shown that the rank and file of Walker's men were in any sense the daredevils fiction calls filibusters. His officers were, in the main, faithful to their duties, insanely courageous and devoted to their leader. But the common soldiers—the hoodlums from New York fire companies, Vigilante fugitives from San Francisco, wharf rats from New Orleans and villains from half the countries of the world— had only the mob spirit. In victory they were tough and brave; in defeat they were craven and drunk. Now, with the ragged, disarmed and terrified remnants of Schlessinger's men to remind them of their peril in these countries, they took to carousing, in defiance of the commander's rule of temperance. From the arrival in Rivas until the end of March it was difficult to keep even the officers sober.

It cannot be said of Walker that he ever lost his head. His errors were the result of premeditated plans, his setbacks due to stubbornness rather than lack of thought. With the disaster at Guanecaste fresh in the minds of his men, with drunkenness increasing every day and with, as he himself phrased it, a possibility that the army would "dissolve from the effects of one shameful panic," he ordered the entire force paraded in the plaza at Rivas, on March thirtieth. His first action was to reduce to the ranks, publicly, his brother Norvell, supposedly for drunkenness and insubordination.

The contrast can be imagined from the bare words that record the incident—Norvell, the glossy blood, eyes red-rimmed and sardonic, lounging as he stood before his brother, and William, in dusty black, his thin face carved in its habitual expression of righteousness, his gray eyes without affection, without feeling.

When the disgraceful ceremony was completed and Norvell returned to his place in the ranks, Walker faced his men. He spoke to them, most briefly, of the "moral grandeur" of their cause. He reminded them that they stood alone in Nicaragua, denied support by every other government on earth; that they were "maligned by those who should have befriended them, and betrayed by those they had benefited" and that they were offered a choice: to yield basely their rights or die nobly in defense of them.

It was an uninspired speech, delivered tonelessly, and at its end it became a temperance lecture; "From urgency," said Walker, "of the danger [surrounding the Phalanx] arose the greater necessity for becoming conduct."

The army was stiffened somewhat by its commander's words. The drinking did not stop, although the drunkenness did. And when a few days later there was brought into the camp a copy of President Mora's latest decree, the *falanginos* summoned from somewhere added courage—for they knew as they read that nothing but courage would save them from dying.

The Mora decree read:

All the filibusters taken with arms in hand will be subject to all the rigors of the law, which in this case is death. But all filibusters who have not used their arms against this Republic, and give up out of free will their arms and persons to officers of the Costa Rica army, shall be pardoned.

VII

ON THE whole, the Americans in Nicaragua had met good fortune. They had seen a few killed and a few more die of cholera, but the mortality rate was no greater than it would have been, say, in the California gold country. They were the adherents of a leader who thought himself (and seemed by achievement to be) the favorite of destiny. And destiny picked this time, fittingly enough, to administer a few defeats. The first of these came not from the arms of advancing Costa Ricans, but from the bluff Commodore in New York, who signed a paper and with the signature all but destroyed the Filibuster.

While Walker girded his loins and drilled an army from which he had expelled all Germans and French because of the conduct of their compatriots under Schlessinger, Cornelius Vanderbilt was bombarding the State Department with protests and demands for justice. But Washington, feeling that he had been hoist with his own petard, and still politically unwilling to declare for or against Walker, replied non-committally to his communications. The Commodore, then, placed reliance as he had for all his life upon the power he had created; he ordered the Pacific steamship *Cortes* to touch at San Juan, take under tow the coaling ship anchored there and proceed to Aspinwall, in Panama. The ships on the Atlantic line were reduced to a few, whose destination was ordered to be the eastern terminal of the Panama railway. This had all been dictated early in March, soon after Vanderbilt was informed of the charter revocation; Walker did not learn of it until All Fools' Day, when young Garrison landed from the south-bound *Cortes*.

Garrison, endowed by his father with full authority to deal with Nicaragua, came at once to Rivas, where Walker was encamped, and informed him of the Vanderbilt order. Morgan & Garrison, he said, had no ships ready at the moment, and would not be able to start service under the new Transit charter for at least six weeks. The dismay Walker knew when this condition was revealed to him may be imagined. Everything he had done until now had been based on the life line to the United States. He had himself cut that line, but he thought he had first obtained a substitute. Now, on April 1, 1856, he was in a corner from which nothing could extricate him but his own ingenuity. He had a potential strength of a thousand Americans, more or less. He had some ammunition, but lacked adequate artillery for any sort of attack. There would be no contact with the United States until mid-May, if then. It was made clear that in canceling Vanderbilt's charter without giving the old Transit Company a chance to negotiate he had overreached himself; the cost of his impatience was now told. But it is in keeping with his character that he did not consider himself to have erred. Every informed observer of the period knew how frightful a blunder he had committed in exchanging Vanderbilt's probable friendliness for enmity; but Walker did not know it. Walker thought only that he had been betrayed by Morgan & Garrison. He called their action bad faith and "timidity—to use no harsher word." And his demeanor did not change, nor did his fanatical belief in himself waver. As though Garrison's son had never come with bad news, he went ahead calmly with the business of the war, heedless of Schlessinger's defeat, Vanderbilt's blow and the lessons that might have been learned from both.

With service suspended, he could see no reason for continuing to hold the Transit route. He decided then to embark upon a course thoroughly illogical. Instead of remaining where he was, safe behind the adobe walls and stout barricades of Rivas, he ordered his army to move north to Granada.

With President Rivas and his cabinet now established in the latter city, Walker was by presidential decree military ruler of the two Departments of Rivas and Granada. But the Filibuster was not relieved of full responsibility to the government. President Rivas wrote him almost every day, from Leon, crying out that the northern countries were threatening an invasion and an alliance with Costa Rica, and pleading for protection. The executive, prodded by the ubiquitous Mariano Salazar, was busy undermining the Walker dictatorship; but the Filibuster, foolishly, did not suspect this and accepted the warnings of a northern menace in good faith. He had no knowledge of the size of General Mora's army and he was forced to base his guesses on the scouting parties which had been seen south of Rivas. He ordered a march, therefore, because he had received false reports from the North and no reports from the South. However skilled he was in the conduct of battle before and afterward, the evacuation of Rivas was a grievous error. He abandoned a line which was effectively protected by redoubts on the mere rumor that other governments would march against him. And he left open to Mora's advancing three thousand the key city of the Nicaragua of that day— Rivas, commanding the Transit.

Only one man, apparently, saw the folly of this northward march. Domingo de Goicouria, who had become quartermaster general, was left in Rivas to settle the affairs of the army. Goicouria learned first of the intention to abandon Rivas when he received an order to furnish transport for the entire command, which was to move to Virgin Bay for embarkation. The Cuban sought Walker at his headquarters, only to be told that the general had gone to Virgin Bay with a small company to obtain the use of the boat. Goicouria followed. He pleaded with Walker that a sufficient number of men be left behind to hold the barricades should General Mora advance. But Walker, actuated by his prejudice against the bewhiskered patriot and his distaste for any unsought advice, told Goicouria to mind his own affairs. "The conceit of Goicouria, excited by his new rank and title," Walker wrote later, "had turned his head; and although he had scarcely been a month in the country he foolishly presumed to thrust his opinion unasked on his general-in-chief. Of course he got a short answer and Walker began to think the shoes and shirts [which Goicouria had brought with him from the United States as a contribution to the cause] might be too dearly purchased. . . ."

Walker recounts his maneuver as a masterly strategem; it was, in bitter truth, a sickening display of military ignorance, reminiscent of the Sonora tactics. The river boat *San Carlos* was commandeered for the dispatch of the soldiers and Goicouria reluctantly watched the Phalanx march on board. Walker crossed Nicaragua to Fort San Carlos, to pick up the garrison there, and then went to Granada.

He achieved nothing by his action; Mora, at the border, had been watching for days for movement behind the entrenchments at Rivas and now, with the entire Department unoccupied by Walker's forces, the Costa Rican advanced.

Two days after Walker left, Mora reached Virgin Bay. He surrounded the Transit Company building and fired into it. Nine United States citizens, employed by the Transit Company, were killed in the first volley. The wounded, possibly numbering as many, were put to the bayonet. Their bodies were plundered, the building wrecked and then burned. When the soldiers had finished destroying a position so easily defensible that a tenth of Walker's men could have held it, they proceeded to San Juan del Sur and Rivas.

Walker learned of the killings at Virgin Bay and the capture of Rivas on the eighth. He ordered his army to return at once and attack the Costa Ricans. Five hundred and fifty marched on the ninth of April to attempt, in what became known as the second battle of Rivas, the seizure of a city willingly given up four days before.

On the night of the ninth the army had reached the Omogocho River, ten miles south of Granada, where it was met by Goicouria and his retreating guard. The next day, through stifling heat and choked with the thick dust of the road, the men plodded on southward. Another river encampment—at the Gil Gonzales— found them that night within striking distance of Rivas and informed that the battle odds would be six to one.

Late in the evening, a stranger was seen lurking near the camp. He was brought before Walker and proved to be a native Nicaraguan—innocent, by the Blessed Virgin, of all wrong. They threatened him and badgered him without learning anything of moment. Walker, the direct and dispassionate, sent for a rope. The Nicaraguan was hoisted gently until only his toes touched the ground; and then, whimpering, he admitted that he had been sent by the army of General Mora, to learn what he could of the enemy. Walker listened to what he had to tell: the position of the houses occupied by the officers of the enemy, the strength of the force, the condition of the barricades—a veritable gush of words, tumbling over one another in their eagerness to be spoken. When the spy fell silent at last, gasping with the effort he had made to tell everything, Walker said, "Hang him," and turned away. He did not look again at the dangling body; he was the only man in the camp so to ignore it.

He made his plans for the entire action of the next day on the information given by the spy. Four companies of rifles were to enter through the northern streets and move at full charge to the headquarters of Mora. Three companies were to detour and reach the grand plaza by the south; other detachments were to take flanking positions right and left; and a large body was to hold the rear and stand in reserve. Walker hoped to take the plaza at once, to capture Mora and to seize the arsenal and magazine, which were opposite the Costa Rican's headquarters.

They hit the town a little before nine, after a march of seven hours. The rifle companies drove in the pickets and advanced at a run as far as the plaza. Orders were to stop for nothing until they reached the house occupied by Mora, but in the middle of the street in which the Costa Rican's headquarters was located they came upon a small brass cannon. They charged and captured it and were so overcome with their great success that they hauled it back to the plaza, capering like children about a new toy. The delay was enough to give the Costa Ricans time to form; they fortified themselves in the houses fronting on the plaza and put a vicious fire into the ranks of the surging Americans. Despite this resistance, the Americans within an hour held every house around the plaza, having driven the enemy back into the streets to the west.

Although this time not deserted by any of his men, Walker again found himself in the sort of self-made trap which had defeated him at the first battle of Rivas. He had won the plaza, but he was all but surrounded there. Further, his troops had lost their first zeal when their headlong charge was halted and many had dropped their rifles and now lay apathetically inside the adobe houses. For the entire afternoon a desultory fight was kept up, distinguished only by a single action—the charge of a dozen officers who volunteered to drive out a hundred Costa Ricans and did it with a blast of revolver fire.

When night came Walker realized that what he had gained was of no value to him. He therefore ordered the town abandoned. The enemy, stupidly officered, permitted him to leave with no

attempt to harass his retreat. Norvell Walker was not to be found
when the column again reached the banks of the Gil Gonzales. He
had been drunk the night before the action and in the heat of the
day climbed into the tower of one of the churches and fell asleep.
When he awakened it was long after dark and the town was quiet.
He made his way to the street and looked into half a dozen houses
before admitting to himself that his brother had led the Nicaraguan
army out of Rivas without taking him along. He escaped without
challenge, skulking through alleys and hiding in the shadows when
figures showed up near him; he rejoined his command some distance
beyond the Gil Gonzales.

Walker's return to Granada was greeted with great enthusiasm:
rockets flared, bells pealed and the populace cheered. But this was
hysteria. The "paralyzing blow" his book mentions as having been
struck against the Costa Ricans does not hold up under examination.
He had weakened his force without dislodging the enemy.

VIII

Whatever William Walker's course of action in Nicaragua had been,
he would have involved himself in a war with another power. It has
been shown that his rise to dictatorship alarmed the other republics
and impelled Costa Rica to the extremity of declaring war, not against
a country but against a man. With a sketchy knowledge of Walker's
outward moves from June, 1855, to May, 1856, the casual observer
would have sympathized with him because he was facing, in a conflict with Costa Rica, unwarranted aggression. But the Filibuster's
behavior on the Isthmus had gone beyond that of an ordinary invader. His forthright executions of Mayorga and Corral added to
the opposition he would have met in any case. His extraordinary
insistence upon dignity irritated other persons—some of his own
men, as will be developed later. And finally, his flight into the face
of Providence, as impersonated by Cornelius Vanderbilt, added the
capstone to the enormous structure of enmity he had incurred, largely
by unwise obstinacy. With the original fifty-eight Immortals and
with saner behavior, he might have captured all of Central America.
By building slowly he might have made himself a supreme dictator.

By treating with Vanderbilt and allying himself with the old Transit Company, he might have made that dictatorship reasonably permanent.

But those would have been the deeds and maneuvers of a normal filibuster. Walker could not be other than he was—and that was as arrogant a little man as ever strode the earth. Obsessed with the conviction of his Providential selection, he went beyond even the extreme limitations of that philosophy and presumed to dictate destiny. Mayorga was an implement to bludgeon Corral, and Walker took upon himself the guise of fate to wield the implement. Corral annoyed him (it would be unfair to say that Walker's impulse in this connection went beyond annoyance, because Corral was by the very nature of circumstances an impotent figure) and he eliminated Corral. Finally, in the case of the Transit, Walker sat as judge, jury, prosecution and defense, examined the portion of the evidence he wished to examine, arrived at his decision and unloosed the forces of a veritable hell.

Vanderbilt rested not in his drive to embarrass his little opponent. On April eighth, three days after the second battle of Rivas, his New York office sent these instructions to Hosea Birdsall, an agent en route to Greytown:

> In addition to the instructions given to you with reference to the company's property, I have further to add that if the Walker filibusters attempt to employ force to rescue the boat [one then in Greytown] from your possession, you are authorized to ask for the assistance of the commander of any Man of War of Her Brittanic Majesty's Navy in the port of San Juan [Greytown] to prevent such rescue.
>
> The object of the Transit Company is to prevent accessions of filibusters to Walker's force pending his hostilities with Costa Rica, and to effect this purpose no pains must be spared or no efforts left untried.
>
> Should an American Man of War have reached the port with instructions, an application to any of Her Majesty's officers will be unnecessary.
>
> Unless our boats are seized by the filibusters on the *Orizaba* and the *Charles Morgan* [en route to Panama] they cannot get into the interior and without large accessions Walker must fail and Costa Rica be saved.
>
> To this result Her Majesty's Officers [in Greytown] can materially contribute by protecting American property in the manner indicated.

The contrast between the Filibuster and the Commodore cannot but place Vanderbilt in the more favorable light. Ruthlessness had built for him an enormous fortune. He would spend great sums gladly—if he could not take what he wanted. And if another sought to take from him, he moved forthrightly in the direction calculated to crush such thievery. Here is the peerless example of filibusterism in the hands of a master: the United States having ignored the Transit Company's protests over the seizure of its property, the Company turns calmly to a nation certain to assist. Vanderbilt must have known, as he dictated the instructions for Birdsall, that the United States Minister in Nicaragua would inform Washington of the instructions, that the bugaboo of England would return to float like a baleful ghost over the State Department and that another blow would have been struck against the sway of William Walker.

The Transit figured again in the Walker saga at this period, when General Mora, as President of Costa Rica, informed Secretary of State Marcy that American ships would be seized by his government if they carried recruits to Walker; further, he would consider any lake or river boat hostile if it carried such troops and fire on it without warning. It was an empty threat, but Walker, learning of it, was worried; presently, however, Minister Wheeler, throughout a prejudiced adviser to the Americans, informed him that Marcy had answered strongly and Mora would not dare to take action. To Walker, the matter of firing on the Transit boats was of no consequence, as the only vessels then in service were the *San Carlos* and *La Virgen,* each of which was in the possession of the filibusters and capable of being sailed cautiously enough not to give Mora any opportunities. But the weeks he spent waiting for Marcy's reply were uneasy ones. With Vanderbilt crying for the aid of Britain and American policy wavering day by day, it was of the greatest consequence that Marcy not altogether disown him.

On the twenty-first of April, Hornsby came down from New York (apparently aboard a boat other than Vanderbilt's) bringing two hundred recruits. The increase was most welcome, for the American Phalanx, since the French and Germans had been discharged, had been shorter of men than Walker wished it to be. Restored to its previous strength, however, discipline improved. The men were well entrenched in Granada. Walker made no move for the rest of the month; spies kept him informed of Mora's situation in Rivas and what he learned made him believe that the war would win itself.

The mad pattern of this man's life is shot through with inexplicable luck. Having lost a significant battle, and the good will of Vanderbilt, he appeared beaten. But cholera came to ravage the Costa Rican stronghold and the tide began to turn.

IX

THE second battle of Rivas, from the Americans' point of view had been a defeat. Nothing had been gained by it, as far as Walker could see, and, when he led his troops through the narrow streets in the darkness and back along the road to Granada, he had little to show for his enterprise. The facts Walker set forth in *The War in Nicaragua* have been accepted by unfriendly historians as accurate: he admitted total losses of one hundred and twenty, and asserted that the Mora casualties must have been six hundred, of whom two hundred were killed.

Upon his return to Granada, though, Walker gave his inept generalship the look of strategy. He made Nicaraguans and his own officers believe he had dictated a Pyrrhic victory for the enemy. That this became true because of outside influences has nothing to do with his conduct of the battle, of course—he merely twisted the facts to convince himself, as well as others, that a quick blow at Rivas and immediate retreat had been his plan from the first.

At any rate, he retired from the city leaving two hundred dead Costa Ricans sprawling grotesquely in the streets and alleys. General Mora's army, while it outnumbered Walker's five to one, was by no means so tempered a military instrument as the Filibuster's. The Costa Rican had infantry and a little artillery, no surgical corps to speak of, no officers worthy of the name. Thus, when it became known that the *Yanquis* had gone, the bodies of the Costa Rican dead were not intelligently buried, but were instead left to rot, many being cast into the wells of the town. The sudden increase in disease (cholera, largely) followed in a matter almost of hours. Within a week Mora saw his army disappearing like a puff of smoke. Soldiers died at all hours, in all attitudes, at all tasks. Sentries did not move when their fellows touched them. Diners slumped over, to be dead in a day. Officers and men alike drank water horribly polluted and epidemic had a merry holiday.

Strict orders were issued that no letters be written to Costa Rica, but in some manner the news of the army's disaster reached San José. Mora on the fifteenth had written a brilliant report of his victory, optimistically describing the number of enemy dead:

> All the time prisoners, wounded and unwounded, are coming up. Up to today seventeen have been shot. In brief, our loss, counting the mortally wounded, will not exceed one hundred and ten men, including the officers; that of the enemy not less than two hundred, including those we have shot.

But the terrible mortality in his ranks could not be kept a secret. San José became more and more uneasy, believing not only that its own army was being decimated, but that Walker was on his way south to invade the capital. As this fear grew, it was put to the customary use of Central American politics: Mora's opponents began to foment revolution against him and to save himself he had to travel southward, leaving his army, before the opposition could grow.

His brother-in-law, José Maria Cañas, remained in command. Cañas tried ineffectually to restrict the spread of the epidemic, but it had gained too greatly for any preventives to be of value. He resolved, therefore, to retreat lest the entire army die before his eyes. The proud three thousand numbered no more than a third of that when they started for San José. The retreat was a nightmare. Soldiers fell out of line by dozens, every day. The column moved with the irregularity and slowness of a snail and, like the snail, left on the country through which it passed the mark of a slimy trail. The disease spread throughout lower Nicaragua and Costa Rica; even Walker's men, in Granada, were not spared. Cañas, reaching San Juan del Sur, buried five hundred on the beach there; the dead were covered with mere scoops of sand and for months afterwards passengers on the Pacific boats were horrified to see a beach paved not with the gorgeous seashells of the Pacific, but with the whitening skeletons of what had been men.

Walker watched the progress of the plague, his carven face reflecting ever so slightly his satisfaction with a new manifestation of his destiny. His brother James died of fever, but he grieved not, listening abstractedly to the news and attending the funeral with no more emotion than he would have displayed for anyone else. He was traveling too fast now to consider trifles. Costa Rica had been his main concern—James Walker was only another soldier in the army who fell ill and died.

If any further proof of Costa Rica's utter defeat was needed, Walker found it in this message, sent by General Cañas:

> Obliged to abandon the plaza of Rivas, on account of the appearance of the cholera in its most alarming form, I am forced to leave here a certain number of sick it is impossible to carry away without danger to their lives; but I expect your generosity will treat them with all the attention and care their situation requires. I invoke the laws of humanity in favor of these victims of an awful calamity, and I have the honor of proposing to you to exchange them when they get well for more than twenty prisoners who are in our power, and whose names I will send you in a detailed list for making the exchange.
>
> Believing that this, my proposal, will be admitted, according to the laws of war, I have the honor of subscribing myself, with feelings of the highest consideration. . . .

The request of Cañas is a clear and typical demonstration of the thought processes which brought about in Walker's time events defiant of all laws of reason and logic. There was no stability, no consistency, in any of the Central American countries of the middle Fifties. While San Salvador was officially exclaiming its approval of the works of Walker, men of high standing within that very country were appealing to England for aid in the suppression of the filibusters. While President Rivas with one voice was urging Walker to protect the North from invaders, with another he was inviting such invasion. And while Costa Rica, in April, could through its President promise no quarter for the Americans, it could in the middle of the next month ask quarter for its own troops. Perhaps the labyrinthian thought and process of Central American politics had a larger share in the discomfiture of Walker than history generally credits; from such incidents as the Cañas appeal to an enemy's humanity, it would certainly appear so.

There is good reason to suppose that Walker believed himself to be a just man. However cruel and wrong his individual actions sometimes were, he obeyed with rare fidelity a code of his own. In the case of the Costa Rican sick, he placed them in hospitals already over-filled with his own men and gave them the same treatment. Whether they were exchanged after recovery is not made clear; it is likely, however, that they were set free, to find their way home as they might.

As a contrast to his behavior toward Cañas' men, Walker demonstrated his unswerving passion for what he called right in the direction of punishment. There was brought to him at Virgin Bay a Nicaraguan, Francisco Ugarté, son of wealth and a staunch Legitimist. Ugarté, from his Rivas home, had directed squads of Mora's men to the hiding places of the few deserters and wounded who had not been able to leave the city when Walker, his attack a failure, had marched out through the back streets. Walker listened to the charges against Ugarté. In the same tone he had used to specify humane treatment for the Costa Ricans, he ordered Ugarté tried by drum-head court-martial—the equivalent, in that army, of a death sentence.

James C. Jamison, a Missourian and captain in Walker's forces, heard an exchange between the Filibuster and the traitor the evening after sentence had been passed. Walker was hailed from the barred window of the guardhouse. Ugarté said he would pay for his liberty in gold, twenty thousand dollars' worth.

Walker replied coldly, "I don't want your money, but your life—you have forfeited it."*

Ugarté was hanged the next day.

"This mode of punishment for such offenders," says *The War in Nicaragua,* "being unusual in the country—shooting being resorted to instead of hanging—the execution of Ugarté made a strong impression on the people and infused a salutary dread of American justice among the plotting Legitimists."

X

NICARAGUA again was at peace, but by no means at ease.

---

* *With Walker in Nicaragua.*

The outcome of the Costa Rican foray must have surprised Walker as much as it did President Mora. In mid-April, with the ships of the Transit idle, American discipline gone, President Rivas fleeing to Leon, and an army three thousand strong coming up the Isthmus, defeat rode at the elbow of the Filibuster. In mid-May the threats and dangers had been removed and the dictatorship once again appeared firmly established. What new delusions this extraordinary good fortune brought to Walker may be judged by what followed the close of the war.

Edmund Randolph had wanted to leave the country when his work as adviser on the Transit charter revocation was over, but two circumstances held him in Nicaragua: fever, which kept him in bed for several weeks, and the task of determining, from what few records were available, the total of the debt the Accessory Transit Company owed the government. On May twentieth, Randolph was well enough to travel from Leon (where he had moved when the situation of Granada became precarious) to the capital. He remained in Granada for a day or two, principally to warn Walker against President Rivas. He could not tell, he said, what was brewing in Leon; with the lawyer's conservatism, he summed up his suspicions in the sentence, "Something is wrong there." He went away, having said this much, to Greytown, to board ship for New Orleans.

Six months before, such a warning—even from Edmund Randolph—would have been forgotten by Walker five minutes after he heard it. But the haste with which President Rivas had left Granada, and the contradiction between his pleas for help against the "invaders" from the North and his insistence that he was remaining in Leon only to maintain contact with the northern republics, made Walker wary. Further, Walker had learned that President Rivas, a fortnight or so after the declaration of war against Costa Rica, had written to the State suggesting an amicable settlement. Such a communication, sent without the knowledge of the commander-in-chief of the armies, was more than a hint of treachery; and as he had with Corral, Walker proceeded to give President Rivas sufficient rope.

While the army of Costa Rica had been within the borders of Nicaragua, reports of a Legitimist gathering in the interior had been received. Waiting in Granada, to see what move President Rivas might make, Walker sent parties out to suppress any revolutionary movements wherever found. Goicouria was sent into the hills of Chontales, where he scattered a small band of Legitimists. Vallé, who had been in active command of the troops to the north, reported from Segovia that he had put down the feeble efforts of the aristocrats there; and Mariano Salazar also went into the North "to pacify the Indians." From the succeeding events, it would seem that Salazar did rather more than pacify; when, in a few weeks, he supported President Rivas' declaration outlawing the American Phalanx and its chief, he did so from the region into which he had gone as an arm of the Filibuster's military machine.

The retreating Costa Ricans had left behind them an active enemy in cholera and conditions in Granada became so unhealthy that Walker moved his men to Virgin Bay. While there, the news from Leon made it necessary that he act with decision, to keep the country from what might well prove a fatal division.

He could see that Rivas, until something should be done to direct his actions, would continue to complain from Leon and do nothing to gain the affection of Honduras, Guatemala and San Salvador. Walker himself was disposed to conciliate those governments only because he had not yet reached the eminence from which he could dismiss their protests. Until long after the war with Costa Rica, therefore, he exerted himself to make his presence in Central America more reassuring to the frightened citizens of its five nations.

Among the first acts of the Rivas government, it will be recalled, had been the dispatch of a proclamation to the neighboring republics, asserting a desire for free intercourse with them and declaring the most pacific intentions. San Salvador alone had replied, congratulating Nicaragua on the achievements of its general-in-chief; Honduras, Guatemala, and Costa Rica had remained officially silent. But the one willing friend, as has been shown, had been lost when Walker turned away Trinidad Cabañas. The latter's violent manifestoes had impelled the Salvadorian government to send a commissioner to inquire as to Nicaragua's intentions and to protest against the addition of any more American recruits to the army. This Commissioner, Colonel Justo Padilla, had arrived on the very day that saw Goicouria's two hundred and fifty men land at Granada. He was an absurd little man, Padilla, dressed in faded trousers far too short for him, a military coat, heavily braided but so tight and so short that his fat little paunch was exposed in its nakedness, and a preposterous cocked hat brave with feathers. His sword was the reverse in size of his garments, so long it dragged on the ground behind him as he strode toward the quarters of Walker. Informed of his coming, Walker decided unwisely; instead of reassuring him and sending him happily back to San Salvador, to report on the gentleness of the Americans, the Filibuster chose to line up his entire army, including the new Goicouria recruits. Padilla, then, walked toward Government House across a plaza thick with armed Americans. He paused on the steps before going inside to see Walker; paused, shook his head so slowly that the feathers of his hat barely moved and murmured thoughtfully, *"Muchos soldados!"*

His report to his Salvadorian superiors further widened the breach between the countries. Later, when President Rivas at Walker's suggestion sent commissioners to treat for future amity, they were turned away; and the answer to their message was contained in a formal note to the Nicaraguan government, dated May 7, 1856, in which it was charged that the presence of the Americans "threatened the independence of Central America."

Now added to this were the gestures being made by Guatemala. On June third President Rivas' fears became so great that he issued a proclamation, announcing the advance of Guatemalan war parties into Nicaragua and calling upon all to take up arms for the protection of the Republic.

Walker left Hornsby in command at Virgin Bay and rode to Leon, to hearten Rivas, to make clear to him that treachery would win him a bullet and to conciliate those Leonese who might be drifting away from the filibuster banner.

XI

He rode into Leon on June fourth. No dictator, ancient or modern, could have asked for a more spontaneous reception. Every dignitary in the town was at its outskirts to escort the little party to the temporary executive mansion. With the bearded Goicouria on one side,

Lieutenant Colonel Anderson at the other, and nearly three hundred mounted Rangers and Infantrymen, the general was the symbol of assurance and power. The streets were filled with crowds, gathered to see the great *Yanqui* of whom they had heard so much. The women wore their most brilliant dresses, the men their cleanest cottons, and all waved heartily at the "deliverer." A feast was prepared in the great patio of the house President Rivas was occupying; from its table Walker was called to an inside room to receive the thanks of a delegation for all he had done for the country. "In the evening," Walker wrote appreciatively, "the musicians came to sing songs in praise of American valor, and the local rhymsters of the place—of whom there were not a few—poured forth the sonorous sounds of Castillian verse in glory of the strangers who had delivered Nicaragua from the oppression of her enemies. All seemed to vie with each other in their demonstrations of respect and good-will toward the Rifles and the Rangers."

Cold, intimate with no other mortal, puritanical, inflexible, diseased with the leprous germ of dictatorship, Walker was ideally constituted to believe only part of what he saw. For twelve days short of a year he had been dealing with a people so mercurial that even they themselves could not look ahead to tomorrow and know what their feelings would be, and he did not regard his position among these people as in any degree certain. Because they cheered him on June 4, 1856, he did not assume that they would cheer him the next month, or the next year.

Rivas was the enigma he must solve in order to hold the country; the President seemed poised to jump and when he did Walker was determined to be ready to counter. The executive seemed unwarrantedly concerned over the antagonism of San Salvador and Guatemala; and on the fifth, the day after his arrival, Walker learned the reason for this pretended apprehension.

San Salvador, said President Rivas, had announced its willingness to deal with Nicaragua if the American forces were reduced to two hundred men. If Walker and he could settle this point their fears would be over. He finished talking in his wavering voice and waited, with the naïve confidence of a child, for Walker to agree to the proposal.

From *Frank Leslie's Illustrated Newspaper.*

CALLENDER IRVINE FAYSSOUX

The Filibuster minced no words. Such a proposition could be entertained, he said—but only when the men under his command were paid in full for their services. Rivas wilted. He wilted more when Walker began to discuss the need for a new election. A vote of sorts had been ordered in April, and had been conducted, oddly enough, on a succession of Sundays. Throughout May the vote was cast, but at the end of that month the returns gave no clear indication of who might claim the Presidency. Walker now proposed that the irregularity of this vote made a new one necessary. He did not mention, although the probability was free to be guessed, that he would be a candidate. His journey to Leon, it proved, was only partly to ascertain for himself the condition of affairs and the loyalty of President Rivas. Before leaving Granada, he had been approached by the citizens of the place, who had spoken of their fear that the capital would be moved permanently to Leon if the every-Sunday-in-May election were allowed to stand. To prevent their hated rival from resuming its place in the political sun, Granadinos were eager that Walker seek the highest office they had to give.

President Rivas, Maximo Jerez—who had been with him since the removal of the seat of government—and Mariano Salazar cried aloud that no new election could be called. Walker remained quietly firm. An election would make him President, an election was due and therefore an election must be held. He repeated his points again and again and skilfully touched upon the danger from San Salvador and Guatemala in this negotiation. Although President Rivas did not promise to call the election, he was a more thoughtful man after the conference.

And Walker, irritated by the suggestion of interference (from the legal President of the Republic), occupied himself with a consideration of the Rivas faction and the quickest means of bringing it to heel. Mariano Salazar, the fat and greedy merchant, offered within a day an excellent subject for the Filibuster's discipline. Walker learned somehow that Salazar had sold the government some brazilwood at an outrageous price. The wood had been smuggled into the country and, in addition to its high cost as a purchase, the State had lost the revenue it might have collected at the port of Realejo. Walker acted toward Salazar as harshly as he had acted in banish-

ing Mariano Mendez: he flung the protesting merchant into the
guardhouse, charged him with defrauding the government and
hinted broadly that if the might of the Phalanx was challenged a
military court would try the prisoner.

Walker had no intention of trying Salazar and in fact released
the merchant in a few hours. Graft in Nicaragua, he had learned,
was too virile an octopus to be deprived of even one tentacle so early
in the fight. Nevertheless he threw a mighty fear into the hearts of
the government's leaders. Their protests that what Salazar had done
was no more than the custom of the country were weak and frightened. The simple action won Walker respect—but only for the balance of his stay in Leon.

In visiting Leon, Walker claimed that his intention was to solidify
the ranks of the Democrats. His demands for an election and the
arrest of Salazar cast doubt upon this claim; it is more probable that
his impatience made him chafe at the delays he was meeting and
sought to hasten his seizure of the country by stirring up further discord in the traditional capital of the Democrats. Certainly his own
actions while in Leon did nothing to endear him to Rivas, Salazar
and the rest; and when Domingo de Goicouria had concluded a
speech—on June sixth, the Sunday after Walker's arrival—there was
still another weapon to be used by the conspirators opposing the
Filibuster: the charge that he meant to destroy the Church.

No charge could have been more false. Not now or at any time
did Walker underestimate the Church. Roughshod he might ride
over everything else; against the power of Rome he admitted himself
to be too small to fight. But an innocent remark of Goicouria's destroyed for him much of what this respect for the clergy had built
up. Goicouria's suggestion was made to the city's leaders, at a conference held to discuss thoroughly everything pertaining to the condition of the country. He delivered what Walker called "a rambling
discourse on his ideas—most crude they were—of reorganizing the
country." Goicouria, said Walker, "labored under the delusion that
he knew the natives, whereas he always underestimated the capacity
of the leaders and the virtues of the people." Toward the end of his
talk Goicouria mentioned the wisdom of obtaining a Bishop for the
country who might be free of the Metropolitan of Guatemala. Con-

sidering the hostility of the latter country and the close connection between Church and State in the period, the remark is not the unutterably stupid one Walker later made it appear. But present at the meeting were Nicaraguans eager to be rid of Walker, who seized upon Goicouria's plan, distorted it into a plot to destroy the Church and so presented it to the gullible peasants. The harm done by this was great; and the unfortunate Goicouria, already sustaining himself in the Walker forces only by what seems to have been a magnificent control of temper, was cast further into the shadows.

On Tuesday, the tenth, the steady pressure on President Rivas and his cabinet resulted in a reluctant decree, ordering a new election immediately. His task done, Walker started from the city for his headquarters at Virgin Bay. He left behind him the companies of Rifles and was escorted by the Rangers. President Rivas, Salazar and others high in the Democratic councils accompanied the general to the outskirts of the city, where there was a touching leave-taking: "Don Patricio affectionately embraced the General-in-Chief, remarking, with moist eyes, that he might be depended upon in every emergency." Walker reached Masaya on June eleventh. Before he could start from that city on the following morning, a courier overtook him, to describe dangerous happenings at Leon.

XII

BRUNO VON NATZMER was an experienced, uninspired Prussian soldier. At the end of a year of service under Walker, he understood what was required of him and obeyed whatever orders he was given without questioning or altering them from their literal sense. Trained in the European military school, he knew the meaning of obedience perhaps better than any other officer in the American Phalanx.

His orders, when Walker rode away south, were to remain in Leon with the Rifles, to guard against any surprise attack by Guatemala or San Salvador from the North and to keep watch on President Rivas and his crew. Almost before Walker was out of sight, the administration at Leon requested a detail of Americans to guard the *Principal,* a storehouse for arms and ammunition on the grand plaza. Von Natzmer obliged with a squad of sentries. The request was a

Rivas-Salazar trap to force the Americans into a position which might be misrepresented; as soon as the guard was in place, the trap was sprung by the spreading of false alarms.

The people in the streets lost their somnolence and grew tense. The officials in the house of President Rivas left hurriedly, carrying bits of baggage and wearing the air of unhappy fugitives. Mariano Salazar, his round belly swelling over a pommel, rode furiously through the streets, crying that the Americans were about to assassinate President Rivas and all his friends, burn the town and destroy the churches. From all sections armed men began to drift toward the plaza and their muttering contained the suppressed menace of any mob. The women closed shutters and barricaded doors, moving heavy articles of furniture against them; they said to one another, "It is the revolution," in tones of resignation. And Von Natzmer, standing off at a distance and watching the excitement, saw in it no more than the bare truth: the Americans were in disfavor and blood might well be spilled. He ordered his two hundred riflemen into the plaza, where they crouched behind the permanent barricades and waited for whatever might happen. A rider was sent to Chinandega, where there was a company of Rifles; a second courier rode south, to ask Walker for instruction and reinforcement.

The commander of the Rifles at Chinandega marched immediately for Leon. On the road he came upon two horsemen, riding rapidly away from the city, whom he recognized as the President and Mariano Salazar. He thought as they came abreast of his column that he should arrest them as a matter of precaution, but he was no more than a lieutenant, standing in some awe of such a dignitary as the President; and the two Nicaraguans were allowed to sweep by, their horses at the gallop and their strained eyes fixed upon their distant destination.

The courier from Leon who overtook Walker at Masaya was matched by another from Realejo. Walker had advised President Rivas to fortify that harbor, and the works had been going up on the beach for several weeks. The second courier brought word that Rivas had ordered the fortifications dismantled. Walker decided to return to Leon. As he rode, at the best speed his horse could give him, additional messengers came up, to report the growing tension in the city and an order from the remaining functionary of the Democratic government, Maximo Jerez, for the *falanginos* to withdraw their riflemen from the towers of the churches. Walker sped the rider who brought this last message with the instruction that Von Natzmer obey and take his entire force out of the city to the village of Nagarote, twenty miles south.

Walker waited at Nagarote. A spy came down from the North to report that President Rivas and Salazar had reached Chinandega and dispatched thence a rider to invite the armies of Guatemala into the country "to protect it against unlawful resistance to authority." Jerez's order to Von Natzmer was intended to be disobeyed, Walker knew, so that the Democratic officials would have grounds for a charge that the Americans were no longer a co-operating body. Riding fast, hearing news in gasped snatches from the couriers who met him, Walker conducted himself in this crisis as he should have conducted himself always. He ordered a withdrawal from Leon and placed the blame for whatever might happen squarely upon the government supposed to be his own. He concentrated his forces—scattered in small bodies from Segovia to Castillo Viejo on the San Juan River—and waited what might come.

When all the troops from the North had joined him, he marched at their head for Granada. Vallé the faithful, his guitar silent and his finger playing hungrily with the trigger guard of his rifle, arrived among the last, riding a lathered horse from which he had beaten the last ounce of speed and spirit. The Indian leader was a little complacent that affairs had taken this turn; he may well have recalled to Walker that in the beginning he had advocated the simple casting-out of all Democrats, with a new government to be started from scratch.

In any consideration of Walker, one is impressed with the odd discrepancy between character and mien. From the moment he learned of the death of Helen Martin, six years before, nothing about him (that could be seen with the eye) changed. He received news of defeat and victory alike, he commended and condemned in the same monotonous tone, his singular gray eyes looked upon what they saw with chilling directness. But he was deceptive, this clerkly little man. Inside him, on every day of his life, were conflict and disorder and change. His progression from hired soldier to president and dictator, judged outwardly, is a steady, inexorable growth—the spread, say, of a poison through the veins. To his contemporaries he was a commander who knew what he wanted long before he set out upon his elected road and who went after it with the best weapons he could master. But this is only partly true. Many evils flourished in his mind. A touch of success may not have altered his manners, but it did frightful things to his thoughts. His body walked primly along the path of justice, and his brain wallowed in a gutter running with humanity's most noxious filth—ruthless ambition and treachery. In truth, he was no paradox. He was the dictator, the complete lecher after the bawd, Power. It was only in the way he looked and walked and talked that he violated the dictator's tradition: he was a dispassionately clicking machine whose power derived from a white-hot flame in his vitals.

With the defection of President Rivas, he cast off the last of his pretence. In a finger's snap he ceased to be the general under orders and threw about his shoulders the mantle he had so long coveted. He became the law and the arbiter of death for those who might resist him.

XIII

To THE United States, he was the supreme embodiment of what an American should be.

When news of the defeat of Costa Rica reached New York, the public again applauded. Forgotten was the tragic blunder of the Transit conspiracy, gone were the unkind quips about "the little Napoleon." Mass meetings were held, a dozen or so of them, in various parts of the country. Congressmen spoke at them, proudly discussing their cynical conviction that the Union deserved what it could steal. Transparencies were hung before the meeting halls in New York and the lamps behind them lighted up such declarations as: "The Boundaries of Liberty Must Expand" and "No British Interference on the American Continent."

While resting his men at Granada after the Costa Ricans had evacuated Rivas, Walker had turned to one of his most faithful shadows, Padre Augustin Vijil. French had been disgraced and cast out and the country still lacked recognition from the United States, which must be obtained as an evidence that William Walker was backed by the powerful land to the north. In the search for a new minister-delegate to the United States, Walker's eye fell upon Vijil. The priest had the theatrical qualities—profundity of manner, thrilling voice, handsome stature—believed necessary in a diplomatic representative. He was thoroughly converted to the value of American domination in his own country. He was schooled in the law and might be expected to act cunningly for his government. So Vijil was appointed by President Rivas and, before the latter could turn against Walker, the good Padre was accepted by Washington. Thus Nicaragua under William Walker was officially recognized at last.

Vijil reached New York to find the city populated almost entirely by adherents of the Filibuster. As he waited over for a day or so before traveling to Washington, he heard the hoodlums before the firehouses lifting their voices (but not yet derisively) in one of the several songs* about the new conqueror. Proceeding to Washington, he was given as mixed a reception, perhaps, as any diplomat ever received. Marcy, the same Secretary of State who had refused to open the doors to French, was cordial, as was President Pierce. But Vijil's fellows of the diplomatic corps treated him harshly. The representatives of three governments—Costa Rica, Guatemala and San Salvador—protested against his recognition as soon as he reached Washington. One of these protests, by the minister who served both Guatemala and San Salvador, boldly accused the administration of seeking to sustain an outlaw even then on the point of

---

* From Fred Shaw's *Dime Songster*, a contemporary publication, are reprinted verses of two typical ditties:

I'M OFF TO NICARAGUA	I'VE BEEN TO NICARAGUA

Have you heard the way
  That's out today,
To better your condition O?
  Those who delight in
  Blood and fightin'
Join Walker's Expedition O.
There you can have all you can steal,
Without the chance of getting a meal;
  Your names will live in books of story,
  And you will live on martial glory.
	At close of day we marched away,
	  To the Army in Nicaragua.
	Not a bit of breakfast did I see,
	And dinner was the same to me:
	  Two fried cats
	  And three stewed rats
	  Were supper in Nicaragua;
	Marching all day with sore feet,
	Plenty of fighting and nothing to eat,
	  Way down in Nicaragua.

being overthrown and charged that Walker's filibusters meant to increase their sway over Mexico, Cuba and Panama, "leaving the task of extending their dominions as far as Tierra del Fuego to a later date." After the first outburst, other countries, notably Peru, New Granada (now Colombia) and Chile, filed protests. The condemnation heaped upon him by his own people gave Padre Vijil pause; he began to doubt, ever so slightly, the wisdom of going along with Walker.

But in spite of the efforts of the Latin American countries, and the more powerful secret negotiations of England and Spain, Vijil was minister. While he endured in Washington a multitude of humiliations, the man he represented climbed higher in the esteem of Americans. A gigantic meeting was held in New York the week after Vijil's recognition, at which Governor Rodman Price, of New Jersey, E. A. Pollard, the traveler and journalist, and Esaiah Rynders, Tammany chieftain, exalted the Filibuster. Letters were received from a number of gentlemen who could not attend: Thomas Francis Meagher, the Irish patriot, sent one; and Lewis Cass, of Michigan, a major contender for the Democratic Presidential nomination wrote: "The heroic effort of our countrymen in Nicaragua excites my admiration while it engages all my solicitude. . . . He who does not sympathize with such an enterprise has little in common with me. The difficulties which General Walker has encountered and overcome will place his name high on the roll of the distinguished men of his age. . . . A new day, I hope, is opening upon the States of Central America."

The sudden reversal of feeling among the officials of the United States followed the calendar with the timeless fidelity of politics. Vijil reached Washington on May fourteenth, three weeks before the Democratic convention in Cincinnati on June second. President Pierce, angling desperately for the Southern vote, was forced from the stand-pat position he had maintained for nearly a year and required by the necessities of his ambition to declare for Walker. In his explanation of the recognition of Padre Vijil, Pierce told Congress that the United States could not continue to ignore Nicaragua, and that the Rivas-Walker government then appeared to be the one desired by the people.

His efforts strengthened him in the convention. Southern delegates—seeing in Walker a new prop for the collapsing institution which was to plunge them into bitter warfare in so few years—rallied to Pierce as the champion of "manifest destiny" and American individualism. But the North swung to James Buchanan, who won the nomination. And even Buchanan, choice of the anti-slavery delegates, made his bow to the clamorous Walkerites in the statement: "The people of the United States cannot but sympathize with the efforts which are being made by the people of Central America to regenerate that portion of the continent which covers the passage across the interoceanic Isthmus."

Not until late in June was news of the latest discord in Nicaragua received in Washington, and by then Padre Vijil, disillusioned by his poor success in the field of international politics, had resigned his diplomatic position.

XIV

WITH his return to Granada, Walker plunged immediately into the responsibilities of his position. He resurrected the treaty of October 23, 1855, in which he and Ponciano Corral had agreed to guarantee naturalized Nicaraguans and natives alike the same privileges and placed this alongside President Rivas' proclamation from Chinandega to prove that the executive had violated a solemn oath. His own part in the events that followed was most logical to Walker; feeling that he was the sole surviving protector of the government, he revived in its literal form the document empowering him to rule absolutely over the Departments of Rivas and Granada and under its provisions (as well as the rights he assumed because of the Corral treaty) he prepared to order a new election. Meanwhile, the position held by President Rivas was declared to be vacated and Fermin Ferrer was named Provisional Director.

Before anything of importance happened in the one-sided struggle for control of the country, both Walker and Rivas issued manifestos. The first of these, dated June twentieth, was by Walker and read:

I, WILLIAM WALKER, GENERAL IN CHIEF OF THE ARMY OF NICARAGUA: *Whereas,* by the Treaty of the 23rd of October of the last year, D.

Patricio Rivas was appointed Provisional President of the Republic, and that the power with which he was invested was but an incident of the powers conferred upon me, by the Supreme Government, as General of the Expedition;

Whereas, the Provisional President, at the time of transferring himself from the city of Granada to that of Leon, in March last, delegated to me all the powers which had been entrusted to him to maintain order in the Eastern and Southern Departments of the Republic and watch, in its whole extent, over its security, guarding against foreign invasions and, in consequence, establishing martial law;

Whereas, the Provisional President, appointed the Secretary of the Treasury, D. Fermin Ferrer, a Commissioner in said Departments, investing him with all his own powers to assist my administration on all proper occasions;

Whereas, D. Patricio Rivas, the Provisional President, betraying his trust in a manner detrimental to the rights and welfare of the Republic, has clandestinely removed to Chinandega for the purpose of dismantling all the frontier fortifications of the West and delivering the Country to Carrera's [Guatemalan] forces which are on the point of invading; and subserviently to which end he has commissioned Mr. Mariano Salazar;

Whereas, on the 14th instant Mr. Rivas published a decree, issued by him four days before, calling upon the people of Nicaragua to elect, by direct suffrage, the individual who is to succeed him in power;

Whereas, the Treaty of October 23rd explicitly stipulated that both the contracting Generals guaranteed the maintenance of peace and order over the Republic; whilst Mr. Patricio Rivas is not only fomenting anarchy at home, but is also inviting invasion from enemies abroad, and lastly,

Whereas, the safety of the Republic is entrusted to me and that it is a sacred duty to save the country from anarchy. . . . I have deemed it expedient to decree, and I hereby

Decree

Article 1st. The Commissioner of the Government, Secretary of the Treasury, D. Fermin Ferrer, is appointed Provisional President of the Republic until the people shall have gone into an election in conformity with the Decree of the 10th instant which remains in full force in all its parts.

Article 2nd. All the provisions, whether in the shape of decrees, decisions or orders, issued by D. Patricio Rivas from the 12th instant thenceforward, are consequently declared to be null and of non-effect, said Rivas having removed from the trust which was confided to him in pursuance of the aforesaid treaty of the 23rd of October.

Article 3rd. All authorities, civil or military, of the Republic, yielding obedience to Mr. Rivas, as also all individuals, whether Native or Foreign, furnishing him with any kind of assistance whether by means of loans or by civil contracts, shall be held as traitors to the country and as such tried by Martial Law.

Article 4th. This decree shall be communicated to all parties interested and solemnly published among all the settlements of the Republic.

On the twenty-fifth, Patricio Rivas, who had returned to Leon, countered with a blanket order to Prefects of all Departments:

REPUBLIC OF NICARAGUA
DEPARTMENT OF RELATIONS
Government House, Leon,

The Supreme Executive Power has deemed it expedient to issue the following decree, through the Department of War:

The Provisional President of the Republic of Nicaragua to its inhabitants:

Whereas, General William Walker has since the 9th instant, given out his intention in the most explicit manner, to the Executive Provisional Power, and in the presence of the Secretary of War, and others, of subverting the public power by force; which intention, thus expressed, together with other serious incidents, induced the flight of the Government and its transfer to the city of Chinandega—a measure which was adopted with the view, at all hazard, of saving the dignity and sovereignty of the Republic and preserving the freedom necessary to meet the pestilent requirements of Mr. Walker, looking to immense grants of lands to foreigners, as a means to be used in the political and religious regeneration of Nicaragua, to the annulment of the election of the Supreme Authorities made by the people, and to the investment, in his person, of indiscriminate power with which he required to be entrusted for the purpose of raising means, even going so far as the confiscation of individual property and the sale and transfer thereof to foreigners; and also

Whereas, it is a notorious fact that said General is endeavoring to carry out such determination, *ipso facto* that he has repudiated the authority of the Government, and raised D. Fermin Ferrer to the Presidency, without any authority but that of force and with the absurd and guilty intent of subjecting Nicaragua and the other States of Central America to his absolute dominion;

Therefore it has been deemed expedient to issue the following

DECREE

Article 1. Said General William Walker is hereby declared to be an
enemy of Nicaragua, attainted of treason and he is, in consequence
hereof, divested of the authority with which he had been honored by
the Republic.

Article 2. The Chiefs, Officers and Troops, composing the American
Legion, who, yielding honorable and dutiful submission to the Government of the Republic, shall disconnect themselves from said Mr.
Walker and present themselves to this Government, will be recognized
in their service; their passages will be paid to them and, should they
see fit, they may continue to reside in the Republic, in the character
of Nicaraguans.

Article 3. Those, on the contrary, who may continue under the orders
and participate in the attempts of said Mr. Walker, and those also,
who may assist or abet him in any manner, directly or indirectly,
whether they belong to the American Legion or, unfortunately to the
country, shall be tried as traitors to the Republic, in conformity with
the Ordinance.

Article 4. Every Nicaraguan, without any exception or privilege, from
fifteen to sixty years, is required to take up arms against said Mr.
Walker and his followers; and also to serve the Government by such
employment as may be assigned to him, in defence of the liberty, the
independence and the sovereignty of the Republic.

After he had written this, Rivas, for some reason, decided to soften
it with a second decree. "Wishing to dispel any idea of hostility
toward the forces now under Mr. Walker's orders, because he held
them guiltless of the treasonable acts which the former has committed; desirous, on the contrary, of giving additional proof of his
benevolence, the President" clarified the provisions dealing with the
falanginos. He left open to them several courses: they might leave
the Republic without hindrance for any destination they chose; they
might remain within boundaries as civilians; or they might earn
rewards if they elected to present themselves to the Rivas government, with what arms and ammunition they could surrender. It is
needless to say that none of Walker's soldiers took advantage of this
last, and typically Latin offer; the Filibuster was too obviously the
superior in the struggle for even the stupidest of his men to suppose
that any profit might be gained by abandoning his cause for the
futile one of Rivas.

Between the second and third manifestos of Rivas, the election ordered by Walker was held. It started on Sunday, June 27, 1856, and continued for two days following. In a country lacking railways or telegraph, and with nothing but the most primitive roads connecting the major cities, it was impossible to inform the interior of the forthcoming election; but it was held, nevertheless, on the date specified. *El Nicaraguense,* which had been publishing regularly, revealed the results: For Walker, fifteen thousand, eight hundred and thirty-five votes, for Ferrer, four thousand, four hundred and forty-seven, for Rivas, eight hundred and sixty-seven, and for Salazar, two thousand and eighty-seven. Editor John Tabor (or Walker—each wrote for the paper and often the identity of an editorial's author was uncertain) asserted that returns had been received from all but a few sections of the country, including a heavy vote in Leon and ballots from nineteen Segovia and ten Chontales precincts. *Falanginos* returning later to the United States said that the vote was almost entirely cast by the army, and that they had voted several times, but Editor Tabor, in the first edition of *El Nicaraguense* following the election, made out elaborate tables intended to represent a full expression of the people's will. The Leon, Chontales and Segovia reports were obviously frauds, for President Rivas was installed in the first named place and had outlawed, by decree, this very election; and at the other points near the northern frontiers, Guatemalan, Honduran and Salvadorian soldiers were already encamped.

Nevertheless, William Walker was proclaimed by Provisional Director Ferrer as the duly elected President and his inauguration was scheduled for July 12, 1856. In the interim three things happened: Ferrer revived a plan approved by President Rivas for the sale of five hundred thousand dollars in Nicaraguan bonds in the United States, and Walker sent E. J. C. Kewen (brother of the dead Achilles) to New Orleans to dispose of them; more than one hundred new recruits arrived at Granada, having been carried to the country on a Garrison ship; and a third decree was issued by Rivas. This document revealed that a treaty had been signed by San Salvador and Nicaragua, under the terms of which the latter country agreed to reduce its foreign armed forces to two hundred men. In return for this concession, San Salvador agreed to form an alliance with Honduras, Guatemala and Costa Rica, and hold the vanguard of its armies on the "frontiers of Nicaragua for the purpose of conferring respectability and strength" on the government of President Rivas. Article six of the treaty read: "The government of Nicaragua, forgetting the past with respect to those Nicaraguans who have not recognized its authority, and wishing that they should live in perfect concord with their fellow citizens, spontaneously holds out the most efficient and trusty guarantees to all parties, whatever their opinions and political past may be, or may have been; and it will recognize the damages which the Democrats and Legitimists both may have suffered, decreeing the means to indemnify them in a certain and efficacious manner, and restoring to them the existing portions of their property which has been sequestered or in any manner confiscated, and all these under the guarantee of the government of Salvador and its Allies."

Here at last was the alliance Walker had anticipated, and Rivas had so diligently sought. From the date of its drafting—June seventeenth—Walker knew that negotiations must have preceded his visit to Leon, when "all seemed to vie with each other in their demonstrations of respect and good-will." Awaiting his inauguration, the new President could look beyond it to the sort of war Costa Rica had tried to wage—a war to the death, Americans against Central Americans, with empire as the prize he might win. He went calmly about his preparations for the assumption of the presidency and for the reform of the entire governmental structure. As he labored, so did his enemies. All Central America—excepting the portion he held— became one. Old party differences were forgotten, old wounds instantaneously healed and the hand of every man (except the few he commanded) was turned against the Filibuster.

BOOK FOUR

The Road to Rivas

BOOK FOUR
The Road to Rivas ...

...The army has yet written a page of American history which it is impossible to forget or erase. From the future, if not from the present, we may expect just judgment. ...

I

WILLIAM WALKER took the oath as President of Nicaragua on a platform in the grand plaza of Granada, at noon of July 12, 1856. A great throng, which had been collecting throughout the morning, watched almost in silence as he came to the precise peak of his career. The men of the Phalanx (hereafter to be called the rightful Army of the Republic) swaggered about in little groups, gigantic against the small-statured natives. Armed with revolvers on their hips and bowie knives in their belts, they were confident, cynical, unmoral and as dangerous as drunken Irishmen. The fondness with which they looked at their commander was only one of the fleeting emotions of that day; the Democratic Nicaraguans watched Walker with gloating hope, for he was (they believed) their hireling; the Legitimists, still present by thousands although perforce secretive about their politics, concealed with varying success their black hatred.

It was a bright day. The sun struck dazzling reflection from the white walls, the sky was a flawless blue. Breezes blowing in from the lake mitigated little the heavy heat of noontime. The spectators were sated with what they had seen: a morning devoted to political claptrap more Yankee than American, with band music, a parade and drinks for all comers. An hour before the oath was to be administered the parade achieved some cohesion; led by the filibusters, with Walker on a white horse, a great company marched to the platform set up on the west side of the plaza. There were native troops, an indifferent band, consular and other diplomatic officials, headed by Minister Wheeler, and every Nicaraguan who could lay claim, however slight, to municipal distinction.

The flowers so lavishly offered by the nearby jungles had been brought to Granada by the cartload and now hid from sight the raw lumber of the platform. Flags decked the railings: displayed were the Nicaraguan device of a seal and seven volcanoes, the Stars and Stripes, and, in subtle promise, the banner of Cuba, half hidden by the others. Against the brilliance of his background, the Filibuster was colorless. His men moved in the throng, boastful, assertive in their power; but he, whose creatures they were, looked to the reporter for the New York *Tribune* like "a grocery keeper from one of the poorer localities of the Sixth Ward." He was dressed in a rusty black coat, nondescript trousers and a felt hat. His face was the color of his flannel shirt. His expression, as he waited for the preliminary addresses to end, was the unanimated blank of a derelict on a morgue slab.

What William Walker thought of this culmination must be imagined, from the tone of his inaugural address and the fragmentary accounts of the ceremony itself. He has been introduced here as at "the precise peak of his career"; subsequent events were to prove the exactness of the phrase. Thus far his record had been one of progress—remembering always that his own ambition was the criterion by which he estimated his results. In this account of his life no effort has been made to spare him, either for the oblique impulses which dominated him or for his many blunders; but, considering him as he stood on the threshold of his presidency, one can pity his appalling blindness. In slightly over a year—or, if the Sonora fiasco be used to date his beginnings, in less than two—he had projected himself from the obscurity of a minor, migratory adventurer to the dictatorship of a sovereign State. No man could know certainly that he was nearly at the end of his incredible accomplishment and had he been any other person it is likely he would not have been finished. Unfortunately, however, he attempted to advance too quickly for his medium and his time. He saw in the inauguration ceremony in the

FORT SAN CARLOS

plaza at Granada much more than was actually there. The election whose result he had dictated and the powers he now claimed were no more than incidental in a struggle of infinitely wider scope than he could comprehend. There were Great Britain and the United States to be reconciled. There was the slavery issue to be decided, for the South was even now losing ground in this tremendous controversy and, to retain its support, Nicaragua as governed by Walker must take a definite stand. There were other concerns, every one calculated to embarrass and perhaps depose him: the factions among the people he hoped to govern, the need for money, the vacillation of native loyalty. But he apparently saw none of the obstacles; instead he blithely set out on his path with a few hundred hoodlums to support him and a Central American inauguration to give him authority.

Fermin Ferrer spoke first and his voice went on and on, a gush of bombast in the liquid beauty of the Spanish tongue. When he had at last finished, and the *vivas* died down in the plaza, Walker went to his knees to be sworn. The plaza was absolutely still, so that the soft voice of the President carried to the farthest limits of the throng:

"You solemnly promise and swear to govern the free Republic of Nicaragua and sustain its independence and territorial integrity with all your power, and to execute justice in accordance with the principles of Republicanism and religion?"

"I promise and swear."

"You promise and swear, whenever it may be in your power, to maintain the laws of God, the true profession of the Evangelists, and the religion of the Crucifixion?"

"I promise and swear."

"In the name of God and the sainted Evangelists, you swear to comply with these obligations and to make it your constant guard to fulfill all that is herein promised?"

"I swear."

"And for this, the succession is committed to you, firmly, by these presents, by authority of the secretary of the Government, charged with the general dispatches."

He stood up, to face the still silent spectators. As the President of Nicaragua, the man who had sailed from San Francisco fourteen months before advanced to the railing, rested one woman-like hand upon it and began to make, in English, his inaugural address. What he said and what Editor John Tabor prepared to be' hurried into the print of *El Nicaraguense* was high-minded and political; but the words could not obliterate the one great truth present on that day— he had robbed and killed to reach this place and, to sustain himself in it, he must yet rob and kill.

He spoke of the responsibilities he had assumed, of the dangers besetting the State from within and without. He pleaded—somewhat unnecessarily, inasmuch as he meant to exact loyalty by decree—for the co-operation of the people. Peace lay ahead, he said, and he implied that without his Americans the country would revert to its former dark confusion. And he went on:

"Not only is internal order required for the advancement of material wealth and prosperity, but also for the proper defense of the Republic from the external enemies which threaten its repose. The other four States of Central America, without reason and without justice, have undertaken to interfere in the domestic affairs of Nicaragua. Conscious of their own weakness and fearful lest the prosperity of Nicaragua should detract from their wealth, these neighboring States are enviously endeavoring to interrupt our progress by force of arms. The imbecile rulers of these States, too, feeling that they have failed to perform their duties to the people they undertake to govern, dread lest their impoverished countrymen may finally fly for refuge to those who have redeemed Nicaragua from anarchy and ruin. Moved by such ignoble sentiments, these miserable relics of a once powerful aristocracy are striving to impede the march of events in this Republic. But the impotence of their efforts is beginning to be made manifest to themselves and to the world; and they are now appearing as blind instruments in the hand of an all-wise Providence, which, out of the bad passions and unworthy motives of men, educes good and improvement.

"In our relations with the more powerful nations of the world, I hope they may be led to perceive that although Nicaragua may be comparatively weak, she is yet jealous of her honor and determined to maintain the dignity of her independent sovereignty. Her geographical position and commercial advantages may attract the cupidity of other governments, either neighboring or distant, but I trust they may yet learn that Nicaragua claims to control her own destiny, and does not require other nationalities to make treaties concerning her territory without asking her advice and consent. While pursuing a course of strict justice towards foreign citizens and foreign governments, we only ask that the same equity may be granted to ourselves."

The promises he gave the people included the usual ones of a new governor: education, liberty of speech and action, freedom of trade and the encouragement of religion. He spoke very briefly, concluding his address with the prayer: "And for carrying out these intentions with success, I humbly invoke the aid of Him without Whose assistance all human exertions are but as a bubble on a stormy sea."

He had known no Spanish when he first came to the country and what he had learned in the year of his occupancy did not seem to him enough to justify an attempt at speech-making in that tongue. Therefore, he talked in English, and was followed onto the rostrum by Colonel Lainé, Goicouria's agent, who translated the address into Spanish, adding to it what adjectives were necessary to make it palatable to the natives. Twenty-one guns were fired, Walker went to the Cathedral and sat in a canopied, throne-like chair while the priest blessed him. His Presidency began.

In the evening, the perplexities facing the new government were forgotten while the officers of Walker's command and the municipal officials banqueted. Walker offered the first toast, to the President of the United States. Hornsby offered another to Walker, calling him "Uncle Billy" and causing him to laugh heartily—an unprecedented occurrence, probably never again repeated. In all, fifty-three toasts were drunk and there is nothing to indicate that Walker did not respond to most of them: on that evening, and that only, did he behave as a normal man in the company of convivials. But although he stayed late with his officers, he was up in the morning at six, for there was work to be done.

Government was an immediate and pressing problem. Three claimants to the Presidency now opposed one another: Walker in Granada, Rivas in Leon, and Estrada, the Legitimist incumbent when Granada fell, at Somoto Grande, in Segovia. Rivas, recognized by the Allies as the lawful chief executive, was busy with the war he had created to drive Walker from the country. Troops from the north poured into his capital; the wrangling of the generals went on constantly, morning and night.

José Maria Estrada was rather less a threat. Upon his flight from Granada he had gone to Honduras, where he had issued a proclamation denouncing Walker and outlawing the treaty of October 23, 1855. He had enough supporters to make him of value to the Allies and, as soon as Rivas broke with Walker, he crossed the frontier into Segovia. The Allies invited him to join them, then, to present a united front against the Americans; he accepted, although without relinquishing any of his claims to office. On July eighteenth Honduras, San Salvador, Guatemala and the remnants of President Rivas' government signed a formal alliance for the "defense of their sovereignty and independence." Their total armed force was estimated at eighteen hundred troops. Costa Rica, still licking the wounds inflicted by the first attempt to defeat the Americans, could offer nothing immediately to support this alliance but encouragement and promise.

For the first few days of his regime, however, Walker paid little heed to the army massing in the North. He needed men and artillery badly, but he needed more the support of other governments. Padre Vijil had returned and there was no representative in Washington to further the cause of "manifest destiny" on the Isthmus. But, five days after the inauguration, Minister Wheeler, who had been a daily visitor to Walker's office in Government House, came to extend to the new authority the recognition of the United States. Wheeler again was inspired by zeal and premature: his instructions had been to recognize the Rivas government, which had sent Padre Vijil to Washington. Secretary Marcy was still unaware of the bloodless revolution which had seated Walker.

Walker accepted Wheeler's proffer as official and at once sent Appleton Oaksmith, promoter of the gigantic mass meeting in New York which had celebrated the recognition of Padre Vijil, to Washington. At the same time, he appointed Domingo de Goicouria Ambassador to the Court of St. James's, again using the technique originated for French: disliking Goicouria and wishing to be rid of him, he made him the second most important Nicaraguan diplomat.

Coincidentally with his attempts to establish his government firmly, the Filibuster added to his armed strength, with the acquisition of a one-ship navy. The schooner *San José,* memorable as the Immortals' engine of retreat after the first battle of Rivas, appeared in the harbor at San Juan del Sur late in June. She flew the flag of the United States and Walker's men at the port boarded her to investigate her apparent change of registry. It developed that the original owner of the ship had sold her to Mariano Salazar, who had obtained from the American vice-consul at Realejo a sailing letter and had boldly sent his ship into Walker's country in the belief that this, and the Stars and Stripes she flew, would protect her and make her smuggling revenues as fat as his paunch. The ship was seized, "condemned by a court of admiralty jurisdiction" and ordered forfeited to the government of Nicaragua. (Her cargo of wine was drunk.) Minister Wheeler ignored a formal protest against the seizure; and the *San José* was armed with two six-pound guns, rechristened the *Granada,* manned with those soldiers who had had some experience at sea and placed under the command of Lieutenant Callender Irvine Fayssoux.

Lieutenant Fayssoux had served in the Texas navy and was one of the best officers ever to take orders from Walker. He is described as a small man, much on the order of Walker himself, except that when excited the French in him overcame his innate dignity. A Missourian, he served first in Texas, joined the second expedition of Narciso Lopez against Cuba and made the landing of Lopez's ship possible when he swam ashore at Cardenas with a mooring line in his teeth. When the Walker saga was ended (and in the excitement of the times all but forgotten) he appeared again as an officer of the Confederacy.

Fayssoux conditioned the *Granada* for sea in a matter of days. He was as strict a disciplinarian as Walker himself and, because the men under him were beneath his eye at all hours, there was nothing but stern duty on the one-ship navy. Julius de Brissot was assigned as second-in-command and about July fifteenth the schooner set out from San Juan, under orders to cruise in the Bay of Fonseca and prevent, if possible, the movement of troops by *bongos* from San Salvador.

Captain Fayssoux, on the twenty-eighth, made the most important capture of the new Walker government up to that time. With all the irony of war, Mariano Salazar, traveling to San Salvador with dispatches, was taken by the vessel he had only recently bought for the conduct of his most dishonest business. He was brought to the deck of the *Granada,* and there gave his name as Francisco Salazar; and he might have escaped had it not been for the presence of De Brissot, who had seen him at Realejo when the Immortals were licking their wounds after the battle of Rivas. Fayssoux confined the merchant, transported him to San Juan as fast as sail could push the schooner and sent him under guard to Walker at Granada.

Salazar received the portion Walker so willingly gave. On August third he was executed in the grand plaza. It was Sunday; a great crowd gathered to watch him die. There was less mourning for Mariano Salazar than there had been for Ponciano Corral, slain on the same spot; Salazar was known to have profited greatly from the constant wars in the Republic and, in the minds of the Legitimists, he had never ceased to be a stalwart of the opposing party.

Among the dispatches seized with Salazar was one from Thomas Manning, who had been reappointed British vice-consul at Realejo, in which the trader complained: "If this man [Walker] receives forces and money, I assure you it will not be so easy to drive him out of the State; for as the forces come from the other States in handfuls of men nothing is accomplished, and the expenses and sacrifices are made in vain. I am much afflicted to think that under these circumstances no more activity is used in so serious an affair." For this outspoken expression of British policy, Walker revoked Manning's exequatur and undoubtedly would have executed the critic, if he could have laid hands on him.

The forces of President Rivas were quick to retaliate for the death of Salazar. Dr. Joseph W. Livingston, the same gentleman who had visited Walker at Realejo during the disagreement with Castellon the year before, was seized as hostage at Leon. Minister Wheeler acted promptly, promising terrible consequences if an American suffered injury, and obtained Livingston's release.

Fayssoux, meanwhile, was busy attempting to obey Walker's order for a complete blockade of the coast. A French frigate, the *Embus-*

cade, hovered in the Bay of Fonseca, serving as rather more than an observer: her presence helped San Salvador move troops across the bay in small boats. Also, the British navy entered the scene in force, thirteen ships anchoring in or off Greytown harbor on August fourth "to protect nationals." With a single schooner Walker could do little to maintain sovereign rights, but he hoped its patrol would persuade the British and French commanders that his government existed more actively than on paper. He still could not see, apparently, that the great governments of the world were dedicated already to the side of the Allied armies.

II

IN DEFIANCE of discretion, Patricio Rivas bestowed upon Ramon Belloso, a Salvadorian, the command of the entire Allied army. Immediately, the Guatemalans, at that moment submerging their hatred for all Salvadorians only in the greater hatred for William Walker and his *Yanquis,* engaged in bitter dispute with their fellows in arms. Also, the soldiers infected Leon through the exercise of insanitary practices identical in results with those of the Costa Ricans in the previous war; cholera spread to the proportions of a full epidemic. Morale in the Allied camp, when the execution of Mariano Salazar became known, ebbed; courage became a weak flame; and there was no harmony. Spies arrived in Granada almost every day, reporting fresh difficulties in the camp of the enemy and leading Walker to conclude, with contempt for the native inability to co-operate, that the war was sufficiently distant for him to postpone its first battle. He concentrated, therefore, upon what he considered bigger things: the first, the matter of the Accessory Transit Corporation.

Since the Transit charter had been revoked, in the previous February, the property of the company had been held pending an adjustment of claims. After months of justifying work, a commission appointed by Rivas had prepared its report. On August 2, 1856, this body of investigators found that the company owed Nicaragua a total of more than four hundred thousand dollars, estimated on a net revenue of fifty-eight thousand dollars per month from August, 1851, to March, 1856, plus interest. The figures were, of course, inaccurate, largely because the commissioners lacked records on which to base their claims, as the Transit Company had seen to it that no books were kept in Nicaragua. Further, although the passenger revenue was based on two thousand passengers per month at thirty-five dollars each, the Vanderbilt auditors contended that the actual fare was much lower than that. The company maintained that a passenger bound from New York to San Francisco bought three tickets: one on the Atlantic line, one for the Transit crossing, and one for the Pacific passage. By this system, the company could charge high rates on the Atlantic and Pacific ships and virtually nothing on those engaged in the crossing of Nicaragua and so technically claim that the revenue on the latter section was little more than equal to the cost of operation, if as great.

It is not to be supposed that Vanderbilt was altogether without sin in the conduct of the Accessory Transit Company's affairs. It has been said that the figures arrived at by Walker's commission were exaggerated. If they had been accurate, they would have represented a return of nearly one hundred per cent on an investment of about seven hundred thousand dollars* for ships and structures in Nicaragua alone. It is significant, however, that long after the revocation of the charter and the seizure of the company's property, Vanderbilt entered into an agreement with the Pacific Mail Steamship Company whereby he agreed not to compete against them, for a retainer of fifty-six thousand dollars a month. Some figures must have been used to arrive at this sum and it is so close to the fifty-eight thousand dollars monthly profit claimed in the Walker report that it tends to authenticate it. Secondly, Vanderbilt offered a Nicaraguan delegation, sent to dun him before the arrival of the Immortals, thirty thousand dollars in payment of his full debt; the Nicaraguans had asked thirty-five thousand dollars and the financier's willingness to pay nearly the full sum indicates that the actual obligation must have been far more.

Walker approved the report and ordered the Transit properties sold to Morgan & Garrison. He thus made final the break with Vanderbilt, in that day the one man in the United States certain to have helped him substantially, had he bargained a little. Vanderbilt,

---

* Vanderbilt's valuation.

although furious with Walker for his interference, was primarily a business man and, even after his properties were ordered sold to his former partners, he still attempted to deal amicably with the Filibuster. But in subsequent negotiations, in which Goicouria was a prime mover, Walker exhibited to an absurd degree the stubbornness which was so much a part of his character; and to this obstinacy may be traced almost every disaster that came to him.

Goicouria received his appointment as minister-designate to the Court of Saint James's on August 12, 1856. His instructions were to go first to New Orleans, to seek a loan for the Walker government. Thence he was to proceed to New York for conversations with other financiers. Before the close of the year he was to present himself in London.

Goicouria remained in New Orleans only a few days, because the prospects for raising money in that city were poor and the work could be done as well by agents. But before boarding ship for New York, he wrote to Walker asking additional diplomatic information. He knew that to be an envoy to England, one of Walker's most powerful opponents, he must be familiar with the form of government his chief proposed to establish. In his months of service under Walker, he had never been informed of the Filibuster's ultimate intentions: antagonism had formed a barrier between the men from the moment of their meeting. But in seeking to obtain the information he felt he must have, he apparently forgot the displeasure which had been his lot in the past, when he had sought to give counsel. He opposed the Transit agreement with Morgan & Garrison, on the ground that it gave them a monopoly on the Nicaragua crossing and suggested an obstacle to free trade; moreover, he believed a stricter financial accounting should be demanded of the new company, with the revenues to be pledged as security against any loan he might obtain in the United States.

He arrived in New York a few weeks after leaving Nicaragua. His vast circle of acquaintances in the city included virtually every financier of any consequence and he called on those first, to discuss Walker in all his phases. What he learned convinced him that his letter from New Orleans had been a wise one; none of the men with whom he talked felt that Walker could succeed while Vanderbilt remained unappeased. Nor would they offer any loan on what they considered an "extraordinarily hazardous" risk.

Edmund Randolph was in the city at the time. The doubts which had assailed Goicouria (without once shaking his loyalty) were made graver when he discovered that Randolph also was seeking a loan, with full powers from Walker, and planned to take a commission if he obtained it. Believing that Randolph intended to profit without the knowledge of Walker, whom he still considered an idealistic liberator, the Cuban continued his investigations and at last prepared a lengthy report for submission to Granada.

He found that Morgan & Garrison, until then merely attempting to give steamship service to the Nicaraguan terminals of the Transit route, were not heavily enough financed ever to make the line a success. This discovery led him to the dingy offices of his old patron, Cornelius Vanderbilt, where he was made welcome and was gratified to be told that the Commodore, although willing to fight Walker indefinitely, would prefer to call a truce, pay for the restoration of his Transit privileges and start running his ships again. There was a concrete and generous offer attached to Vanderbilt's desire: he promised to pay one hundred thousand dollars in cash the day his first ship sailed, and an additional one hundred and fifty thousand in the first year of the line's operation.

The Cuban, excited about the offer and proud that he had achieved so much so quickly, added this information to his report. He mentioned that Vanderbilt would be a friend instead of the most dangerous of enemies; the filibusters would have sufficient money to win the war with the Allies; and between the two—Walker on one end and Vanderbilt on the other—Nicaragua could not fail to be recognized by all governments.

He received a prompt and discourteous answer. He was curtly informed that he had been given no powers to deal with Vanderbilt's Accessory Transit Company and could promise nothing on behalf of the Nicaraguan government. He was ordered to restrict his activities to those required of the minister-delegate to England. And his information about Edmund Randolph was dismissed with the remark: "As to anything you say about Mr. Randolph, it is entirely thrown away upon me."

Discouraged, but not yet despairing, Goicouria remained in New York, determined to serve in the best way he knew. His only reason for declining to give way to anger under the succession of rebukes he received from Walker was the hope of liberating Cuba. This hope, however, died in the interchange of letters which followed, for revealed to him then was the mad, self-centered and unacceptable character of the man he had tried so hard to help.

Because the United States had not recognized Nicaragua (recognition having been withdrawn after the departure of Padre Vijil and upon the outbreak of the Walker-Rivas war), Goicouria thought that an immediate journey to England would be unwise. He wrote again to Walker, informing him that he would remain in New York for a time, both to do what he could toward raising money and to await a more propitious time for approaching England as a diplomat. The reply he received was a furious letter, informing him that if he would not operate in absolute obedience he could relinquish all part in the Nicaraguan government. In addition, Walker returned to the Vanderbilt negotiations, bluntly accusing the Cuban of acting as the Commodore's agent and spy.

Goicouria's magnificent patience was at last broken. He replied bitterly, reminding Walker that he had pacified Vanderbilt in the hope of guaranteeing the Americans sufficient ammunition and supplies to remain on the Isthmus and also to make an ally of a dangerous enemy "who already has caused you much difficulty and even loss of reputation." He recalled the discourtesy and opposition which had been his portion from the day he joined the Filibuster's forces and remarked that he had been treated as a subordinate when in fact he was, by virtue of their agreement, an independent associate. He concluded his letter with a complete analysis of the Walker failing: "You have shut your eyes to the truth—whether it is that you look upon yourself as divinely infallible and are determined to pursue your course at all hazards, or whether it is that a third party has filled your mind with false suggestions."

Walker then inserted in the columns of *El Nicaraguense* this notice: "Brigadier General Domingo de Goicouria has been dropped from the army rolls." The Nicaraguan newspaper was a major source of news for the New York press, and the notice was reprinted as soon as copies of *El Nicaraguense* arrived from Granada. Moreover, before Goicouria could reply, Edmund Randolph published a card, calling the Cuban an "intruder with a treacherous and dishonest intent" and frankly inviting him to take offense at the words and challenge.

There was no duel, however; Goicouria fought with shrewder weapons. In this instance recurs the circumstance of Walker's obstinacy and its cost: from Sonora to Truxillo, he followed a routine of impressing worthy associates, antagonizing them and engaging in disputes which almost invariably redounded to his hurt.

Between the time Goicouria wrote from New Orleans, asking information on policy, and late November, when he struck back viciously at Walker because of the accusations of treachery, the Filibuster had given the United States a somewhat clearer view of his intentions. The keystone of a great arch of decrees which he constructed was a legalization of slavery, which will be discussed more fully in the succeeding chapter; Goicouria made use of this decree with damaging effect. Crucifying Walker with his own words, the Cuban published letters containing such sentences as:

"With your versatility and, if I may use the term, adaptability, I expect much to be done in England. You can do more than any American could possibly accomplish, because you can make the British Cabinet see that we are not engaged in any scheme for annexation. You can make them see that the only way to cut the expanding and expansive democracy of the North is by a powerful and compact Southern federation, based on military principles.

"Cuba must and shall be free, but not for the Yankees! Oh, no! That fine country is not fit for those barbarous Yankees. What would such a psalm-singing set do in the island?"

It had been believed generally in the North that Nicaragua, and possibly other Central American republics, would be added to the Union as soon as Walker could accomplish their subjugation. Even the fact of the slavery decree had not done too much harm in the abolitionist States, because the North's first interest was manufacture; and greed, in that day as in this, was more universal than principle. Merchants and industrialists had foreseen the opening of new territories for their exploitation, new markets to sell and new products on which to profit. It was thought, too, that the tropics were a sort of hell, wherein free labor could not be expected to maintain any reasonable level of production and Northerners tried to consider the slavery question as two: one affecting the United States, and the other (entirely different because of climatic conditions) Central America.

But when Goicouria published the letters, and it became clear that annexation was no part of Walker's plan, his popularity waned. The South clung to him, because the South saw the dissolution of the Union as inevitable and cared only whether Nicaragua was free or slave. In the Civil War soon to be fought (and already in the minds of many Southern leaders a foregone crisis) it would matter only that the slave-holding areas be promised support from outside their boundaries.

What the South thought was well expressed by the editor of the New Orleans *Delta,* who in March, 1856, had written: "The fate of Cuba depends upon the fate of Nicaragua, and the fate of the South depends upon that of Cuba. This is the hour of destiny. We must live now or have no life. We must do or die!" The North, though, felt more earnestly about Walker and annexation. And the North counted in any struggle, for it contained the factories which furnished arms and powder, it had many failures who would make armies for an adventurer, its bankers controlled the sinews of every war. Of Walker, already an object of suspicion because of his rash defiance of Vanderbilt, the North suddenly would have little part. He had betrayed the North on slavery, he had abandoned "manifest destiny," which appeared to the important men of the time the only justification for his conquests and he had shown in the Vanderbilt matter a shocking disrespect for vested power.

The old quips were heard again. The songs were sung with a leer. The editorial pens were no longer friendly. Thumbs turned down and the spectators at the circus watched lustfully for the kill.

III

FROM the time of his arrival in June, 1855, until August 15, 1856, Walker's entire attention had been occupied by the struggle to establish himself and his army on the Central American Isthmus. Consequently, everything he had done until the latter date could have been dictated by the necessities of the moment. After his inauguration in July, however, he found time to work on the reforms at which he had hinted from time to time. The Transit revocation entirely behind him and the property of the Vanderbilt company sold to Morgan & Garrison, his next step was to assure himself of additional recruits; he would never feel secure in his position until thousands of Americans were behind him, well-armed and commanded by a staff of experienced officers. To this end he required Fermin Ferrer to negotiate a colonization contract with William L. Cazneau, of Texas, whereby one thousand able-bodied men were to be shipped to the country, to serve in the army and be paid with land. Cazneau's contract was declared unlawful by the United States District Attorney in New York on the grounds that Ferrer enjoyed no official position in Nicaragua, but in spite of this ruling several hundred Texans migrated to Nicaragua, confident that they would find the sort of adventure they wanted and by loyalty to William Walker win rewards. Other recruiting activities were carried on more or less openly in the United States: S. A. Lockridge worked busily in the Middle West, Norvell Walker was sent to his native Nashville and E. J. C. Kewen operated throughout the deep South. It is not clear whose ships brought the recruits before Morgan & Garrison's line began service.

With the work of recruiting started, Walker left it entirely in the charge of the men he had selected and started upon his legislative program. Then, for the first time, confusion over his motives vanished.

He had been quick to note the advantage to be held by a person speaking both Spanish and English and he had learned much Spanish in his first year. To "regulate the relations between the several races meeting on the same soil," therefore, he decreed that all laws of the Republic should be published both in English and Spanish. This decree seemed fair and wise, until one read it carefully enough to find this clause: "All documents connected with public affairs shall be of equal value whether written in English or Spanish." Walker said brazenly of this that it would not be noticed except by the careful; and by its terms the proceedings of the courts and the deeds of the

State could be prepared in English alone. It was a lawyer's trick and Walker did not attempt to conceal its intention: to give those speaking both English and Spanish an advantage in legal matters over those familiar only with the latter language. "The decree tended to make the ownership of the lands of the State fall into the hands of those speaking English," Walker's book says succinctly.

Another decree ordered confiscation of the estates of the "enemies of the Republic." The confiscated lands were to be advertised in *El Nicaraguense* and, if the owners failed to show cause why they should not be seized, they were to be sold to the highest bidder. The joker here was: "military script is to be received in payment," which enabled Walker's regime to retire the debt due to its soldiery at no cost and at the same time guaranteed the possession of farms by Americans. By late September of 1856, scores of farms had been seized and were advertised for sale, and not a landowner in Nicaragua who could read or listen failed to heed the warning. By this decree alone, Walker forged himself a weapon so powerful that many native supporters turned against him.

Third in the program of land policy was the institution of the American system of requiring all titles to be registered within six months. There were no order to the titles of Nicaraguan lands and no registry laws; consequently, virtually every farm in the Republic could be forfeited by the mere operation of this single law. Further, the Nicaraguans had no knowledge of registry and in any controversy would be certain to lose, competing as they were against men in whose country such regulations had been in effect for years.

The program was admittedly intended to give the American occupants of the country a firmer hold on what they had seized. Walker could see that military possession, while good enough as a beginning, required some stable underpinning to sustain it indefinitely. If he could assign to the greater number of his men thousands of acres of Nicaraguan land and grant them the only titles his military dictatorship would recognize, he felt that he would be in a fair way to guaranteeing the full Americanization of the Isthmus.

He had seized the presidency by force of arms and, under the current circumstances, his claim was as good as those of Estrada and Rivas: being president consisted not so much in having a legal right to the office as in having a sufficient army at one's back to hold off the opposition. His next urgency, then, was the army. He considered his prospects and saw two weaknesses: all the recruits he might get from the United States would not be enough for the pending war and native auxiliaries were necessary; and to bring the lands he proposed to confiscate into production much labor would be required.

So he issued a decree against vagrancy. The natives of the provinces to the north had fled before the press-gangs of the Guatemalan and Salvadorian armies. They constituted a menace to Walker, he felt, because they had been in the service of the Legitimists and could not possibly sympathize with his regime. Until they could be placed under authority, there was always the possibility that they would foment dissension and possibly even revolt. The vagrancy law, then, was advanced as a protective measure against a dissatisfied segment of the population. Actually, it was something more: another phase in the corruption of the *Yanqui* idealist, who upon arrival had deplored conscription and who now meant to impress any man he chose into his army. Some of the peons who were arrested for violation of the vagrancy laws were set to work in the fields around Granada, to furnish food to the Americans; others were given muskets and the opportunity to die gloriously for a cause they could not understand; the majority fled into the interior, where jungle and swamp discourage all men of destiny.

Finally, as his masterpiece of legislation, Walker revived slavery. It will be remembered that in New Orleans and San Francisco he had been an opponent of slavery. In the South he had assumed a conservative tone, in which his sympathies were sufficiently Northern for him to earn the appellation "Yankee editor." In California, where there was nothing to be lost by a bold espousal of a conviction, he had worked actively against the slavery bloc. He professed at that time to be convinced that the Negro should be free; but when he now examined the institution and what it might bring him, he turned whole-heartedly to the opposite view.

His motives were clear. Generally, the United States, despite official indifference, gave him as much support as he could reasonably expect; but elsewhere throughout the world governments were bitterly against him. In his own country he was a creature of constantly altering worth: in victory, a superman; in defeat, a dunce. To eliminate this wavering, he was forced to appeal to one great section of the American people, preferably a section with a principle he could uphold. Slavery gave him the flawless issue. The "irresistible conflict" was approaching and a few astute observers could almost have named the day on which it would start. The cleavage between the North and South had reached a stage in 1856 where there existed two distinct countries, attempting to do business under the generic name "United States." Walker played to what was to prove the losing side, but in his choice he showed wisdom, for had he remained inactive about slavery it would have gained him no aid in the North, whereas by advocating it for the nation he controlled he won the gratitude and acclaim of the entire South.

The decree, like all his other acts, was a lawyer's trick. He did not say bluntly that slaves might be owned, but instead left an option—the sort of option present in the English language regulation. On April 17, 1824, the Confederated Congress of Central America had drawn up a constitution, which abolished the slavery practiced by the Spanish. This prohibition endured beyond 1838, when the Central American Union was dissolved, and in Nicaragua became a permanent part of national policy. Walker sought to destroy this, on September 22, 1856, in this manner:

DECREE

Article 1. All acts and decrees of the Federal Constituent Assembly, as well as of the Federal Congress, are declared null and void.

Article 2. Nothing herein contained shall affect rights heretofore vested under the acts and decrees hereby repealed.

The document was in English, and so that its intentions could not be mistaken by anyone in the United States, Walker appended to it this sentence, "Among the decrees which the foregoing repeals is an act of the Federal Constituent Assembly . . . abolishing slavery in Central America."

This action Walker considered the key to his entire policy. Without slavery itself he did not believe the white race could become and remain the rulers of Nicaragua. The enslavement of African Negroes for the development of the country was proposed (again we glimpse the Filibuster's madness) as the one great progressive step taken by the Americans on the Isthmus. Although willing enough to sign a contract as a mercenary soldier, Walker constantly denied that this was his position in the social and economic scheme of the country he occupied. He cried "Regenerate!" whenever he was given the opportunity and, in the midst of the bitterest battles, reiterated the hollow claim that his presence in a foreign country was the working of a benign fate. Slavery was necessary for Spanish Americans, he said, because their governments had not been given the original freedom Britain had allowed her possessions and so were not securely founded; and only through cheap forced labor was possible the redemption of the natural losses the former Spanish colonies had suffered. His defense was that of a man either blind or pretending to be blind for a purpose. The shining example of the need for slavery, as he advanced it, was the United States itself— where, at the moment his pen touched the paper of the decree, thirty million persons were drifting toward chaos.

The effect of the slavery decision, regardless of the South's increased support, was to isolate Walker. England, already against him, began to work harder to drive him from his eminence. The *calzados* of Nicaragua, who might have been cheered at the prospect of obtaining all the cheap labor they needed, knew that the new policy was intended to benefit only Americans. And the administration in Washington, even after Minister Wheeler had written to defend "this important and necessary" action, was thrown into confusion, with slavery and anti-slavery factions arguing angrily over the attitude to be taken toward the Filibuster.

There had always been the hope on the part of the officials in Washington that Walker would ask for annexation as soon as he had won Nicaragua. The legalization of slavery made clear that what Walker wanted was empire and that he meant to build toward it with every implement he could find.

With his house in order, then, William Walker turned to the war.

IV

HE SHOWED wisdom in making no move against the entrenched Allies until his preliminary legislation was on the Nicaraguan statute books.

Granada was not the healthiest place the Americans had inhabited, but it was safe compared to Leon. Dozens died in the latter city every day, some because they had been brought from the high air of Guatemala to the lowness of the Nicaraguan plain and many more because there was little attempt made to provide sanitation for the massed thousands. In addition to cholera dissension took considerable toll; so bitter did the *pulperia* brawls between Guatemalans and Salvadorians become that it was found necessary to confine all Guatemalan privates to their quarters, to save them from insult on the streets.

On September 1, 1856, William Walker's effectives numbered eight hundred. There were two battalions of Rifles, two of Light Infantry, one of Cavalry—called the Rangers—and a company of Artillery. The First Rifles was the backbone of the army, consisting of two hundred well-trained veterans; the Second Rifles contained largely newcomers and was far from being a full battalion; the Rangers, three companies strong, were cavalrymen of considerable competence. For artillery Walker had two or three small pieces, not in the best repair. Headquarters was at Granada, where all stores and workshops of the army were maintained. Garrisons also held Masaya, Managua, the San Juan River and the city of Rivas. Except for skirmishing in the north, there had been no engagement in the two months since the alliance had begun to move against Walker.

At Leon, Ramon Belloso remained still. He commanded an indeterminate number of men, possibly about two thousand. A few of his officers worked northward out of Leon, picking up conscripts in Matagalpa and Segovia and hampering Walker indirectly, because he was drawing his supplies of cattle from those districts and the peons who herded them, fearing press-gangs, refused to leave what safety they could find in their own huts. Early in September, Walker sent men to drive out a force said to be holding the buildings of San Jacinto, a large cattle estate in Matagalpa. The Americans were beaten at the adobes of the ranch and fell back to the village of Tipitapa, whence a courier was sent to Granada with news of the repulse. Walker took no official notice of the defeat, because the condition of the roads made a reinforcement impracticable, but when volunteers proposed that they go to the aid of the outpost he consented. The company consisted of fewer than one hundred Americans, many of whom had resigned from the army but now wished to re-enter it, and sixty-five regulars from the garrisons at Masaya and Granada. They marched on September twelfth, reached Tipitapa on the following day and there encountered Byron Cole who, although still engaged in the duties of a civilian aide, held a nominal lientenant-colonelcy and so ranked every other officer with the advancing volunteers. He was offered the command of the party and, as the duty that had carried him into Chontales (to exchange military requisitions for what cattle he could round up) was completed, he accepted.

At 5 A. M. on Sunday, the fourteenth, the attackers arrived before the ranch houses of San Jacinto. The main house occupied a slight rise of ground; it was well shuttered and further protected by the nearby corral, which was heavily fenced and offered the defending Allies perfect breastworks. Cole, the hot-blooded New Englander, who had proposed filibustering when his newspaper failed, who had gone to hunt gold when Walker was slow in joining him, who seems to have wanted nothing more in life than to be irresponsible, ordered a ridiculously gallant charge. Armed only with revolvers, his men attempted to storm the house and the corral. Almost before they were within pistol-shot of it, they were reduced to a third of their number by a careful fire from the corral stockade and the house itself, and were forced back. The filibusters drew off, picked up their wounded and retraced their march to Granada. Cole's body they left where it had fallen; it shared ground with that of Charles Callahan, who had traveled from New Orleans to report the war for the *Picayune,* had found Walker the sort of a man he could follow and had exchanged a war correspondent's mantle for a soldier's shroud.

The retreat was so disorderly that, when the remnants of the attack reached Tipitapa, a mass desertion threatened. The men were in so great a panic that they ripped up the bridge leading into town and for hours watched with white faces the road to the North, fearing an attack that never came.

Trivial as the fight had been, it had an important effect. General Belloso, waiting in Leon, was heartened by the beating administered to the Americans and he began at once to prepare his main body for

The Wharf at Granada

a march on the Walker strongholds. The war between the Filibuster, on the one hand, and the allied governments of Honduras,
San Salvador and Guatemala, on the other, at last began to be fought.

As Belloso marched toward Managua, two hundred recruits arrived
in Granada, having been transported on a Morgan ship from New
York. They were dregs unfit for action, Europeans of the poorer
class mostly, who had been persuaded that free food and lodging
awaited them under the renowned Walker. An effort was made to
organize them into companies to be scattered through the army, but
all except a few deserted before the first major engagement of the
war and doubtless straggled back to New York or their native
countries.

Managua, today the capital and one of the chief cities of Nicaragua,
in Walker's time was relatively unimportant. It was inhabited by
ten thousand or so, a restful, minor city whose people lived in the
greatest simplicity, carrying on a desultory trade with the surrounding countryside, where broad acres produced a small quantity of
very fine coffee.

This city was the northernmost American stronghold. Major
John P. Waters occupied it, with a strong garrison of more than two
hundred men, more than half mounted Rangers. The city's construction was similar to that of Leon and Granada: adobe houses, a central
plaza and narrow streets across which strong barricades could be
flung. There was every reason for Walker to have held Managua.
With a couple of hundred men he might have resisted long enough
to have weakened appreciably the Allies, who numbered about
eighteen hundred when they left Leon. But he ordered Waters to
fall back to Masaya, when Belloso had come almost within sight of
Managua, and permitted a key position to fall into the enemy's hands
without firing a shot in its defense.

Belloso paused briefly in Managua, to tighten his lines and instruct
his officers, who included Martinez and Mendez, the commander and
the Indian aide respectively in Walker's first battle in Nicaragua.
Vallé, the invaluable Indian, who had ruled the country's northern
extremities for Walker with matchless success since the end of the
Costa Rican war, had been taken at Chinandega while en route to
rejoin the Americans and, after a short time in jail, had been released

only to be dogged and made profanely impotent by the local police.

When his rear guard had come up and rations for another march had been issued, Belloso advanced again, this time along the road leading to Masaya, one of the oldest cities in Central America.

Although Walker had been reinforced by seventy Californians and one hundred New Yorkers in the first week of October, he was yet unwilling to test himself against the Allied army. The disposition of his forces in the probable area of attack was strategically sound and should have dictated a continuation of his waiting policy: Waters was in Masaya with two hundred and fifty riflemen and the main army, numbering nearly eight hundred, was safely barricaded in Granada. With eighteen hundred men marching against him, however, he lost faith in the small garrison at Masaya. Although he had fought against defenders of cities enough to have known that two hundred and fifty men behind barricades could delay and harass an enemy many times their number, and possibly even stop it in its tracks, he ordered Waters to fall back to Granada.

The instant the order was executed, he regretted it. He had given up an ancient place, founded by the Indians long years before the Spanish came, located high on a promontory and accessible only by tortuous mountain roads. Around it was spread the rich western plain of Nicaragua—the country's granary. Almost any body of efficient soldiers could have held the city indefinitely against any army attempting to reach it from below; but Walker realized this only when the positions had been reversed and the problem of storming the town was one for him to solve.

The retiring garrison arrived in Granada in great confusion, having abandoned arms and a cannon in its flight from Masaya. Walker consolidated all his main forces and planned a counter assault in the twenty-four hours between his order for the retreat and his own advance. In this instance he resembled more a flighty woman than a conquering general—but he never learned that in war it is seldom profitable to change one's mind. Instead, having been guilty of a grave military blunder, he prepared in his mind the glib explanation he was later to commit to paper. His action was thought out, he said, because it was his wish to fight the entire Allied army as a unit instead of weakening himself in guerrilla conflict; and "the best manner of treating a revolutionary movement in Central America is to treat it as a boil—let it come to a head and then lance it, letting out all the bad matter at once."

The lance he now wielded consisted of eight hundred men. Waters led the column with the Rangers; the First Rifles came behind; Hornsby brought up the rear with two companies of infantry. Two mountain howitzers had recently been received from New York, but the shipper had neglected to send their carriages; they went along anyway, resting insecurely on clumsy makeshifts. The men were well armed with Minié rifles and revolvers. Walker had designed a new flag which replaced the device of a chain of erupting volcanoes: a wide white stripe between two narrow ones of blue, with a five-pointed red star in the center. The color-bearer for the Rangers carried, fluttering from a lance, one of the new banners with the addendum, hacked out of a red flannel shirt with a sabre: FIVE OR NONE!

After a quiet and orderly march, the column halted at the outskirts of Masaya, encamping on the high banks alongside the Granada road. Early evening had been misty, but at ten the moon shone brightly, picking out the white of the city's houses and dulling the campfires in the courtyards held by the Allies. There was some irregular firing in the night, between American scouts and enemy pickets, but the battle did not start until an hour or so after daybreak. The howitzers threw a few shells into the nearest small plaza, San Sebastian, and under the cover of this barrage the First Rifles occupied the square. The main body followed and began a movement toward the grand plaza, where Belloso's thousands waited. For the first time since the Americans had come to Nicaragua, an effort was made to advance within the houses, with amateur sappers and miners cutting a path through the walls. The advance was moderately swift, the Rifles edging up on one side of the street and the Infantry keeping pace with them on the other. The artillery was brought up and a few shots fired at the plaza, but the fuses were too short and the shells exploded in the air; also, one of the howitzers blew itself off the makeshift carriage and had to be silenced. But by night-fall the Americans had cut their way to the row of houses fronting on the plaza, where they mounted pickets and lay down to sleep until morning, when an easy victory appeared inevitable.

No man among them finished his sleep. Within a few hours they were on the march again, this time down the winding road toward Granada. For the jealousies of his own officers had saved Belloso.

When Walker began to march northward, Estrada, the former Legitimist president, who was commanding a division of the Allied army, deserted Belloso. Resentful of the Salvadorian's appointment as general-in-chief, Estrada thought to wrest glory for himself by a swift march to Granada. He skirted the road, therefore, as Walker marched along it; entered it when the Americans had passed and pressed southward toward the capital. The two attacks—Walker's on Masaya and Estrada's on Granada—almost coincided.

A Ranger rode up to the house where Walker slept sometime before midnight, to report heavy firing on the lake. Lainé was sent with a squad to investigate and returned very quickly into a plaza hushed except for the snores of the *falanginos* and the occasional discharge of a nervous musket, to verify the Ranger's report: the enemy held a large part of Granada, with every prospect of fortifying it before morning.

To hesitate would have been disastrous. Walker knew he faced the alternative of remaining where he was and winning a battle at the cost of Granada, or giving up his gain and returning to the defense of the capital. He was on the road again in thirty minutes, his officers forcing the column along at the best pace it could manage.

On October thirteenth, a year to the day since he had seized Granada, Walker saved it at the finish of a forced march. He led his army into the suburb of Jalteva, overcame with a charge the resistance of a small force of Allies and proceeded into the center of the city. Estrada sounded the retreat and his six hundred-odd men retired from the south, circled the city and struck out for Masaya.

The damage done in Granada was slight, in point of numbers, but it was to have a profound effect upon the general morale of both armies in the war. Estrada, angered that the few civil officials and the single company which guarded the city could resist him at all, had turned his Guatemalans loose with the tacit understanding that they might kill anyone who came within range of their guns. Two missionaries and a merchant were found on the streets, mercilessly shot, their bodies mangled and disrobed and tossed naked into the plaza. An English boy was killed as he ate a meal. The American flag was torn down from the United States Legation and Minister Wheeler, lying ill inside, heard the mob howl for his blood.

Walker discovered, however, that against any odds there were sections of his army willing to die rather than surrender. Editor Tabor of *El Nicaraguense* had seized from its convenient corner the rifle he held ready and had fought valiantly until a bullet in the thigh had brought him down. Other officials had fought as well; the only absolute craven remembered in the records is the good Padre Vijil, who fled to a swamp and hid there until it was safe to return and who returned only to ask for a passport, so that he might go to the comparative safety of New Granada.

While Walker was clearing the streets of stragglers, Colonel Lainé was moving toward Granada by another road. In the latter march there was much confusion. Lainé came upon sections of the Estrada army in its retreat and was unable to fight because the Rangers under him had permitted the dew to wet their arms. The Rangers scattered and Lainé, pursued by a small company of the Allies, was wounded and taken prisoner. Walker, busily repairing the damage to the civil government done by the attack, heard the following day that he had been executed.

Walker's regard for Lainé was similar to that he had had for Crocker. The Cuban had been a devout and unquestioning follower of the Filibuster. The news of his death was a shock; Walker needed him more at this time than ever before and he took his death more seriously than that of any other officer. And as theretofore, he could think of nothing but retaliation. In the blindness of his passion, he ordered two Guatemalan officers shot in the plaza. He found it difficult to get a squad to carry out his order, because the two Guatemalans had accepted their captivity as gentlemen and had impressed the officers under Walker with their culture and manners. They declined to die seated; after the fusillade, smoke still rose from their casual cigarettes.

Meanwhile, Estrada was assassinated, under circumstances so strange that Walker felt required to publish a lengthy explanation wherein the blame was laid at the door of the Nicaraguan Democrats. Whether the Rivas faction ordered the assassination or whether it was a work of Walker's cannot be decided from the evidence; the suspicion, however, falls on the American, because coincidence enters so prominently.

When Walker relieved Granada he found that prisoners had been flung into dungeons, chained together as they had been at the time of the original seizure of the capital. Among the men he released was Antonio Chavis, a passionate Democrat, who immediately collected a band of fifty men and started for Somoto Grande, in Segovia, ten miles from the Honduras frontier. Walker maintains that Chavis acted independently, but he makes no effort to explain the irregularity which would permit an individual to lead an armed band from the stronghold of one force into the country of the enemy. It seems entirely logical that the commander-in-chief, if he did not actually order the assassination, knew of the plan to commit it; otherwise it would appear that his military control over Granada extended no farther than to the bare limits of his own army.

Estrada had not been able to return to the main Allied army because Belloso was angry at him for his attempt to conduct a personal campaign. He repaired, therefore, to Segovia, his perennial haven of refuge since the overthrow of the Legitimist party. There Chavis found him. In the narrow streets of the little village, in the dark, where the shadows of the thick adobe walls would hide until morning the bright blood, he was seized and knifed and left.

If coincidental, the murder was a fortunate event for Walker. What little cohesion the Allies had was further weakened by it. It was known that Guatemalans hated Salvadorians and Salvadorians hated Hondurans. Now there was added to the suspicions and discords which tore the fabric of Belloso's army the old distrust of Legitimist for Democrat. And if Walker could wait, the Latin temperament might prevail and the so-called alliance crumple into an untidy mass of men, wasting their substance in quarrels among themselves.

V

THE early part of October, 1856, was the most uncertain period of the entire war. Walker had lost many of his most valuable assistants—Cole, Lainé, Gilman and Davidson by death, Padre Vijil through a form of desertion, Minister Wheeler because of recall by the State Department, and Goicouria by his own prejudice. The lack of suitable officers hampered him seriously; he was afraid to move for fear he would lose what he held; and yet he knew he must strike at least one decisive blow against his foes. He had intended Masaya to be a lesson to the Allies; that having failed, he was required to prepare a new lesson.

In his service there were a few really capable officers. Three—Fayssoux, an artilleryman named Swingle and Thomas Henry—were comparative newcomers, but each was to prove of great service. Hornsby continued to occupy the place he had filled since his arrival: he was efficient, uninspired and enduringly loyal. Waters was an able commander of cavalry. But none was a man Walker could tie to. He had always had one aide whose opinions commanded extraordinary attention: Crocker in Sonora, Lainé in Nicaragua, Edmund Randolph in the United States.

To fill this need now came the most famous, and the ablest, of all the soldiers-of-fortune who sought to bring glory to the Walker banner. A British subject, born of Scandinavian parents, Charles Frederick Henningsen was everything a filibuster should be. Forty-two years old, handsome, humorous, he was a cosmopolite and the veteran of many wars. At nineteen he had fought under Zumalacarregui, the Spanish patriot, returning from his fighting to write two books of reminiscences. His literary work was distinguished, but he was not cast in the mold of the modern writing adventurer; war was his business, books merely a by-product. He was off again to the Caucasus, where he assisted an abortive revolution against the Czar; and, when he had written another book or two on Russian life, he traveled to join Kossuth's revolt in Hungary. Defeated there, he fled with a price on his head and reached the United States with Kossuth. He married a Southern belle, a widow and the niece of Senator Berrien, of Georgia.

With position and wealth, Henningsen had no reason to join the army of William Walker—except the unanswerable one: he was a born soldier. He had read of the Filibuster's struggle and talked with the Southerners in whose circle he moved; and at last he abandoned the cushioned ease of Washington for blankets in the tropics. He took with him thirty thousand dollars' worth of equipment, including several thousand muskets which had been converted into Minié rifles under his direction. He also carried the assurance of further support from another shipping magnate, George Law.

Law had acquired the muskets and employed Henningsen to convert them. They were intended for the return of Kossuth to Hungary but when that patriot failed to renew his revolutionary activities, the guns were stored by Law against an opportunity. And the opportunity, as it so soon developed, was Walker. George Law's ships ran to many ports: Havana, Panama for a time, San Francisco. He had watched alertly the progress of the three-cornered battle among Morgan & Garrison, Vanderbilt and William Walker. In the back of his mind was the thought that if Vanderbilt and Walker continued to disagree, there could be no Transit crossing and, while this condition existed, Morgan & Garrison could not operate their line. He knew the financial condition of the latter company as well as its owners, and it was clear to him that unless its Transit charter brought in revenue quickly, it would be unable to fulfill the requirements. Thus, having ships to run, a knowledge of the situation to guide him and General Henningsen to make a first gesture toward Walker by taking him a gift of arms, Law suddenly emerged as the greatest threat to Vanderbilt's final victory.

Henningsen reached Granada late in October. He was immediately commissioned brigadier-general in charge of artillery, his first duty to instruct officers and men in the use of the Minié rifles he had brought with him. For a time he met difficulties because his high rank appeared to other officers an unwarranted favoritism, but his worth soon lessened this jealousy. His instruction made possible for the first time a trained handling of the rifle among the rank and file and he also brought the artillery Walker had—mortars and howitzers principally—to a point of high efficiency. His knowledge of engineering was sufficient for him to see, when he had no more than glanced at the construction of Granada, the need for sappers and miners and he formed a company which in future battles concentrated on breaking connecting walls in the houses to clear the way for a protected advance.

Until the first of November the army did nothing but drill and prepare for another attack from the Allies at Masaya. When October had gone, it did not appear that the Americans were in any danger; Belloso declined to leave his stout barricades for the time and there was no other threatening force in the Republic. But then Costa Rica entered the alliance. For months the country had been recovering from the costs of the first war against Walker, both in money and in victims of disease, and by November 1, 1856, President Mora felt he was strong enough to attempt to throw a barrier across the Transit, which he called the "highway of filibusterism." On that date he proclaimed a blockade against San Juan del Sur and on the second sent General Cañas with a small body to seize the port and close the Transit Road.

Lieutenant Fayssoux was the first to learn of this new threat. He had been cruising in the *Granada* for all of October, touching at a dozen points a week to keep uneasy whatever enemy might be lying in the brush. On November second, when a ship from California docked, he was at San Juan. Hornsby with nearly two hundred men came from Granada to escort the specie train across the Isthmus and, when they had seen the treasure safely aboard the lake boat, they remained at Virgin Bay, leaving the defense of San Juan entirely to the one-ship navy. On November seventh, Fayssoux received a note signed by General Cañas, dated "One Mile from San Juan—4 P.M." and demanding the surrender of the town without the firing of a shot. If the demand were met, Cañas said, the "citizens should be protected, if not, no protection would be given." Fayssoux ignored the message and remained where he was, anchored off the main wharf. At five Fayssoux received word that Cañas was in the main plaza with six hundred men and would demand the surrender of the *Granada*. Again the threat to butcher the inhabitants of the town was voiced, and again Fayssoux ignored it. In prudence, however, he ran out of the harbor and anchored in the Pacific.

On the eighth, Fayssoux entered in his log: "Lying-to off the harbor. At 3:30 P.M. received letters from the officer in command of San Juan, Guardio, offering protection to all citizens that would deliver up their arms to him, and from Mr. Rozet [United States vice-consul] praying me not to come in, that if I did all Americans would perish. My answer to Rozet was that I did not intend to come in and for him to say to Guardio that I would not communicate with the enemy." Fayssoux hazarded no attack, but he did remain in sight of San Juan, skeptical of the rumor that two brigs and a bark, all Costa Rican, were making for the port.

On the tenth, Walker, learning of the capture of San Juan, sent reinforcements to Virgin Bay. Hornsby, with two hundred and fifty men and a howitzer, began a march over the Transit Road, intending if possible to drive Cañas from San Juan and fortify the city. Cañas, anticipating him, moved all but a few of his men to the very spot where Walker had waited more than a year before for Corral to fall into an ambush. His position was a commanding one, on a hill overlooking the road about a mile closer to San Juan than the Halfway House. Near the hill on which the Costa Rican main body waited the road entered a deep ravine and crossed a small bridge; a few of Cañas' men barricaded this bridge and awaited the assault of Hornsby's troops.

A detachment of Rifles hit the bridge quickly, driving the Costa Ricans to the hill. When Hornsby came up, his vanguard was already before the principal position. He waited there pending a reconnaissance and the repair of his lines, which had been disordered by a fairly accurate fire both from the bridge and the hilltop; but, when he saw the impregnability of Cañas' position, he determined to fall back to Virgin Bay. He reported at once to Walker at Granada, insisting that a greater force would be needed to dislodge the Costa Ricans and also complaining at the uselessness of the howitzer battery which had been sent to him.

Walker, as ever, needed the Transit. Although he was still confident he would defeat the Allies, the advance of the Costa Ricans was a blow he had not anticipated and one which might prove costly. He determined to retake the Transit at once, demoralize the Costa Ricans and if possible drive them back to their borders. On November eleventh he set out from Granada with two hundred and fifty Rifles, a howitzer, a mortar and (should the Costa Ricans barricade San Juan) a company of sappers and miners. General Henningsen was second in command, in charge of the artillery and engineers, and at Virgin Bay the balance of the Hornsby force was added. Shortly before daybreak on the twelfth, the army reached the Halfway House, where Walker laid out the plan of battle in the few minutes he allowed the men for rest.

Cañas had retaken the bridge and his men again were behind its barricades. His eight hundred troops on the hilltop were well concealed and in a position to sweep the road with artillery and rifle fire. Walker directed the flank movement of Hornsby's command repeated and the bridge again fell to him; and then he paused to block out the advance toward the hilltop.

Colonel von Natzmer, who had covered this ground in June of 1855 when acting as aide to Vallé, was familiar with the condition of the country back of the road. He suggested that the sappers and miners be sent in a long arc to the right, to cut a path through the thick jungle. Walker agreed to this, covering the work of the engineers with a Rifle company in the brush and a howitzer at the curve of the road.

For an hour and a half Walker, by maintaining an artillery duel, concealed Von Natzmer's advance. There was little damage done on either side in this period; the howitzer once was withdrawn and replaced because its men were under direct fire from the Costa Rican barricades, but aside from inflicting a few casualties neither side gained an advantage.

When Von Natzmer had nearly cut his way through to the position he sought, however, Cañas discovered his movement. He left the hilltop and retreated. When Walker's men reached the barricades they were deserted. The Costa Ricans dropped down onto the Transit Road and set out swiftly for San Juan, closely pursued by the Americans.

Henningsen, his artillery no longer needed, mounted a horse and set out in charge of a party of Rangers. For most of the six miles to San Juan the Costa Ricans retreated well, falling back in order and occasionally making a stand. But as they reached the outskirts of the town, Henningsen, backed by a handful of officers and men, charged wildly and the enemy broke and fled. By the time Walker and the foot soldiers reached San Juan, the army of General Cañas was scattered throughout the immediate countryside, some fleeing through the bush toward Guanecaste, some retreating in disorder along the road to Rivas.

Walker remained in San Juan only until the next morning. Confident that Cañas was thoroughly beaten and could do no more than barricade and attempt to hold the city of Rivas, he decided to return and seek an engagement with Belloso in the North. He marched back over the Transit Road again, leaving Fayssoux and the *Granada* to watch San Juan, embarked his men on the *San Carlos* and reached Granada the same night. The First Infantry was left to hold Virgin Bay and to harass any company that might attempt to occupy the Transit Road.

VI

THE FILIBUSTER massed for his attempt two Rifle companies, one of Infantry, one of Rangers, a detachment of engineers and five assorted field guns. With a strength of five hundred and fifty men, he marched for Masaya on November fifteenth. The day was hot, the mules carrying the army supplies slow, the road dusty. By mid-afternoon he had not covered more than half the distance to Masaya. During a pause beside the road a courier came up with information that Maximo Jerez, at the head of eight hundred Allies, was on the march to Rivas, to reinforce Cañas.

Once more Walker was forced to interrupt his campaign to take Masaya in order to relieve another point. He sent his infantrymen back to Virgin Bay, to join the Rifle company there and to be ready for a march along the Transit Road if Cañas should attempt its capture; and with only three hundred men, the artillery and the supplies, he moved on toward Masaya.

The march was so slow that some of the lustier spirits broke away from the column, passed the advance guard and ventured into the enemy territory on their own. One of these was Major Henry, who had been wounded in the first assault on Masaya. Mounted on a mule, his head bandaged where he had been grazed by a ball in a duel on the beach at Granada, he reached the Allied picket line with one companion. With a yell, they charged the pickets, firing so enthusiastically that the startled Guatemalans broke and ran for the shelter of the town. It was an irresponsible act and did Walker no service; when he reached the huts at the edge of the town the enemy was waiting for him, and gave his main body momentary pause.

The Rangers met the first fire. Walker, as soon as the guns spoke, ordered the bulk of the column into the undergrowth beside the road and sent the Rifles in to support the cavalry. After a bitter fifteen minutes, the Americans advanced into the Plaza of San Sebastian, covered by Henningsen's splendidly directed canister-fire. The Allies dropped back into the center of the city, but the Americans did not follow; spent and dispirited they remained in the Plaza of San Sebastian. Walker discovered that the war of the Allies was not, as he confidently had believed, a triviality.

Darkness came on. He ordered pickets set out, but his army had disintegrated into a languid, undisciplined mob. There were at least six Americans dead and more than fifty wounded and the encampment was so confused that the surgeons had to go from group to group, seeking the injured and binding up their wounds without light. The officers, with the exception of Henningsen and Hornsby and a few others, had found *aguardiente;* many were drunk.

Walker stalked through the scattered companies like an outraged matron in an unruly orphanage. It is some tribute to his personal magnetism that he was able to get any order at all, because his was a beaten army and none but himself refused to accept the fact. The condition which had so suddenly burst upon him was the result of an imperceptible decline in the calibre of the men who had come to Nicaragua. The Immortals were fighters, from the first to the fifty-eighth, as were the recruits who immediately followed. But as the Walker legend grew in the United States, and as his actions began to meet with the disapproval of his intelligent compatriots, the standards lagged. Throughout the latter half of 1856 he had no means of examining the men who offered to serve him until they were on the ground; and when they reached Nicaragua he was forced to accept them, although they might be diseased, criminal, lazy or cowardly. Not until the night in the Plaza of San Sebastian did he see the danger in this. Until that night he was arrogant, considering himself the director of an invincible army . . . and after that night he became desperate, marching as quickly toward his inevitable defeat as he had toward dictatorship.

Morning found his army slightly refreshed and with the iota of added courage daylight lends the weak. The artillery threw a few shells into the houses occupied by the Allies, the wounded were installed in the Church of San Sebastian, a breakfast of sorts was prepared and the sappers went to work.

For all of the sixteenth and seventeenth, the engineers did the fighting, with pickaxes and spades. Wall after wall was broken through, house after house occupied. Occasionally the Allies attempted to retake the Plaza of San Sebastian, without success. On the evening of November seventeenth, Walker had reached a point thirty yards from the main plaza, where Belloso's men lay in wait, their rifle barrels thick in the windows.

The American line was so thinly spread by the time Walker had covered the few blocks between the two plazas that no portion of it could have withstood a major attack. He abandoned the Plaza of San Sebastian, then, burning the houses around it and moving his entire force up to the head of the sappers' operations.

Once more, by tremendous sacrifice, he had gained a position of no value to him. Henningsen tried futilely to drive out the Allies with his howitzers but the fuses again were too short and the precious shells he fired exploded in the air. The army had been traveling on its second wind and now was utterly overcome with lassitude; even the pickets slept in the night, not caring much whether they lived or died. The losses in the three days' fighting totaled one hundred, a third of the entire command. And now, as he had from Rivas, Walker retreated in the dark, his army divided into two parts for the assistance of stealth, his wounded on mules, his rear guard consisting of the imperturbable Henningsen and one mortar.

They marched throughout the night of the seventeenth, arriving in Granada shortly after daybreak. The Filibuster was shaken by his failure. Expecting to strike a paralyzing blow against the Allies, instead he had suffered self-paralysis. And from that moment to the end of his deeds in Nicaragua, a new element entered into his

character. He felt the first gnawings of panic, he tasted desperation and he learned there could be such a thing as fear. The mere
fact of defeat was nothing, for he had suffered defeat before. But
he saw for the first time that the army in which he had placed such
exalted faith was composed only of men: it was a wall of sand, which
under the pressure of Masaya had shown a crack. And as the days
passed it began to crumple, bits of it running off in a fine stream
and greater chunks breaking away to vanish. The men showed an
uneasiness they had never before displayed. Circumstances were
against them, they mumbled; their luck had run out. There was
disease—cholera, yellow fever, dengue, dysentery—selecting a dozen
or so every day for its frightful work. Granada was hot and unhealthy—not so unhealthy as Leon, true, but nevertheless no climate for a large foreign army. Recruits from the United States
were few, and those few worthless. Masaya was gone and with it
much of the hope that the broad acres about it would furnish more
food for the Americans. Small wonder that the desertions increased.
The men of Walker were mostly amateur soldiers, in the tropics for
adventure and booty—and what adventure or booty could there be
in a guarded city ridden with disease and already lacking sufficient
food for the hundreds penned up in it?

A company of Rangers which had been sent north of Managua
on patrol never returned. A report was received that mounted Americans had swept through the hills of Chontales, killing and robbing
as they rode and making for the Bluefields River. Still later a French
trader came into Granada, telling a grim tale of the Rangers' fate.
They had tied up a miner in the hills and flogged him when he refused to reveal the cache of his gold. The French in the region had
banded together and fought the Rangers for hours; and when the
deserters ran out of ammunition they had pleaded for a truce and
safe passage. They were marched farther into the hills and at a
signal were butchered, all but two.

This story was true, but there were many false ones (each as
grim) whispered about the campfires in Granada. Sentries jumped
at a sudden footfall. Scouts went into the brush and hid there
safely, returning with fictitious reports after spending a plausible
time away from the town. And from Henningsen to the lowest pri-

vate, they all looked for salvation to Walker, the quiet, the dignified. Nothing altered his countenance. He remained a block of ice
carved in the figure of a man. But he was uneasy, as a cornered
rat is uneasy, and he tried to find in the recesses of his mind some
resource which would serve two vital ends: give his men a vision
of victory and persuade Belloso that the Allies could not win.

He found a solution of sorts. It was born of desperation, panic and
some hatred. None but an outlaw with the warped mind of all
outlaws could have conceived it; few but the granite-hard Walker
could have executed it. When it was done he had nakedly revealed
what he was and could nevermore lay claim to the name regenerator.

Doubting that Belloso had the strength or the courage to advance
against him and realizing how untenable his position in Granada
was becoming, he resolved to take Rivas and fortify it. He could
assemble all his soldiers and hold the town against any comer. His
decision was sound, because although he was electing to stand siege
it was only partial siege, as long as the *Granada* held the coast open
to his recruits from California.

But the vicious part of his decision earns no forgiveness. He ordered
Henningsen, when the army had been moved from Granada, to
destroy that magnificent city.

VII

THE prevailing wind sent a surf against the beach below Granada as
rhythmic as that of the Pacific shore. Walker's recruits, landing
from the lake ships, were carried ashore in launches, or on the
backs of bare-legged natives. One wharf, the remnants of a deserted fort, built of masonry and with its inland walls still strongly
standing, was to be seen at the lake's edge. Above was the city
itself, reached by a road which climbed a series of terraces, paved
and shored to thwart the wasting of the rains. On the outer edges
of the city there were the cane huts of the poor, white-washed
and very clean and beyond, the adobe, tile-roofed houses. On the
road were three great churches: the Guadaloupe Cathedral, nearest
the lake, the Esquipulas, a block away, and the Church and Convent
of San Francisco, called the Parochial, on the corner of the plaza

itself. It was an ancient city, for centuries the stronghold of the aristocrats.

This city Walker destroyed. Although Henningsen performed the actual destruction, the blame is Walker's: his brigadier was an officer who would have obeyed with the same quiet determination any order given him—and Walker knew this when he ordered Granada reduced to dust. General Henningsen was to leave no stone upon another, nothing unburnt that would burn, no adobe houses or cane huts or churches of God. Nothing was to remain . . . and three hundred men were assigned to carry out the execution.

Granada was razed because it was more a symbol than a city. To wipe it from the earth would strike thousands with full terror; again the intention was to infuse "a salutary dread of American justice among the plotting Legitimists."

On the nineteenth, the sick and wounded were placed aboard the two lake boats. So widespread had been cholera, dysentery and dengue fever that the hospitals in the city had become impossible. The surgeons recruited from the States were mainly drunkards and incompetents, who could not be depended upon to enforce the simplest measures of hygiene. Immediately before the evacuation of the city they had possessed so long, at least one-fifth of Walker's men were incapacitated. Housed in two large buildings on the main plaza, they suffered in unspeakable filth. The sick lay on cots thoroughly infected with the diseases of others who had died on them, without linens, garbed in their woolen breeches and flannel shirts. There was often insufficient water, flies in millions crawled on the faces and festering wounds of the unfortunates, indifferent attendants watched as the delirious shrieked and fell to the floor. The odor overpoweringly seeped through the windows and onto the plaza, causing well men to walk extra blocks to avoid passing the hospitals. It was the consensus of the surgeons that, under the conditions they were leaving, every American in Nicaragua would have been dead in six weeks.

As a new hospital base, Walker selected the little volcanic island, Omotepe, ten miles off the western shore of Lake Nicaragua and thirty miles south of Granada. The island had been for years a reservation for the Indians of the region and they held it under the agreement that no white man would occupy it without their consent; but Walker was in no mood to consider regulations he had not made (or even regulations he had made, for that matter) and the sick were landed at Muigalpa, a village on the western shore.

The island itself was crowned by the volcano for which it had been named and by another, smaller peak, Madera. The wounded and ill had to be landed on an old barge and many of them suffered severely from the crude handling the crew of the vessels gave them.

No provision had been made for the reception of the casualties: the small beach was deserted and the jungle behind it, wherein lay overturned the idols of the ancient civilizations, appeared all but impenetrable. With the greatest difficulty the company at last was quartered in the village, which had been abandoned by its inhabitants.

Nine able-bodied men were left to help care for the invalids. They carried sick and wounded men to the village until they collapsed from exhaustion, leaving twenty-four lying on the beach, exposed to a pitiless rain. Six of the twenty-four died in the night; five more died in the village. Within a week forty were dead and possibly half as many, emaciated and delirious, had plunged off into the jungle and were not seen again.

On November twenty-second the third boatload of refugees from Granada was landed. It consisted of civilians, American women and children and the families of other foreigners who had been residents of Granada. Conditions were somewhat improved after this arrival, as many of the women cleaned the huts of the village and did what they could to nurse the invalid soldiers.

Meanwhile, Walker had completed his arrangements for the destruction of the capital and, with all of his force except the three hundred left for Henningsen's work, he embarked for Virgin Bay. He encamped there, expecting only a short wait until Henningsen and Colonel Fry (who had taken a guard of sixty men to Omotepe) would rejoin him; then he planned to march either to San Jorge or Rivas and establish a new base.

It was late November, near the close of the rainy season. Virgin Bay was a desolation, having suffered much in the various battles fought for its possession. The spirits of the army were low and, except for a few of the more talented officers, there was no great effort made to maintain discipline. While the Americans had been supreme in Nicaragua, it had been easy to control the men, but now they absorbed some of Walker's desperation and, lacking his conviction of destiny, were disheartened at their outlook. He could no longer conceal from them the fact that he was on the defensive and stood a better than even chance of being deposed from the presidency he still claimed. A victory was needed to restore in the minds of his men the fact that the "Gray-Eyed Man" was still fortune's darling. And, in the unvarying and almost monotonous manner, a courier came to Virgin Bay to report a conquest so decisive that the army to a man was converted to the philosophy of success.

Lieutenant Fayssoux and his *Granada* had done nothing but patrol the coast since Costa Rica's entrance into the war. For a time there was nothing to be done by a "navy"; an occasional innocent vessel was overhauled, examined and permitted to resume her course, but the *Granada's* frequent pauses in San Juan did not, as they had a month before, uncover anything so alarming as a concentration of hostile troops. On November twenty-second, however, Fayssoux saw from his place at anchor the rigging of a brig. He went out to challenge her, gallantly trustful of his seventy-ton ship, his crew of twenty-three and his two six-pound guns.

The inhabitants of San Juan lined the beach and watched the ships. They came together at six o'clock and the quick darkness of the sea soon covered them. For more than two hours there was a distant sound of an engagement; and at the end of that period a terrific explosion, which lighted the western sky and made the darkness more absolute when it was over. The spectators turned from the beach and went to their homes, believing that they had seen a gallant little man with an insufficient ship die before the superior power of a brig-of-war. A message to that effect was sent to Walker at Virgin Bay.

But in the morning, the *Granada,* her decks black with nearly three times as many men as had sailed out in her, returned to the harbor, casual, cocky and with no more than scratches to show for her adventure. A second courier was sent to Virgin Bay, carrying an extract from Fayssoux's log:

At 4 P. M. saw a sail off the harbor; hove up anchor and stood out to her. At 5h. 45m. she hoisted Costa Rican colors. At 6 within four hundred yards of her; she fired round shot and musketry at us. At 8 we blew her up. At 10 we had taken from the sea her captain and forty of her men. Her name was *Once de Abril,** Captain Antonie Villarostra; crew one hundred fourteen and men and officers; guns four, nine lbs. calibre. The captain states that he was about surrendering when she blew up. All were lost and killed but those that I picked up. I had one man . . . killed and eight wounded. Light breezes; stood in for the harbor.

Walker seized upon the lucky shot Fayssoux had fired, which had struck the *Once de Abril's* magazine, and turned it skilfully to his ends: it was reported and believed that the Americans had developed a shell so powerful it could destroy a ship in a single explosion. Costa Rica, hearing of this marvelous shell, made no further effort to engage the *Granada,* either to remove her from the sea or to avenge the *Once de Abril.*

The survivors of the enemy brig, most of whom were badly burned, were treated by the surgeons at Virgin Bay. When they had recovered they were given passports and permitted to return to San José, a circumstance so startling that they hastened to their own country loud in praise of the humane Americans. They were silenced at last by orders of their government, but they are supposed to have refused later to fight against the Americans.

As soon as his ship was at anchor, Fayssoux was summoned to Virgin Bay to give a personal report of the battle. He was commissioned a captain by Walker and given an estate, Rosario, near Rivas, as a reward for his efforts. The record does not make clear who owned the estate or whether Fayssoux ever profited from the acquisition of it.

With something to talk about, the filibusters forgot the poor food and living discomforts of their station. Their renewed cheerfulness was not lessened, either, when on the night of November twenty-fourth they learned that the destroying Henningsen and his crew had been attacked at Granada and were desperately trying to hold back a superior force.

---

* "Eleventh of April"—so named to commemorate Costa Rica's initial victory over Walker.

VIII

WHAT Henningsen did at Granada becomes, in the account of the
Filibuster, the one great military achievement of the campaign.
Given the disgraceful task of destroying a city which had survived
for three centuries, commanding men with no conception of discipline, assisted by officers with infinite courage and little intelligence, he withstood a siege for three long weeks, never once neglect-
ing the work he had been set to do.

He started obliterating Granada on November twenty-second.
Dividing his three hundred men into squads, he sent them to various sections, to blast down adobe walls and burn whatever was in-
flammable. Before nightfall the city was an obscene sore: flames
licked the sky in half a dozen places, smoke hung over the plaza like
a black velvet drapery and the destructionists were howling drunk.
As the torch-bearers and sledge-swingers moved from house to house
they plundered what they thought they might use and, as this
plunder consisted largely of casks of fine wines, jugs of *aguardiente*
and an occasional bottle of real whiskey, reason died.

Henningsen established headquarters in the abandoned Convent
of San Francisco, on the main plaza. He expected the job of razing
Granada would be a laborious but not necessarily a difficult one; but
when the first day was over, he knew that upon him alone depended
success in the execution of the Filibuster's order. The officers as
well as the rank and file were drunk. Groups of men reeled through
the streets, their faces black with smoke, their voices hoarse from
constant shouting, their breaths foul from the quantities of liquor
they had drunk. As the first day passed, and the second, they gave
up their mood of conviviality for undirected fury and, as do all
men when the weapon of destruction is placed in their hands, concentrated with a terrible singleness of purpose on leaving nothing
of the city.

Although he was pleased with the vigor of their assault upon the
huts and mansions of Granada, Henningsen yet knew that their
safety became more doubtful with the hours. The drunker they
got and the more they destroyed, the weaker they became to repel
an attack. And Henningsen was the only man in Granada to realize

that the Allies unquestionably would attack; the city was the stronghold of Legitimacy, and it would be folly not to suppose that at
least one resident had fled to Masaya with a tale of helpless debauchery to encourage the enemy.

Some leaders of the Allied army advocated an advance on Granada
on the very afternoon Henningsen began to tear it to pieces. But
the mere suggestion turned Belloso against it, because he and every
other Allied officer lived always with jealousy. For forty-eight hours
the high command bickered; and it was not until the twenty-fourth
that some sobriety was pounded into the skulls of Henningsen's
wreckers by the sound of rifle fire coming from three points at once.

One Allied body attacked the Jalteva, northern suburb; another
the Church of San Francisco; a third from the vicinity of Guadaloupe
Cathedral, on the street leading from the lake to the main plaza.
Major Swingle, Henningsen's ablest aide, manned a gun and disposed of the Jalteva forces with half a dozen rounds of solid shot,
while the other officers tried to gather together enough of the sober
soldiers to assault the enemy in the churches. Several charges on
the Guadaloupe Cathedral failed, and at nightfall the Allies were
fortified both in that edifice and in the smaller Esquipulas Church.
Henningsen and the main body were cut off in the plaza and could
not reach the lake until the street had been cleared; and twenty-
seven men on the wharf, who had been assigned to the task of
handling stores preparatory to sending them to Walker at Virgin
Bay, were completely isolated.

The company making a stand at the San Francisco church could
not be dislodged by long distance firing from the Americans and a
Calvin O'Neal, whose brother had been killed in the first minutes
of the engagement, suddenly appeared before Henningsen, who was
crouching at the window of a house studying what he could see
of the situation. O'Neal was beside himself with grief for his dead
brother and asked that he be allowed to charge the Guatemalans in
the vicinity of the church. It was an insane request and one which
Henningsen resisted; but when he saw that O'Neal meant to charge
with or without orders, he allowed him thirty-two riflemen.

Barefooted, shirt-sleeved, O'Neal mounted a horse and led the
charge. His thirty-two men followed him into the very center of

From *The Story of the Filibusters*, by J. J. Roche.

CHARLES FREDERICK HENNINGSEN

the Allied troops and for long minutes there was a carnival of slaughter in the shadow of the San Francisco church's quiet walls, The Guatemalans, altogether unprepared for the attack, fell, in the words of Walker, "as heedless travelers in the path of a simoom." Henningsen had great difficulty in recalling O'Neal and his gallants, for after the first assault they were carried away with the lovely lust of killing and could see nothing but men to be slain. It was full dark before they returned to the plaza. From the tone in which this incident is described by Walker, it appears that few of the Americans were killed in the charge, although to return they had to pass through "streets almost blocked with the bodies of the Guatemalans they had slain."

By the morning of the twenty-fifth, Henningsen had arranged a sort of order. His men were concentrated on the adobe houses of the plaza, and could communicate with one another regardless of the severity of a future battle. He had two hundred and twenty-seven able to bear arms, seventy-three wounded, seventy noncombatants and twenty-seven isolated on the wharf. He had lost twenty-two in the various attacks on the Guadaloupe. He possessed cannon but very little shot for it; later in the siege the resourceful Swingle improvised cannon balls by using wet sand as a mold and concocting missiles of one part lead and three parts scrap iron.

The street to the lake was closed off at the plaza end by breastworks built between the parish church on one side of the street's mouth and the guardhouse opposite. Throughout the twenty-fifth, the Allies made several attempts to break this defense. They were beaten back, however, as much by the effects of the burning buildings near them as by the rifle-fire from the Americans: embers filled the street and fired several huts. Late in the afternoon, Henningsen ordered a charge toward the Guadaloupe and succeeded in reaching the Esquipulas Church after he had driven the enemy from several huts in the vicinity which they had strengthened and loopholed.

The night of the twenty-fifth and the next day were spent in further futile attempts to drive the Allies out of the Guadaloupe. Henningsen's men, sobered by the shock of the first attack, had gone back to their jugs and could not be marshaled in sufficient force to storm the Cathedral; also, the work of destruction, in the orderly mind of the General, was as important as the battle and as he moved forward a painful foot at a time he burned the foot behind. By dawn of the twenty-fifth, four days after the destruction was started, he had all but leveled the main plaza into heaps of smoking ruins, effecting a double purpose: obeying the orders Walker had given him to the last letter, and cutting off from his men (likely to turn into cravens as soon as the effects of the liquor wore off) the only possible escape without advancing. At sunset on the twenty-sixth, however, Henningsen saw the impossibility of forcing his men toward the Guadaloupe Cathedral before morning. He installed them in adobe houses, set out pickets and prepared to wait for light.

Meanwhile, Walker arrived off the Granada wharf. Hearing nothing further after the news that Granada had been attacked, he waited in Virgin Bay until the twenty-fifth, when he went aboard the *San Carlos* to relieve Henningsen. Shortly after dark on the twenty-sixth, he ordered the boat halted off shore and sent a launch to the wharf. He could see, from the boat's deck, the red-starred flag flying from the tower of the Esquipulas Church and the clouds of smoke from various sections of the city, and he guessed from the signs that Henningsen was delaying his departure until he had finished his work.

The boat returned from the wharf with the news that Henningsen was cut off, but by no means defeated, that the wharf defenders were in good spirits, needing only food and ammunition to hold their position indefinitely and that no help from the *San Carlos* was wanted at the moment. The twenty-seven, their commander reported, were well protected behind the walls of the old fort from which the wharf had been constructed and believed they could block the Allies until Henningsen could cut his way through to them.

After dark a boat was sent ashore with ammunition and food. Its crew returned with grim tidings. A Venezuelan, Tejada, who had been one of the political prisoners freed from their chains when the Americans took Granada in 1855, had deserted. The remaining defenders feared that he would reveal the smallness of their number to the enemy, who until then had believed the landing to be held by a force several times its actual strength. For some reason, Walker did not seem to regard this circumstance as dangerous; he made no effort to reinforce or remove the landing guard, instead remaining offshore in the *San Carlos*. Shortly after midnight, a vicious burst of musketry was heard from two points: the street leading to the wharf and the water before it.

Henningsen heard this musketry too. He believed himself relieved when the sound came to him; it was not until next morning that he knew his lake outpost had been wiped out. Walker, on the *San Carlos*, saw in the darkness the place where the wharf had been become ringed with fire, heard the shrill shouts of the natives and then nothing but an occasional musket shot. As he was watching for a renewal of the fight, not believing it to be ended so soon, the deck of the *San Carlos* was hailed by a swimmer, who came aboard as the lone survivor of the twenty-six remaining after Tejada deserted.

The Venezuelan had reported to the Allies, the swimmer said, the number of men on the landing, and, also, had shown them how they could overcome the Americans by using an old iron barge on the lakeside as an assault position. Two bodies of men then were sent to storm the pier, one from the barge and another from the street. The Americans fought well enough, but were overwhelmed in a few minutes. The swimmer thought some of the men might have been taken prisoner, in which case the scattered musket shots were likely to have been the sounds of executions.

On November twenty-seventh, Henningsen moved his wounded from the church at the corner of the plaza into huts on the street leading to the Guadaloupe. When the wounded had all been moved, a couple of hundred pounds of powder unsuitable for the guns was set beneath the tower of the church. Riflemen were stationed in the tower as the last of the plaza defenders moved into the street leading to the lake and their careful fire kept the Allies from advancing into the ruined square. When the plaza was cleared, the riflemen retreated, firing the powder train. The Allies, moving into the undefended square at a trot, were caught by the toppling masonry as the powder blew, sending the tower high into the air and raining debris on the entire area.

Henningsen's job was almost done. There remained now the more difficult duty—to save himself and his men. He was locked in a narrow street, holding one church but unable for the moment to take another. Walker was on the lake, but could not land a relieving force until the wharf had been recaptured. And Belloso, commander of the Allies, could see a great victory before him, a vision which impelled him to pour fresh men into the ruins of Granada.

On November twenty-eighth Henningsen felt himself well enough manned to attempt still another assault on the Guadaloupe. He selected sixty riflemen for the attack, and three crews of eight for the guns. When all was prepared, the artillery fired seven rounds each into the Guadaloupe and the sixty Rifles advanced to storm the church. The maneuver was successful without the loss of a man; when the Rifles reached the Cathedral they found that the Allies had abandoned it after the artillery barrage. Henningsen, now in control of the only large building still standing in Granada, moved in at once and fortified his capture, preparing to rest his forces before hacking a pathway to safety.

Major Henry was sent ahead with twenty-seven men, to take and hold two small huts midway between the Cathedral and the lake. He reported a little before dark that the enemy was in strength before him and he could hold only one of the huts; Henningsen ordered him to do this and promised reinforcements, but in the confusion of establishing the wounded in the Cathedral only ten men and one howitzer could be sent. In a brisk battle which followed the coming of darkness, however, the thirty-seven were enough to rout the Allies. Major Henry, watching at a window of the hut, held his fire until the enemy muskets betrayed the main force, then, with a single charge of canister from the howitzer, was able to break and demoralize the advancing enemy.

Henningsen later sent Henry a reinforcement of thirty men, ample to hold the hut against any attack the Allies could marshal. In the Cathedral, he divided his troops (two hundred odd remained fit for service) into a main guard of the forty best, held for emergency and reserve, fifteen at the doors and windows of the church, twenty for the rear enclosure and ten each for the six guns. The Americans had recovered from their debauchery of the preceding days and, with a full consciousness of the seriousness of their position, were more willing to work; acting under Swingle, they completed in a single night a breastwork in the street before the Guadaloupe which Henningsen had not expected to finish in less than forty-eight hours.

For three days Henningsen occupied himself with organization, fighting none but trivial forays. He was completely encircled by the Allies and, although still hopeful that Walker would relieve him, intended as far as he was able to withstand the siege alone. The Cathedral was easily defensible, but it was no place in which to house three hundred persons, including women, children, sick and wounded. There had been little food in the first days of the battle; there was less now and meals consisted of mule and horse meat, bread from bad flour and coffee. The Allied dead still lay in the streets all about the Guadaloupe and from the decomposing bodies arose an overpowering stench.

Without any means of achieving sanitation, the inside of the church became the sort of charnel house the hospitals had been before the evacuation of Granada. Inevitable cholera struck. The incompetent doctors dosed the victims with opium and refused them water. There was no order except that enforced by the indomitable Henningsen, who seemed never to sleep, never to get out of countenance and never to lose hope.

On the twenty-eighth, Zavala, the Guatemalan, and a renegade named Price entered the Guadaloupe under a flag of truce. Zavala came as a spy; he was not blindfolded in accordance with custom and he wandered about in the enclosure examining what he could see. The message he brought, addressed to the "Commander-in-Chief of the remains of Walker's forces" urged an immediate surrender for the sake of humanity, mentioning that three thousand Allies ringed the Guadaloupe and without surrender no American could hope to survive. Price walked about among the men, urging them to desert to the enemy. Henningsen treated the entire matter with contempt: he ordered Price arrested, insolently told the Guatemalan he might examine all the defenses minutely and carry back a report to his command, defiantly declined to discuss surrender, "except at the cannon's mouth."

At three that afternoon the Allies tried to storm the church and were beaten back with terrible losses. There was another attack at eight, when a movement toward the rear of the Cathedral reached a point eighty yards short of the breastwork before it was discovered; Captain Swingle, now become chief of the artillery, used two six-pounders loaded with canister with such effect that the enemy was flung back.

The conditions in the church made it necessary for Henningsen to move his wounded. The only direction in which they could be taken was toward the lake, where Henry still held the hut outpost; on the plaza side there was nothing but the black ruins of what had been buildings. In the morning of December first, under cover of darkness, the first of the sick and wounded were carried to Henry's position. By daylight all had been moved, leaving the Guadaloupe in the hands of seventy men. The vanguard rested all day, occasionally beating back small parties of the Allies, and when night came advanced a few feet more. This tactic was repeated daily, with the result that in four days the breastwork had been pushed several hundred feet closer to the lake, and an unbroken line of defense stretched from the Guadaloupe—toward the end held by thirty of the best riflemen—to the front line.

Conditions improved somewhat as soon as the sick were evacuated from the insanitary Cathedral, but the deaths continued. Dozens had succumbed by the fifth. Of these, one was a courageous and unfortunate victim of William Walker's madness, Mrs. Edward Bingham. Her husband's career on the American stage had been halted by severe illness and he had gone to Nicaragua to take up one of the grants of land the Regenerator was making available for Americans. The Binghams arrived in the midst of war and saw none of the peace they had expected to find in a new country; the husband died and the widow found herself in the center of the disease and agony through which Henningsen took his men. For days, in the Cathedral, she worked as hard as the commander, tireless in her patience, caring for the sick and remaining inflexibly brave in the face of sights no woman should witness. She died quietly, in the night, soon after the Guadaloupe had been evacuated.

IX

WILLIAM WALKER, almost constantly on the lake, hovered off shore for two weeks, aboard *La Virgen*. His knowledge of Henningsen's plight was sketchy; he could be sure only that a great force opposed his ablest officer. Something of the predicament into which he had got himself must have come to him, in the days before Henningsen reached the lake shore with the pathetic remnant of his three hundred; but as always he revealed no weakness. He never ceased thinking of himself as President of Nicaragua and his blind belief in his destiny kept him from despair when the evacuation of Granada became, instead of a tactical maneuver, the great battle of Nicaragua.

While he hovered, hoping that some fortune would clear the wharf and let him land a force to extricate Henningsen's, trouble developed in a new quarter. The refugees at Omotepe had warned him that guns were being transported from the mainland, presumably to assist an Indian uprising. The camp at Virgin Bay, manned by a handful of riflemen, also was apprehensive of an attack from Cañas, who was still in Rivas. There was every indication, to the commander, that the ship he rode must soon or late speed to the assistance of one of the three threatened points: Henningsen's Granada, the refugees' Omotepe, or Walker's own Virgin Bay.

On December second, a canoe bumped against the side of *La Virgen*. Three men came aboard, shivering and unable to speak, either from cold or fear. Walker on the deck failed to obtain a connected story from any of them; he took one, then, into the cabin, dosed him with a tumbler full of whiskey and learned that the Indians had attacked the hospital settlement at Omotepe and probably had butchered every person on the island.

La Virgen turned for the island at the best speed her old boilers could muster. Two miles from Omotepe an iron barge, one of several used by the Accessory Transit Company for lightering cargo and passengers on the lake, was sighted; it was filled, crushingly, with men, women and children. Few were fully clothed and when Walker had taken them aboard his boat they said they had been adrift all night, without sail or rudder, hoping that the wind would carry them away from the accursed island. The Indians had attacked the evening before, firing into the huts and driving the entire company into a panic. Fry's command of sixty men had driven the Indians off and remained on shore; but Walker never knew how many who had fled into the jungle died there.

Walker landed the refugees, dropped ammunition for Fry's force and left the island for Virgin Bay. He paused briefly off Granada, to observe that the Henningsen line had been pushed another fifty feet closer to the lake, and then went to his base, where he ordered an immediate removal to San Jorge, three miles from Rivas. Nearly three hundred recruits, from New Orleans and California, had arrived since December first, giving him a total of seven hundred soldiers, exclusive of what might remain of Henningsen's command. When the base had been established at San Jorge, without opposition of any sort from Cañas, the island of Omotepe was evacuated and all the sick and wounded concentrated with the main army.

The larger body of recruits, two hundred and thirty-five from New Orleans, were under the command of Lockridge, the recruiting officer, who delivered them to Walker and returned at once to the United States. The new men were eager to see action and Walker determined to attempt the relief of Henningsen. For this rescue one hundred and sixty men were organized under the command of Captain Waters, chief of the Rangers. With Walker aboard, they sailed from Virgin Bay to Granada, where the entire afternoon of December twelfth was spent at anchor, the men concealed and the officers attempting to determine through glasses the exact state of the siege. The Allies, who worried whenever La Virgen hove into sight, made a great demonstration on the beach, parading a small number of men in an obvious effort to suggest an inexhaustible supply of troops.

With nightfall La Virgen extinguished her running lights, dropped a canvas curtain to conceal any gleam from the cabin and moved up the shore. Precisely as it had a year and more before, when Granada fell to the Filibuster, the vessel made a landing, launches were hauled ashore on cables and Waters' one hundred and sixty set down. Walker remained aboard the ship; his last order to the relief was not to leave the shoreline in the event that a retreat should be made necessary.

The Filibuster's expectation was that Waters would succeed and the combination so effected would be enough for Henningsen to reach the lake. If this could be accomplished, the entire army could be massed at San Jorge, Rivas taken, Virgin Bay fortified and the

Transit assuredly retained for the further reinforcement of the regime. With Henningsen freed, with recruits by the hundreds arriving from New Orleans and San Francisco and with the discord in the Allied command reaching new peaks of excitability, victory would be a matter of days.

Walker waited on the ship for Waters to get through. Shoreward little could be seen; it was dark and dead Granada had no more lights to show. After the reinforcements had been landed the boat puffed back to her anchorage of the afternoon and those aboard her lined the rails, watching. Occasionally a musket went off, or one of Swingle's six-pounders, hurling its improvised ball of scrap iron and lead at the Allied barricades. Otherwise there was no action for hours.

At midnight there came a succession of volleys from a point north of the Henningsen breastworks. Walker could distinguish between the brutal thud of Allied muskets, and the shrill reply of his own rifles. The guns hushed, renewed their bickering and then were silent again. Walker, leaning over the rail and peering intently toward the shore, heard a splash beneath him and a muffled voice. He looked down into a pair of dark eyes and a matted head; he ordered a rope overside and the swimmer was pulled aboard.

He was young, swarthy and, except for a breech clout, naked. For a few moments he could offer no replies to Walker's hurried and concerned Spanish; he had been in the water a long while and was winded. But when he could speak it was in English and Walker recognized him as the Hawaiian who had come with the Immortals and who was known only as "Kanaka John." He had been swimming in the lake for several hours looking for *La Virgen,* he said, to deliver a sealed bottle with a note from Henningsen, reporting on the condition of the defenders and giving the signals to be used if a rescue was to be attempted. Walker ordered the signals to be given immediately, but the fighting had broken out ashore again and they were not seen.

Waters, when he had organized his force, had traveled along a narrow strip of beach, with the lake on one side and a lagoon on the other. He had approached to within the limits of Granada when musket fire stopped him; the enemy, in force, waited behind the first barricades. Waters ordered a charge; the men hesitated and hung back; then a few ran forward and swept over the breastworks. Their first victory seemed to give them heart and they continued an advance so sweeping and so swift that the Allies believed themselves to be attacked by a much larger army. By daybreak Waters was past the suburbs and in the midst of the ruination Henningsen had wreaked. Encumbered now with thirty wounded, and having lost fourteen killed, Waters reached the high ground overlooking the lake. Here a halt was called while a scout, an Indian called "Cherokee Sam," went ahead to ascertain the number of barricades yet to be forced. The Indian reached Henningsen, returned to Waters with his report, remained as before in the forefront of the ensuing action and was killed at the very door of the Guadaloupe, when the rescuers reached it.

Henningsen waited for them there. Waters was of much help, but the situation remained desperate: there was virtually no food left, ·the original company was reduced to one-third of its number, cholera was still an enemy more dangerous than the Allies and the road to the lake remained blocked.

But by noon the Allies, disheartened by the surge of Waters' advance and fearful that in another battle their triumph would become black disaster, abandoned the lake wharf, firing the wooden sheds which the Transit Company had built upon it. Unopposed at last, after one of the bitterest sieges in Central American history, General Henningsen moved with his remnant of a battle force toward the lake. Throughout the early evening and until midnight the well helped the weak down the stone-paved terraces and into the launches of La Virgen. The record of the three weeks in Granada was a grim one: on November twenty-fourth there had been four hundred and twenty-one persons in the capital; on December fourteenth one hundred and twenty-four had been killed or wounded, one hundred and twenty had died of cholera and other diseases, forty had deserted and two had been taken prisoner. One hundred and eleven fighting men were left of two hundred and seventy-seven originally under arms.

Henningsen was the last to leave Granada. He returned to the Guadaloupe, alone except for an aide, and walked past the great church to the ruined plaza. The work he had done was awful to contemplate. He had destroyed well and as a military man he could not but have prided himself upon his thoroughness. But the shame of the man must have fought with the pride of the soldier; for when he had looked upon the desolation he had created, he reached down and found a piece of rawhide, partly burned. A charred stick gave him his pencil, a shattered lance his standard. He wrote *"Agui Fué Granada"* ["Here was Granada"] on the rawhide and stuck it among the ruins. He walked quickly down the terraces and joined his commander.

The epitaph was as much for a cause as for a city. When Granada had been burned, defeat rode at the shoulder of the Filibuster and would not be shaken off. There entered now into the scene the great adversary, Cornelius Vanderbilt, who after months of furious planning elected to cut the Transit, leaving Walker to withstand alone and unaided whatever might come.

X

FROM the day he had received notice of the revocation of his franchise, Vanderbilt had not relaxed his fight against Walker. He was a man of infinite ingenuity: when the United States had failed to help him recover his confiscated property, he had appealed to England; and when England had offered no substantial assistance, he had communicated with the officials of Costa Rica, San Salvador, Guatemala and Honduras, urging them to unite and drive Walker from Nicaragua. There is no question about Vanderbilt's influence; the Allies had found encouragement in the beginning of the war in the thought that one of the richest men in America stood behind them and that he was inspired by a hatred of Walker greater, if anything, than their own.

It also developed that Vanderbilt had negotiated with President Rivas before the defection which led to Walker's assumption of the Presidency. Walker, learning of this negotiation when he received an old copy of the New York *Herald* from an Atlantic ship's captain, tried vainly to find (for execution) the man in his own ranks said to have carried Vanderbilt's offer to old Topsy-Turvy.

In answer to his suggestions to the Central American Republics, Vanderbilt received one reply sufficiently receptive to suggest further action. The President of Costa Rica, Mora, expressed willingness to co-operate in defeating Walker, and Vanderbilt employed two men to go to San Jose and complete the details. One of these agents was an Englishman, William R. C. Webster, and the other an American, Sylvanus Spencer.* His selection was wise: Webster, because of his nationality, was opposed to Walker, and Spencer had become bitter against the Americans in Nicaragua because his investments in Accessory Transit Company stock were made worthless by the seizure of the line's property and the revocation of the charter.

The two agents reached San José on November 18, 1856, and entered into conference with Mora. Between the original discussions with Vanderbilt and the arrival of his representatives, the Costa Ricans had suffered a crushing defeat in the attempt to take San Juan del Sur and the Transit Road. Mora was more eager than ever to achieve a victory over Walker somewhere along the route followed by the Transit passengers. The defeats were largely responsible for his hatred of the Filibuster, but cupidity also entered; for years Costa Rica had laid claim to certain portions of the San Juan River and Mora thought that if he could now seize part of the stream he would enjoy a share in any revenue it might produce in the future.

The plan revealed to the soldiers was for Spencer and Webster to command a force to be sent against Hipp's Point, the American garrison near the juncture of the San Juan and Serapiqui Rivers. From San José to the headwaters of the Serapiqui was a distance of only fifty miles, three days' march. Thence the expedition was to sail down the Serapiqui in *bongos,* form on the banks of the river short of Hipp's Point, capture the garrison and take all the steamers on the river. Spencer was delegated to lead the campaign, for he had been an engineer on one of the old Transit Company's boats and knew virtually every American sailor on the river. When the march had begun, however, the men made for the headwaters of the San Carlos River, which enters the San Juan about twenty-five miles above the Serapiqui.

---

* A son of John Canfield Spencer, one-time Secretary of War, and brother of the only American naval officer ever hanged for mutiny.

The plan worked without flaw. So well was it executed that it was days before Walker knew he had lost the Transit and with it what service Morgan & Garrison had given him.

On December sixteenth, the expedition of one hundred and twenty men reached the San Juan. They embarked on canoes and rafts and began to float down the river towards Hipp's Point. There were many rapids on the San Juan River and the progress of the rafts and *bongos* was swift. Nevertheless, it required six days for the soldiers to reach striking distance of Hipp's Point, because they camped along the banks of the river every five miles or so to reconnoiter. On the twenty-first, when they were within ten miles of the Serapiqui junction, a river steamer passed them. The Spencer expedition was, in that moment, as close to failure as it ever got.

Aboard the steamer were two of Walker's most important officers: S. A. Lockridge, en route to the United States after having delivered recruits to his chief at Virgin Bay; and William K. Rogers, unofficial commander of the filibuster foraging companies. In his haste to destroy Granada, Walker had permitted only food, arms and ammunition to be carried from the city; the printing equipment of *El Nicaraguense,* through an oversight, went up in the flames set by Henningsen's madmen. Walker required a publication for the quick dissemination of propaganda in the United States, and he remembered that Colonel Kinney had edited a paper called the *Central American* in Greytown. Rogers was traveling only as far as the Atlantic port, to obtain the press and type of the *Central American* and return them to the new base at Rivas.

Both Rogers and Lockridge commented on the extraordinary number of rafts and boats traveling on the river. They exchanged idle suspicions about the great bodies of natives aboard them. But with unforgivable stupidity they neglected to investigate and sailed blithely on to Greytown; and, before the boat on which they rode reached that place, Hipp's Point, inefficiently garrisoned, fell to Mora.

Spencer left forty men to hold Hipp's Point and proceeded to Greytown. He arrived there at 2 o'clock in the morning and by daylight had possession of the four river boats then in harbor. The crews made no effort to resist and, when Spencer offered them good Vanderbilt money for their services, they willingly agreed to work the boats for a new master. The Costa Rican flag was hoisted over the vessels, and the hapless agent of Morgan & Garrison, who had no United States vessel to which to appeal, was told by the commander of the big British squadron then at anchor that the latter was not prepared to pass on the merits of the controversy over Transit ownership. His apathy recalls Hosea Birdsall, the Vanderbilt agent, whose instructions were to "ask for the assistance of the commander of any man-of-war of her Britannic Majesty's navy in the port . . ."

Meanwhile, Spencer's support, eight hundred Costa Ricans under the command of José Joaquin Mora, brother of the President, was on a march more difficult than any other in the entire Walker period. From San José this comparatively great body of men had to cut its way through the stupendous growths of the jungle to the San Carlos River's mouth. The trail they followed was one used infrequently by Indians and, since the last passage, the jungle had flowed over it with the slow, steady surge of lava. Squads went ahead with machetes, hacking doggedly at vines and foliage which seemed actively to resist their progress. The movement was slow and difficult; the trailblazers worked for an hour or two and then fell back into the main column, exhausted with their efforts. Others relieved them. For days the army went ahead a foot at a time, through a country utterly uninhabited except for wild things. There was no sustenance in this land and more than three hundred of the soldiers toiled along like beasts, carrying great burdens of food and supplies on their meek shoulders. In spite of the magnitude of the struggle needed to cover thirty or forty miles, however, Mora reached the San Juan at precisely the right moment.

One of the boats Spencer had seized waited at the mouth of the San Carlos as the first of the rafts containing the Costa Ricans floated into the San Juan. The eight hundred, less the dozen or so who had died of fever and accident on the march and had been shallowly buried where they fell, were embarked and moved upstream at once. Off Castillo Viejo two more river boats were captured. Mora remained there, sending Spencer closer to the lake to effect what captures he could; the American, at a point thirty miles from the San Juan's beginning, took *La Virgen,* resting there in innocence and peace for Rogers to return from Greytown with the printing equipment. There remained only one stronghold left to Walker: Fort San Carlos, on the terraces overlooking the juncture of Lake Nicaragua and the river. Spencer, unhesitating, sailed against this fort.

It was an ancient stronghold and the parent of a gallant legend. In 1780, when England, in the pursuit of her hostility toward Spain, sent a squadron to the Nicaraguan coast, a young captain named Horatio Nelson went up the river with a company in small boats. His expedition, traveling much as did Sylvanus Spencer's, came within sight of Fort San Carlos; and the cravens who watched the bright uniforms advancing up the stream fled incontinently into the bush, leaving only the commandant and his beautiful daughter to hold the walls. The commandant was too ill to leave his bed; his daughter too brave to leave her father. As Nelson's boats lost way in the river, the beauteous heroine of the legend ran fleetly from gun to gun with a lighted match, to create a formidable bombardment. A ball or two struck—the legend has it that Nelson lost his eye as the result of one shot striking splinters from his boat.* The hero of Trafalgar is supposed to have fallen back in some confusion before the onslaught of the 16-year-old beauty's martial energy. Her name, ironically enough, was Mora—Donna Rafaela.

Spencer boldly brought his ship to within earshot of the fortress and waited until the commandant of the garrison, a Captain Kruger, came out in a small boat, expecting to welcome Rogers. Kruger was taken prisoner and forced to sign an order instructing the sergeant in charge of the garrison to surrender the fort. Thus, in two weeks and almost without the firing of a shot, Vanderbilt regained the main link of the Transit route, again isolating Walker from all Eastern reinforcement.

There remained the lake to be taken. Walker's forces (still ignorant of the happenings on the river) possessed the *San Carlos,* biggest and fastest of the lake vessels. Spencer hesitated to venture upon the lake with his smaller boat, but instead lurked in the concealment of the river. He had not long to wait. A few days after the fort was captured, the *San Carlos* appeared off the head of the river, carrying passengers for Greytown and New York; the fort

---

* Horatio Nelson, says history, lost an eye at the battle of Calvi, in Corsica, fourteen years after the attack on San Carlos, when a shot plunged itself into the ground and peppered his face with gravel.

gave her the signal learned by Spencer's men from the commandant and she innocently entered the trap. When she had passed the fort, she was confronted by Spencer's boat, armed and waiting. Her captain could not go forward because of the other boat nor could he retreat safely because of the guns of the fort. Spencer demanded the ship's surrender; the captain, a Dane named Ericsson, declared instead he would run the gauntlet of the fort to the lake; but a son-in-law of Charles Morgan, one Harris, ordered him to surrender, so as not to jeopardize the lives of passengers.

So the *San Carlos* fell into Spencer's hands. He permitted the eastbound passengers to be transported to Greytown, where they continued to New York on the ship which had just reached there. The California-bound passengers were carried to Panama and from there to San Francisco on a Pacific Mail Steamship Company's boat, at a cost to Morgan & Garrison of twenty-five thousand dollars—an unexpected expense which had much to do with their subsequent retirement from the Nicaraguan scene.

General Mora, meanwhile, brought up his rear guard, crossed Lake Nicaragua and took Virgin Bay. By using lake boats, as Walker had done, he was in a position to maintain contact with the Allied army at Masaya, with ruined Granada as his landing. And Walker, as soon as the enemy could come down from the north, would be all but surrendered, probably in Rivas.

XI

UNAWARE as yet of the staggering loss he had suffered, the President of Nicaragua was not surprised when, a few days after the relief of Henningsen, the Allied army moved out of Rivas. Maximo Jerez's Nicaraguans, José Maria Cañas' Costa Ricans, and the men of Honduras and Guatemala marched unresisted to Masaya, to make a junction with the main body under Belloso. Walker occupied Rivas on December 20, 1856. With the artillery hitherto used by and for the destroyers of Granada, he felt himself capable of pursuing the war as long as the enemy had stomach for it. By January 2, 1857, what had been the American Phalanx, now grown to nine hundred men and purportedly Nicaragua's official army, was well established in Rivas and prepared to withstand assault and siege.

The architecture and general appearance of Rivas was that of all other cities in the Republic: Spanish and Indian influences dominated in its structures. It was laid out with the usual squares terminating in plazas and with the major activities centered in the grand plaza, around which stood the finest buildings. Ringing the city proper were many suburban villages, with cacao groves separating them. In another day it had been subject to earthquake, and the walls of many of its structures bore commemorative cracks. On the principal plaza stood the unfinished walls of a great cathedral, intended originally to have been the heart of all religion (which meant all life) in the region; but a quake had damaged the adobe before the roof could be applied and the project had been abandoned, the interior being converted for use as a graveyard.

From this city forces of the enemy had twice thrown Walker's men back. He believed, therefore, that it would be impregnable in his hands. Also, it mattered not if all the rest of Nicaragua fell to the Allies, for insofar as Walker's progress was concerned there was only one thing in all the country worth the holding: the Transit Road. It crossed the Isthmus a few miles south of Rivas, easily close enough for occasional mounted companies to patrol it and keep it clear. And at San Juan del Sur, Captain Fayssoux's two-gun *Granada* guaranteed safe arrivals and departures of California ships.

The war with the Allies was six months old when the Americans marched into Rivas and they had prosecuted it altogether without vigor. Managua had fallen with no more resistance than the casual shots of the retreating Rangers; Masaya had been idiotically abandoned, then attacked and reattacked without success; Granada had been obliterated. From the moment of his inauguration, his absolute pinnacle, William Walker had gone downward. Not realizing it, either. Even in Rivas, he clung to his conviction of ordained success and until a month after his occupation this belief persisted. Then he heard the first murmurs of the Transit loss to the Costa Ricans—and Vanderbilt.

Mora's campaign in the capture of the San Juan River was effected with generalship. Much of the early success was due to Spencer,

the agent, and Vanderbilt, the principal; but the fact remains that
Mora counted no chicken hatched until he had fortified San Carlos
and made his prize secure. Then, and then only, did he communicate with the Allies under Belloso; and then for the first time the
singular luck which had given Walker's arm a giant's strength
failed him. Belloso, Jerez, Cañas and all the other uncertain generals, encamped in Masaya, and tremblingly awaiting Walker's next
move, were prepared and eager to return to their own countries and
resist or lead in revolution, depending upon current circumstances.
The six months of war had been as exhausting to them as to Walker;
there was a striking difference between the armies, however—
the men. Belloso held the "granary of Nicaragua," but he commanded quaking peasants, more accustomed and inclined to fields
than to the cannon. Walker at Rivas was faced with the possibility
of a food shortage, but his troops in the main were men of courage.
And then, within a few days of the virtual abandonment of the war
by the Allies, Belloso was told of the victory on the river. Heart
returned at once to the officers in Masaya; Belloso gladly gave up his
command to Cañas, because now the Costa Ricans, by virtue of their
magnificent triumph, stood highest in the councils. Topsy-Turvy
Rivas was informed, in glowing prose, of what had happened and,
in joyous prediction, of the success which lay ahead. Two days after
the report of the victory was confirmed, Cañas at the head of virtually the entire Allied army marched into Obrajé, a village three
miles north of Rivas.

The Americans, meanwhile, worked busily. With the return of
Henningsen to the main force and his promotion from brigadier to
major-general, the days grew full with constructive occupation.
Walker depended for success largely upon his uncanny power over
the men in the ranks, but Henningsen was a professional soldier who
built upon no such sand: to him an army meant guns, fortifications,
ammunition and the essential weapon, preparedness. He enlarged
the corps of engineers, and for days before Obrajé fell was laboring
to make Rivas secure against attack. Huts at the northern extremity
of the city were burned and the tropical growths in the fields around
them cut down, leaving a broad exposed area in which no enemy
might find concealment. The stronger houses of the city were con-

stituted into a system of small fortresses and those with whole walls were attacked by the sappers and miners, who drilled concealed passageways for the length of every strategically important block. The barricades in the streets were rebuilt. Captain Swingle, the armorer, obtained from San Juan del Sur an old steam engine, used in handling cargo from the Pacific ships, adapted it, placed it in a suitable building and created the first cannon-ball factory in Nicaragua. The vociferous churches in Rivas, and in every village as far as San Juan, were silenced, the tongues torn from their throats to be cast into solid shot. Climate at Granada and San Jorge had increased the number of sick in the army, but with the removal to Rivas there came an improvement. A house on the outskirts of the city, called the Hacienda Maleaño, became the hospital. Great care was taken of the incapacitated and for the time the supplies of medicines, instruments and food were sufficient. Otherwise in the army there was a stiffening of discipline and a more rigid enforcement of the prohibitions which to Walker's temperate mind seemed ideal in fighting men.

Then, to the revelation of the Transit's fall, there came the exclamation point of Cañas' advance into Obrajé. Walker realized at once the gravity of this advance and would have moved against Cañas immediately, but Henningsen dissuaded him, arguing that the town was not important enough for the risk and that its fortifications made an attack a gamble. On January twenty-ninth, however, the advance was resumed and Cañas took San Jorge; Henningsen then agreed that the enemy must be driven out. San Jorge was two miles from Rivas, Mora was across the lake and the Americans were surrounded except for the passageway to San Juan, where Fayssoux's ship lay at anchor.

Henningsen was sent with four hundred men to take the town. Serving as his second in command was Brigadier General Edward J. Sanders, who had arrived in Nicaragua many months before Henningsen. He was "of a jealous disposition," Walker said, and he chafed that his service had not given him Henningsen's rank. He did not co-operate with the leader of the attack, therefore, but permitted the subordinate officers and the men in the ranks to get drunk on the march. When Henningsen arrived at San Jorge he found that the Allies already had constructed barricades. (Walker's remark on this talent offers another of his few flashes of humor: "The rapidity with which Central American troops throw up barricades is almost incredible and they are more expert at such work than even a Paris mob.")

With a drunken army at his back, Henningsen threw himself at the barricades. Sanders (wilfully, Henningsen charged) disregarded orders and an entire company of riflemen became separated early in the engagement. Thrown back, with a loss of forty killed, Henningsen retreated to Rivas. So far as could be learned, none of the several thousand Allies had been hit by the ill-aimed bullets of the Americans.

On February fourth, Walker tried to take the village, this time with two hundred men. He was repulsed at the point Henningsen had reached, losing twenty-five men in the attempt. One of the mortally wounded was Calvin O'Neal, the hero of the charge against the Guatemalans in Granada. "Young and enthusiastic, he was not without the quick perception and rapid decision which fit a man for command in moments of danger. . . . He lingered for several days when carried back to Rivas, and probably his gallant spirit would have preferred to go forth from the world amid the storm of battle."*

On the night of the fifth, a sentry in the eastern part of Rivas heard a noise, called a challenge. A voice said, "Don't fire; we're Rangers." The sentry fired nevertheless; cannon were brought up and the plantain field sprayed with canister. The reassuring voice had been that of a renegade, the body in the plantains part of Cañas' army. Elated with the successive defeats of Walker's men at San Jorge, Cañas had decided to try a charge at the city of Rivas. There was a brief, brisk engagement and the Allies withdrew.

The army then settled down to a defensive program. By constant vigilance, a pathway of retreat—to San Juan and the *Granada*—was held open. Walker had no intention of using this avenue, however, until the last of his hopes, the one least likely to fail him, should be gone. At Greytown he knew there were reinforcements: the recruits Lockridge by now would have brought from New Orleans. He did not know their number, but the schedule of the Morgan & Garrison

* *The War in Nicaragua.*

boats on the Atlantic was as familiar to him as his name; and he was certain that men would be aboard the *Texas,* due from New Orleans, or the next vessel from New York.

Hemmed in by the enemy, handicapped by dwindling supplies and the constant weakening of morale, he yet believed that Lockridge would get through, either running the gauntlet of the San Juan River, or actually seizing that artery and restoring it to the services of filibusterism. Therefore he played the only game he could, a waiting one, and his men played it with him; but where they despaired, the Filibuster fixed his cold gray eyes on tomorrow and waited for the fulfillment he knew must come.

XII

In the long months that Walker had been losing ground in Granada, on the lake and river, and in Rivas, the naval branch of his forces had been successfully performing its limited functions. Captain Fayssoux, in the harbor at San Juan or on patrol along the coast, had been in a position to watch the outside forces assailing the army of the Filibuster; he had seen much, enough to convince him that defeat was the only possible outcome of the war. If he developed any such conviction, however, it failed to show in the manner of his conduct. In February, for instance, Fayssoux had been in San Juan harbor when H. M. S. *Esk,* commanded by Captain Sir Robert McClure, came in. The *Esk* was a large and heavily armed steamer, ostensibly on a routine patrol of the coast. Fayssoux ignored her; some weeks before, in the Bay of Fonseca, he had attempted to exchange courtesies with the commander of a French warship only to involve himself in a controversy over maritime etiquette; the memory of this made him wary of the *Esk.* The British ship had been in harbor only an hour, however, when her captain sent the gig across, with a lieutenant sitting in the stern sheets and a squad of marines manning the oars.

Fayssoux received the lieutenant courteously and informed him (for Sir Robert) that the *Granada* was a schooner of war and the red-starred flag she flew the ensign of Nicaragua. The lieutenant returned to the *Esk* and was seen in conversation with his commander; and when he returned, an hour or so later, it was with the peremptory demand that Fayssoux go aboard the British ship, taking his commission with him. Fayssoux suggested in answer to this that Sir Robert go to hell. The lieutenant went off with that message. The log reports that Sir Robert "at 6 p. m. again sent on board, using threats that he would take me prize or sink me if I did not proceed on board of him with my commission."* Fayssoux piped his men to battle stations, manned his two six-pound guns and waited for the engagement to begin. He had twenty-five men against hundreds on the *Esk*, seventy tons of rotting timbers under his feet and two pathetic little cannon; but he was quite willing to be sunk rather than obey any orders given by the master of a foreign ship. There was a long strained silence, while the *Esk's* gig bumped against her side and the two commanders regarded each other across sixty feet of water. Sir Robert must have been surprised at the doughty responses he received from Captain Fayssoux, but a little knowledge would have saved him from any surprise whatever: he was dealing with a man who had, in the brief span of a month, suppressed two mutinies on American ships in San Juan harbor, once knocking down the leader of a disturbance on a Morgan & Garrison vessel. In any case, he thought long before deciding upon a course of action. When his decision came it was a prudent one: "After making me three visits and threatening everything," says the log of the *Granada*, "the lieutenant insisted upon my making a friendly visit to the commander, which I did."

A typical sequel to this incident was furnished by William Walker in Rivas, three days later. Sir Robert traveled to the headquarters of the Filibuster, to protest against Fayssoux's impudence, but when he entered Walker's room he was given no chance to speak. Walker stood up and said in his toneless voice, "I presume, sir, you have come to apologize for the outrage offered to my flag and the commander of the Nicaraguan schooner of war *Granada?*"

Traditional imperturbability abandoned Sir Robert in that moment. Impressed with Walker's manner, the cold gray of his eyes and his imperishable dignity, the Englishman apologized; chatted briefly; then went outdoors, where he mopped perspiration from

---

* Quoted in *The War in Nicaragua*.

THE HOSPITAL AT GRANADA

his brow and said in wonder, to whoever might be listening, "If he had another schooner I do believe he would declare war on Great Britain."*

The *Esk* departed from San Juan, to continue her patrol of the coast. Another warship, however, remained in harbor, seriously hampering Fayssoux's efforts. This was the United States sloop-of-war *St. Mary's,* under command of Charles H. Davis, which had arrived four days after the *Esk.* For a time Davis contented himself with acting the part of neutral and observing the action as he could see it from the deck of his ship; later he became more eager to involve himself, unofficially and with great skill, on the side of the Allies.

Meanwhile, the situation at Rivas became daily more serious. Walker did not believe his plight to be a necessarily fatal one, but he was forced to pursue a waiting game and watch impotently as the enemy strengthened the positions they had taken. The advantage clearly was all on the side of the Allies and would remain there until Lockridge got through with reinforcements.

The loss of the lake boats was the greatest handicap and most disruptive to morale, for it gave the Allies free passage from point to point and it also permitted them to transport bodies of troops quickly, thereby creating the impression of a much larger force than was actually available to them. Early in February an attempt to recapture the boats was considered. A schooner, which once had belonged to the King of the Mosquitoes, lay at Virgin Bay. Walker posted a large garrison there and sent for Fayssoux, who, although ill with fever, came at once. As a naval expert he was asked to pass upon the merits of a plan whereby the schooner would be armed with land artillery and sent in the night to Omotepe Island, an anchorage of the lake boats. The captain journeyed to Virgin Bay, poked at the rotten hull of the schooner and advised against the plan; and Walker, obeying counsel in this case, ordered the schooner burned and the garrison withdrawn.

Fayssoux returned to San Juan del Sur, to guard the landing place of possible California recruits and to hold open a final way of retreat if for any reason Lockridge failed to force a passage up the San Juan.

* *The Story of the Filibusters.*

Late in February a messenger was sent to Lockridge by way of Panama, confirming him in his command of the recruits and urging an immediate junction with the main army at Rivas.

Walker's orders were to seize the river forts if they could be taken or, failing this, to cut a path through the jungle and reach the lake shore overland.

Losing little of his hope, the Filibuster tried to hold the army together, depending too much upon luck and the precedent which had been established in the conflict with Costa Rica. For while disease did reduce the Allied force from a high strength of seven thousand to a low of two, Providence also visited the American camp. And the disease which ate at the center of the army was not the only cause of loss: there was the dwindling at the edges from desertion, and the general disintegration because of a diminishing food supply. Before Walker's eyes, a thousand men became, by mid-March, five hundred.

Oddly, the staunchest support came from those least likely to give it—the natives. Nicaraguan fathers and sons manned Walker's works together, resisting the blandishments shouted at them by the visible soldiers of the enemy. The women and children of the city pursued their daily lives with only casual regard for the armies opposing each other at the edges of the town. The Democrats who had remained in the city, or who had come from the outlying villages to assist the *Yanqui,* gave up their beef to the Americans and ate fragmentary meals cheerfully. To the Leonese who had been stationed by the Allied high command close to the northern part of the town they issued proclamations, calling for loyalty to Walker as a guarantee against tyranny; and were told that the Allies had impressed Nicaraguans who would have preferred to fight under the red-starred flag. From some sections of the enemy barricades, Walker said, there came no firing; the soldiers were tied to their posts and forced to stand guard, but nothing could persuade them to kill men in the American strongholds. Although for the time there was a reasonably adequate supply of food, the rank-and-file lived under constant threat of starvation. What happened in March, then, was the beginning of panic. Unlike Henningsen's rapinists, the men at Rivas remained all too sober. Life in the besieged city was almost austere, for Walker and his officers discouraged any conduct which might lighten the peril of tomorrow, and what drinking and sexual adventure occurred were surreptitious. Lying behind their barricades in the night, the Americans who a few months before had been arrogantly supreme in this country knew themselves to be desperately placed and probably marked for early death. From the Allied camps came laughter, the music of guitars, fires which suggested bountiful mess-times. As early as February, desertions were a serious problem; the morning report of the sixth showed that twenty men had gone over to the enemy in the preceding twenty-four hours.

On March fifth one hundred and sixty Americans, moving along the Transit Road after having been to San Juan, were attacked by two hundred Allies. They were badly beaten and forced to run for Rivas; and their report was to Walker an astonishing shock, for heretofore his men had been able to oppose five to ten times their number successfully, whereas suddenly an almost even fight ended in defeat.

For three days he thought about the dwindling of his soldiers' zeal, which by now had become his greatest asset. He cast about in his mind for a means whereby he might recreate the magnificent prowess the Immortals had displayed. He was ill at this time, suffering from a mild fever which puffed out his cheeks and caused his head to ring; but on the afternoon of March eighth he left his sick room and walked suddenly to the middle of the grand plaza. The filibusters were scattered about in groups, morosely discussing their hunger, the "goddam jiggers" which entered their feet through the cracks in their boots and bored tormentingly, the equally "goddam Greasers."

When the square had fallen into silence, and Walker stood alone in its center looking at his men, he began to speak. His voice was no more toneful than it had ever been; but he believed what he said— the fire behind his eyes told how very firmly he believed.

"Soldiers!" he cried. "We are engaged in no ordinary warfare. A powerful combination surrounds us on every side. A hatred to our race has united adverse States and reconciled the most hostile and repugnant factions. The object of this league is to expel us from the land with which we have identified our lives, but through your fortitude and courage the effort is destined to defeat. . . .

"Notwithstanding all the sacrifices we have made, all the dangers we have encountered, all the suffering we have endured—sacrifices not only of our blood in battle, but of our lives to the pestilence—bear witness, the graveyard at Granada!—are we to be driven from this country merely because we were not born on its soil? Never! Never!

"No, soldiers! The destiny of this region and the interests of humanity are confided to our care. We have come here as the advance guard of American civilization and . . . with the help of that Power which never deserts the brave and the just, victory and honor will be our sure reward."

It was neither a lengthy nor a reasonable speech. Yet, oddly, it brought some profit. There was a decline in the desertions and a rebirth of ferocity (conversational) on the part of the rank-and-file. It is significant that Walker, ill and all but defeated, could so easily imbue his ignorant followers with some of his own spirit. The devices he used—"Soldiers!" as a salutation, reiterated throughout the address, the assurances that the Americans were the chosen of God to perform a sacred duty, the mealy-mouthed insistences that no wrong had been done but by the enemy (with the ashes of Granada barely cooled!)—were the time-tried of the dictator, valid in Caesar's Rome, valid in Walker's Nicaragua, and thrice-valid in Mussolini's Italy and Hitler's Germany.

Not until a week later—on March sixteenth—did Walker test the strength his words had infused into his army. On that day he led four hundred men, almost his full command, on a march to San Jorge. His hope was to strike one stunning blow, breaking the ring of Allied fortifications and possibly beginning a campaign whose momentum would increase. Henningsen, with seven guns, marched as second in command; Swingle, the talented armorer, remained behind with one hundred men, to hold Rivas.

Walker reached the outskirts of San Jorge just before daybreak. The enemy, estimated at two thousand, was alert and waiting for him; his advance was held up for a few minutes until Henningsen, firing grape and canister, could clear the plantain fields on either side of the road. Then he moved into town, battling against the stubbornest resistance thus far met in Central America. The fight lasted for hours, the Americans gaining ground by inches until they were within three hundred yards of the main plaza. There sharpshooters in church towers and strong bodies of men behind adobe walls halted them. Walker, still in a black frock coat but wearing a gray flannel shirt instead of his customary linen, called for forty volunteers to storm a house. Fifteen responded. He led them, running with insane courage almost to the windows. A spent ball struck him in the throat (the second in his career) and its force knocked him down, but he was up again in a moment, attempting to hold his foolhardy fifteen together for the finish of the charge. It was too late. The army was spent and discouraged by the extraordinary courage of the Allies. A retreat was ordered and the Americans filed out of San Jorge as they had, in the past, filed out of Rivas and Masaya; and as at Masaya, they were met by a courier, who reported Swingle attacked and fighting desperately in Rivas.

They made the best time they could on the road back. At Cuatros Esquinas, a plantation, dusk overtook them. In Walker's eagerness to relieve Swingle and save the only city he still held, he proceeded incautiously. The road narrowed between two adobe buildings, wherein the Allies Swingle had defeated were hidden. As Walker, mounted now on a horse he had obtained in San Jorge, came abreast of the houses there was a blast of musketry and the dusk was pierced by streaks of flame. The horse jerked; the column broke and hovered on the brink of panic. Walker glanced back once, while he was bringing his horse under control; then, deliberately, he drew his revolver and fired six spaced shots into the window nearest him. He turned his horse toward Rivas, and rode on, erect and disdainful.

Behind him followed a Captain Dolan, also on a commandeered horse; and, as the balance of the men wavered between courage and flight, Dolan with an Irishman's passion for being brave, followed his general. He too paused before the house and fired six shots; and just before the answering blast of musketry swept him from his horse he hurled his revolver into the nearest window, making the air rich with his curses. He was hit in several places and fell, but his foot in the stirrup saved him. His horse dragged him beyond the line of fire and when, in the following month, the siege of Rivas became most difficult, he was about again, carrying his scars like medals.

They reached Rivas at last, having left twenty-five dead at the enemy's lines, to find that Swingle had been attacked at about the same time the Americans lunged at San Jorge. Artillery had held the Allies at a distance, but they had built and manned a barricade inside the limits of the town and were dislodged only after hours of vicious fighting.

On March nineteenth, Waters went with one hundred men to meet the California steamer. There were only twenty recruits on board, no supplies, no ammunition. The packet of letters for Walker included one from an informant in California, announcing that Charles Morgan and C. K. Garrison no longer wished to contest with Vanderbilt for the right to operate the Transit line and planned to dock their ships after another voyage or two.

An effort was made to keep the news from the men, but they whispered among themselves of fresh disaster. They had been told too often that Lockridge with a great company was coming to revive them. Cholera was increasing and the hospitals, although cleaner than Granada's charnel houses, were overcrowded centers of misery and unspeakably wretched death. The Allies, immediately after Walker's return from San Jorge, closed off the roads to the north and thereafter the Rangers found it all but impossible to bring in cattle from the farm regions. On March twenty-seventh, the beef supply consisted of two oxen attached to the quartermaster's department; they were slaughtered, together with several mules, and the indiscriminately mixed meat served to the unaware men. Mule meat was eaten for several days before it was discovered; when it was, the apathy of the camp had so increased that there was little or no complaint. Plantains and mangoes were gathered in the fields and groves to the north; the little salt remaining was mixed with sugar and used sparingly as seasoning. Almost overnight, the supply of normal food vanished and the horses of the cavalry were turned into corrals, for slaughtering.

There had to be desertions. President Mora, who a year before had promised death to every armed filibuster he could capture, now scattered handbills about the outskirts of Rivas, promising food, protection and a free passport to deserters. The wind would pick up a leaflet, carry it into an adobe house or over a barricade, drop it like a satanic smirk at the very feet of starving men. Sentries, bearded, dirty, with eyes taut from the gnawing in their stomachs, peered over the barricades at the bright camp fires a scant half-mile away, looked shamefacedly at the next sentry a dozen paces away, slipped over and ran stumblingly toward the Allied lines. A single sentry deserted one night, returned the next to a point where his shouts could be heard and persuaded "Charley" or "Frisco" to "come on over; we're eatin' like kings and all the likker you can drink." Two went that night, and six the next, and a company the next. A brass band departed sometime in March, carrying their instruments and trading Walker's patriotic anthem, "The Blue, White and Blue" for Castilian airs and the anthems of the aristocrats. Parties set out to forage for food and never returned. A courier sent to San Juan on foot came back mounted; his horse was in the stewpot within the hour.

Only the officers, and a percentage of the rank-and-file motivated by the same queer loyalty the Immortals had exhibited, continued brave and cheerful. A few riflemen, more for amusement than for military gain, left the barricades every night, to wander about in the plantain fields and fire into the Allied camps; the Allies, retaliating, fired up the few streets of Rivas not protected by breastworks and made the already difficult life of the non-combatants even more perilous. Henningsen sauntered about within the lines, inspecting guns, jesting with the gunners, rolling a succession of cigarettes with a master soldier's casual disregard for the empty stomach they were meant to ease. He watched the food diminish and is reported to have remarked one day, as he paused by a battery, "A little more of this and we'll have to eat the prisoners." Fayssoux paced the deck of his little ship and waited for Walker to order action; he would gladly have fired on a grand fleet at the Filibuster's word. Waters, onetime commander of mounted Rangers and the savior of Henningsen at Granada, gave up his horses and led bands of foragers on foot, bringing back edible plunder from civilians and even from the camps of the shiftless Allies.

Walker wrote Edmund Randolph, who was in New York, that a slight blow would break the strong ring of Allied armies, but he did not wish to strike it. Until the fighting was carried to him and he was driven to offensive moves of his own, he preferred to watch his army dissolve. He was told of men who went to the mango groves north of the town and failed to return. He learned that to "gather mangoes" meant, translated, "to desert." The desertions required some action, but for a long time he could not decide what form it should take; then he issued a proclamation, informing all in the army that they were free to go and would be given passports on application. Five applied. They started for the barricades, to cross the open field between Rivas and the enemy. They were cursed, spat upon, hissed. One lost his courage when he was still short of the freedom he had asked; he turned to come back, but Walker, small and cold and determined, told him dispassionately to go on.

And the faithful went about their duties, their eyes fixed on the one beacon of hope: Lockridge.

XIII

THE private soldiers who served William Walker were hoodlums, poor misfits, unimaginatives with no greater inspiration than their dream of rich farms to be had for the taking. Some of the officers, too, fell into this category, but few; the spirit of the times, the color of Walker's deeds, or the desire of men for action brought to his banner vivid and forthright figures. At Rivas there were Henningsen and Swingle, the one a great soldier, the other an ingenious one. At San Juan there was Fayssoux. And at Greytown, marooned by the skilled machinations of Vanderbilt's creatures, there waited and plotted a full roster of competents.

There was Charles Doubleday, the Englishman who had listened to Walker's plans but had not been able to follow this "bold and capable, but not sagacious man." Returning to the United States via Panama, Doubleday had watched with quiet satisfaction the upsurge of Walkerism in Nicaragua. Remembering his talks on the beach at Granada, he had desired nothing of the victory but the small warmth of having once been close to its possessor. Then Vanderbilt struck back, the Allies marched and every day's news in the United States added another defeat to the many Walker had endured; and for Doubleday "the crisis had arrived. I could read of his successes and those of my countrymen without regretting that I was not with them. When the story of hardships, reverses, the opposition to overwhelming numbers, came to be chronicled, I could only feel that my place was with them."*

There was Frank Anderson, one of the Immortals who had been invalided home, now recovered and impatient for fresh wounds.

There was General Robert Cheatham Wheat, one-time school-mate of James Walker, veteran under Lopez, prisoner of Spain when the Cuban campaign failed, revolutionist in Mexico, Military Governor of Vera Cruz.

There was the faithful Hornsby, who with the flat of a sabre might have beaten into the cravens in besieged Rivas some of his own granite courage.

There was Norvell Walker, returning nonchalantly to help William to take his beating.

There was Lockridge, recruiting agent and master of transportation for the army, Rogers, the "confiscator-general," J. Egbert Farnum, another veteran of the Mexican war and of Lopez's Cuban expedition.

Backed by about three hundred recruits, these talented gentlemen were eager to report at Rivas but temporarily without means of getting there. They were quartered across the harbor from gloomy Greytown, on a spit of land called Punta Arenas. The shanties they constructed out of waste lumber leaked badly and there was much misery, for the rains already had begun on the East coast; and also there was cause for worry in the presence of H. M. S. *Cossack*, Captain Cockburn commanding, whose broadside frowned over the encampment.

Captain Cockburn, intent upon withdrawing from the force such British subjects as he could identify, ordered Lockridge to parade his men. Walker's aide was no military man, but more properly a recruiting and civil officer of the army. Serving voluntarily under him were the veterans of many battles who, had they received Cockburn's demand, might have defied him; but Lockridge, fearing the British

* *The "Filibuster" War in Nicaragua.*

guns and otherwise uncertain of himself, obeyed the order. Cockburn came ashore in full uniform. He painted a grim picture of what the men faced: participation in a war being waged solely for William Walker's personal gain and being opposed not alone within Central America but by the world at large; an almost impossible passage up a river heavily guarded by the enemy; probable death and certain suffering. To those who wished to claim the protection of the Crown, he offered transportation away from Nicaragua.

A good number of Lockridge's privates were recruits from the slums and alleys of New Orleans. Some twenty of them appealed for the offered protection, a few in foreign accents which made their claims to British citizenship ridiculous. General Wheat, a contemptuous observer of the proceeding, told Cockburn sardonically that Doubleday was an Englishman and should be saved; and when Cockburn asked Doubleday if he would accept haven on the *Cossack,* he was answered with a vivid blast of profanity. Wheat listened grinning to Doubleday's outburst, and then suggested that Captain Cockburn had been insulted and should demand satisfaction. Cockburn ignored him and Wheat, mounting the prow of the gig which had brought the officer ashore, made a mocking and derisive speech, offering to fight for Doubleday if Cockburn hesitated to meet a Nicaraguan officer and advancing himself as a dueling companion in the guise of an American gentleman. When Cockburn, red-faced and miserable at the titters Wheat's challenge brought, turned to go back to his ship, Wheat remarked ruefully that it was tragic to witness the spectacle of an English tar taking refuge in his rank at the expense of his courage.

With the *Cossack* within gun range and the glasses of her officers almost constantly trained on his camp, Lockridge bought a condemned steamboat, the *Rescue,* which was open-decked and had machinery so ancient it had been deemed unsafe for operation on the Transit line. Into this were herded the New Orleans recruits for an attack on the river defenses.

The boat, little better than a launch, puffed upriver to Hipp's Point. A hail of bullets met the party there, and from the sound were identified as the projectiles of Minié rifles—Vanderbilt's gift to Costa Rica. A landing was made on the opposite bank of the San Juan and log defenses thrown up. Anderson and Doubleday urged an attack upon the works at once, preparing for it by selecting an assault force from the recruits. Wheat spent the afternoon casting shot for the small brass cannon, connecting balls with chain as the most murderous projectile he could conceive.

At midnight Anderson and Doubleday set out, crossing the river in the boat, cutting their way through the jungle along the banks and arriving in position shortly before dawn. The plan of action called for an infantry charge by the Anderson-Doubleday command, with Wheat's cannon on the opposite bank of the river forming the second point of the triangle. For an hour the Americans fought a difficult battle; then the firing slacked and the charge was blown. The fort was deserted when they reached it and the number of Costa Rican dead testified to the skill with which Wheat had manned his little gun.

Lockridge and the main body then crossed the river. The American dead were buried, but Lockridge ordered the bodies of the Costa Ricans thrown into the river, to float down to Greytown as a reminder to Captain Cockburn that all filibustering was not necessarily marked for defeat.

A shrewd and effective blow had been struck for Walker. Although Lockridge did not know it, the Costa Ricans were finding it difficult to hold the river they had taken. Great numbers of troops were withdrawn from the San Juan's defenses, to assist the army besieging Rivas, and the usual fever was taking an added toll. General Mora needed fresh troops; he so stated in a letter addressed to the Allied high command, which was intercepted and delivered to Walker at Rivas. But Lockridge, as has been said, was no military man. Having been given a convincing demonstration of the capability of some of his officers, he now outlined the next step in his advance—the taking of Castillo Viejo—and selected as commander of it a worthless and conceited fellow, Colonel H. T. Titus.

Titus had been a Kansas landholder of the "border ruffian" class. In August of 1856, a company of abolitionists, commanded coincidentally enough by a Captain Walker, besieged him and a few sympathizers in his house. When their ammunition ran low they offered to treat for surrender and Captain Walker promised Titus a fair trial and his life. The prisoners were taken to Lawrence, where a Committee of Safety sat on Titus' case, condemning him to be hanged; Captain Walker marshaled his three hundred armed men and announced that he had promised Titus safety and intended to fight, if necessary, to guarantee it. John Brown, with other abolitionists, harangued the mob with the demand he always made—death for the pro-slaver!—but Titus was pardoned. He was impoverished, however, and with what followers he could gather—upwards of one hundred and fifty—sailed for Nicaragua to rebuild his fortunes. He was a poor commander and a poor man; he went to Nicaragua ostensibly to serve the cause of slavery, but he really wanted profit and was of little help to William Walker.

To this incompetent and his ruffians was given the task of taking Castillo Viejo. The command of one hundred and eighty sailed upstream in the decrepit steamer, arriving before Castillo Viejo in the afternoon. The lower defenses—those almost immediately on the river bank—were undefended, and when the attackers had occupied them, they looked above to where the old castle stood on the brow of a hill.

An English soldier-of-fortune, Captain Cauty, who was serving in the Costa Rican army, was in command of the garrison, numbering barely thirty men. At the sight of Titus' ship moving upstream, Cauty concentrated on saving the river boats, four of which were moored below the fort. Two were sent upriver successfully; the others were set on fire. Titus's men boarded both of the latter, saving one, the *Scott*, and tying the other to the opposite bank where it burned to the waterline.

To Titus's demands Cauty replied that he could surrender only with the permission of his commanding officer at Fort San Carlos, and Titus agreed to a twenty-four-hour truce, thereby earning for himself the right to be remembered historically as a military imbecile. Within twenty-four hours Cauty was reinforced with men and guns from San Carlos, and Titus barely had time to retreat down the river, his only prize the ship *Scott*.

What little morale Lockridge had maintained vanished when the Titus expedition returned. Anderson, Doubleday and Wheat, thoroughly disgusted with the commander's inefficiency, watched the

Kansans construct rafts and float down the current toward Greytown by dozens. For a day or two the encampment was within a hair of complete disintegration, but a fresh reinforcement arrived, lending Lockridge new courage. Numbering one hundred and thirty well-armed men, the "Alamo Rangers" from Texas came upstream on a chartered boat. Added to those already in camp, four hundred answered Lockridge's next call, for a new attack on Castillo Viejo.

Using the same boats in which Titus had returned, they moved to a point in sight, but not within gunshot, of the fort. Cauty was armed to the teeth, his fort bulged with men and he was as wary as a fox. Scouts searched for a possible attack point and could find only one space sufficiently covered by the jungle to offer protection; but this was bisected immediately below the walls of the fort by a deep ravine, which the defenders could close off with both artillery and muskets. The attempt was abandoned and the entire force went back to Hipp's Point.

It was obvious to every member of the expedition that no success could attend any further efforts to ascend the river. At a conference of war, the veteran officers—Hornsby, Doubleday, Wheat, Anderson and Norvell Walker—decided to return to Greytown on the *Scott*, obtain passage to Panama, cross the Isthmus and reach Walker from the Pacific side. The "Alamo Rangers" were quick to join the new organization, but the balance of Lockridge's force had no such high courage. Even before the company headed by Hornsby and the others could get away from the base, panic descended upon the poor misfits left to Lockridge and they stole what small boats were available to flee downriver. Others departed on rafts; still others on single logs. The ones who had hooted at Captain Cockburn's offer of British assistance appeared in Greytown in ones and twos and dozens, pleading to be taken back to the United States.

The *Scott* moved into the stream, with the stalwarts aboard it. From the deck the officers watched the loading of the *Rescue*. More than two hundred sick were carried abroad and Hornsby is supposed to have remarked, when he had taken one last look, "I have been a soldier twenty years and this is the saddest sight I have ever witnessed."

The *Scott* dropped downstream. Near the Serapiqui a reconnaissance was deemed prudent and the ship's prow was beached on a spit while a company went ashore to seek Costa Ricans in the region.

The engineer of the *Scott* was an amateur, as were all its crew. As they waited, this worthy, no one knows why, pumped cold water into a hot cylinder. There was an appalling roar and the entire front of the boat disappeared momentarily, to return to the water in splinters. Those who remained aboard were hurled into the air by the explosion and fell back into a torturing welter of broken wood, twisted metal, scalding steam and flames. The more seriously injured screamed and pleaded to be shot. Hornsby and his shore party returned on the run and did what they could to rescue those lying in the gravest danger. Even when a voice cried, in the tormented tones of unendurable fear, "The powder!" the rescuers did not hesitate or lose their precision; Wheat and Anderson threw overboard a flaming tarpaulin and doused with buckets of water the three tons of gunpowder on the forward deck.

About twenty were killed by the explosion and double that number hurt. The *Scott* was a complete wreck and was abandoned where she lay. The *Rescue*, which came into sight an hour or so after the accident, picked up as many of the wounded as she could accommodate and took an abandoned barge under tow for the balance. Nothing remained of the San Juan River expedition after the *Scott* blew up; the *Rescue* steamed for Greytown, at the best pace her old engines would allow, in an attempt to connect with the *Tennessee*, known to to be sailing for New York. She arrived late; the *Tennessee* was already hull down on the horizon.

The survivors felt the pent-up bitterness of wretched Greytown as soon as they arrived. Foreigners had dominated the community since its beginning; the villagers had not been encouraged to show charity. The Lockridge party was refused quarters in the town proper and had to erect shelters on Punta Arenas similar to those they had occupied in the period of the controversy with the British naval officers. A band of Costa Ricans came to the port a few days after the arrival of the survivors and made gestures indicative of an attempt to exterminate the Americans; but Cockburn flung a ring of small boats around Punta Arenas and protected the *Rescue* by mooring it to his own vessel.

From *Frank Leslie's Illustrated Newspaper*.

THE NAVY WINS A BATTLE

Cockburn proposed to remove the men and obtained from the Morgan & Garrison agent an order for passage. Three hundred and seventy-five were taken abroad the *Cossack* and carried to Aspinwall, Panama, where the Pacific Mail Steamship Company agent refused to honor the Morgan & Garrison draft. Cockburn then offered to be responsible for two hundred passages at twenty dollars each, suggesting that the arms of the filibusters be sold for the balance of the money, but the representative of the Pacific Mail found a new objection: some of the Americans had measles and he refused to run the risk of contamination aboard his vessels. Finally, Cockburn placed the men aboard H. M. S. *Tartar,* and they were returned to New Orleans, arriving miserably in that city on April 28, 1857.

William K. Rogers was the only officer of Walker to reach his chief. Transported to Panama on the *Cossack,* he left her in the night, at Aspinwall, and made his way across the Isthmus alone. On the Pacific side he waited several days for a northbound steamer. When none appeared he sought out the two owners of a small boat. He was a persuasive Irishman and he convinced the boatmen that he was interested in a voyage to the Pearl Islands, a group fifty miles off the coast. A deceptive bargain was struck, Rogers bought provisions for several days sailing and embarked, sometime in the second week of April, 1857. When the little boat was at sea, Rogers produced the two revolvers he had purchased, took over the tiller and announced that the destination was San Juan del Sur. For two days the cockleshell bobbed over the waters of the Pacific, with the sleepless man in the stern forcing the two cowed natives to handle sail.

But Rogers reached San Juan only to learn that William Walker's cause was a lost one.

XIV

Until just before Rogers reached him, Walker did not know what had happened to the men on the river. He continued to hold Rivas grimly, in the face of serious attacks. He withstood a massed charge on March twenty-third; he lost all opportunity to forage when the Allies filled the last gaps in their lines; and he was assailed with great ferocity on April eleventh. He held on, however, even though the continued silence of Lockridge argued that his sole remaining course was a retreat to San Juan del Sur and escape on the *Granada*. There was still confidence in his heart that the war would end with his own victory. He gambled for this outcome, because while warfare cost the Central Americans men they could not replace, an inexhaustible supply of Yankees would be available to him as soon as he won. Also, he did not want to abandon Rivas until he knew that Lockridge could not reach it, for he was enough of a soldier to realize that the least he owed the men on the river was the protection of a destination.

The attack on March twenty-third was a fair battle, fought largely with artillery. The Allies had one battery commanded by an Italian gunner whose skill approximated Henningsen's, and who threw shot over the barricades with splendid accuracy. For the early part of the engagement, Henningsen stood on a parapet, rolling and smoking cigarettes, ignoring the bullets aimed at him and showing thorough appreciation of the Italian's craftsmanship. He occasionally murmured a direction to the crew of the six-pounder behind the barricade on which he stood; and not until the Italian's piece had been moved to within dangerous distance did he decide to make the affair a personal duel. He tossed aside his cigarette and dropped to the ground behind the breastworks. He loaded his gun, aimed it, fired it. His first shot struck the enemy's four-pounder squarely, demolished it, and killed most of its native crew and seriously wounded the Italian.

Two other cannon which the Allies used, ancient Spanish twenty-four-pounders, threw solid shot into the main plaza; Swingle seized these before they stopped rolling, popped them into his furnace and recast them into the six-pound shot Henningsen was firing back at the enemy.

The battle gained one objective for the enemy: a strong house less than half a mile from Rivas. They fortified this structure and from it sent forth a party, on the twenty-fourth, to attempt the burning of a house manned by Americans. The Allied soldiers, carrying flaming masses of resin on bayonets which were attached to long poles, succeeded in firing the cane upon which the roof tiles were laid. The blaze was extinguished and the next day Henningsen heated round shot and fired it, "a safer and more effectual method of setting fire to the enemy's barricades."

There was a lull of almost three weeks in the fighting, during which the threat of famine became increasingly serious. On April eleventh, anniversary of the second battle of Rivas, Walker instructed his officers to exercise the greatest vigilance, knowing that the Allies would attempt to make use of the psychological value of the rebuff Costa Rica had given him the year before. Reinforcements had been sent into the enemy lines from Guatemala and in the morning every man the Allies could mass was hurled at the Americans. The attack struck four sections of the city at once. Walker's barricades held firmly, however, and in one section, where fresh Guatemalan troops attempted to charge, the Americans almost regretted having to shoot so many down. The Guatemalans had not been warned of the rifles Walker's filibusters used, and hundreds of them were shot long before their muskets could be brought within range of the barricades.

The Allies abandoned the attack before nightfall. With this engagement, the war in Nicaragua was at an end. For Commander Davis, of the U. S. S. *St. Mary's,* took a hand.

Davis was under difficult orders from Washington: he was to protect American lives and property, he was to remain strictly neutral—but he was to do what he could unofficially to get Walker out of the country. He communicated with Walker soon after his arrival, hinting at withdrawal, and was told somewhat curtly that the Filibuster meant to hold Rivas until his supplies ran out and then either move to the Pacific shore or attempt the recapture of the San Juan River.

On April twenty-third, Davis sent a lieutenant to suggest the removal of non-combatants from the besieged city. Throughout the four months of the occupation the Americans had brought peril to a considerable number of natives. Life had gone on in the city, after a fashion, but the women and children had remained indoors, except at night, and the men had skulked from doorway to doorway, never knowing when a stray shot from the Allied barricades would strike them down. Walker agreed, in some relief, to the removal of the women and children from the city and they were marched to San Juan under escort of a file of marines from the *St. Mary's.* For the period of the truce, the belligerents left their shelter and mingled on the contested ground; the desertions were increased, when the truce ended, by the fact that *aguardiente* and tobacco had been given freely to the Americans. Several of the early deserters performed missionary service, also, promising protection to the sick and wounded if the filibusters surrendered.

Four days later Walker made an address to the men, in which he claimed to have heard from Lockridge and promised that support would reach the city within a few days. Although he had received letters that day, he told a bare-faced lie; Lockridge was already in New Orleans, arriving there perhaps at the very moment that Walker was speaking. What he said buoyed the men for a day or two; but when on the thirtieth Commander Davis suggested surrender, even Walker knew that he was without choice.

Davis, convinced that Walker would not hold Rivas for more than a few days and fearful that the Allies would slaughter every man in the city when it fell, sent a message by an aide of General Mora. The Costa Rican, after a full survey of the force opposed to him, had given up all hope of defeating Walker by assault and was prepared to conduct an indefinite siege, trustful that starvation would win; Davis proposed to him that if the Americans were given protection, he would force Walker to surrender.

Henningsen led a delegation to San Juan, to a conference on board the *St. Mary's*. The naval commander told him that Lockridge had deserted and that their position was no longer tenable. Henningsen did not agree about Lockridge; the report he had received from Rogers was that Lockridge remained at Panama and might either travel to New York or San Juan. Further, he remarked to Davis that Walker intended to retreat to San Juan and evacuate his troops aboard the *Granada* when he chose. The intentions of the United States then were brought into the open: Davis said he would not permit the *Granada* to sail, but meant to seize her before he departed from San Juan.

The emissaries returned to Rivas. The army's future was now hopelessly black. The *Granada* was a sure salvation, but without it no escape for the Americans was possible. The matter of Lockridge, although it entered into the negotiations with Davis, was settled even in Walker's mind; not until his return to the United States was he to learn that his master of transportation had abandoned his venture, but the possibility of relief was obviously a remote one. Walker listened to the ultimatum and the suggestions for the surrender: himself and sixteen officers to be transported to Panama on the *St. Mary's* and the balance of the Americans guaranteed safe conduct by another route. The impassive Filibuster, his dreams dissolved, agreed to his only choice; he accepted the ultimatum, specifying only that the natives who had fought for him be accorded the same measure of protection the United States Navy was to give his own men. Henningsen assisted in the preparation of the document of surrender, which was submitted to Davis (and not to the Allied commanders, who entered into the negotiations only indirectly), approved, and returned to Rivas for signature. It read:

May 1, 1857.

An agreement is hereby entered into between General William Walker, on the one part, and Commander C. H. Davis of the United States Navy, on the other part, and of which the stipulations are as follows:

Firstly, General William Walker, with sixteen officers of his staff, shall march out of Rivas, with their sidearms, pistols, horses and personal baggage, under the guarantee of the said Commander Davis, of the United States Navy, that they shall not be molested by the enemy and shall be allowed to embark on board the United States vessel of war, the *St. Mary's,* the said Commander Davis undertaking to transport them safely on the *St. Mary's* to Panama.

Secondly, The officers of General Walker's army shall march out of Rivas with their sidearms, under the guarantee and protection of Commander Davis, who undertakes to see them safely transported to Panama in charge of a United States officer.

Thirdly, The privates and non-commissioned officers, citizens and employees of departments, wounded or unwounded, shall be surrendered, with their arms, to Commander Davis, or to one of his officers, and placed under his protection, he pledging himself to have them transported safely to Panama, in charge of a United States officer, in separate vessels from the deserters from the ranks and without being brought into contact with them.

Fourthly, Commander Davis undertakes to obtain guarantees, and hereby does guarantee, that all natives of Nicaragua, or of Central America, now in Rivas, and surrendered to the protection of Commander Davis, shall be allowed to reside in Nicaragua and be protected in life and property.

Fifthly, It is agreed that all such officers as have wives and families in San Juan del Sur shall be allowed to remain there under the protection of the United States consul, till an opportunity offers of embarking for Panama or San Francisco.

General Walker and Commander Davis mutually pledge themselves to each other that this agreement shall be executed in good faith.

XV

THE army learned that it had lost a war in General Order No. 59, the last to come from the pen of William Walker as President of Nicaragua. He read it to the men, drawn up in the grand plaza, his soft voice still unafraid:

The commander-in-chief, in communicating to the army the following agreement, thinks it proper to state that he enters into it on the solemn assurance from Captain Davis that Colonel Lockridge with his whole command has left the San Juan River for the United States.

In parting for the present with the brave comrades who have adhered to our cause through evil as well as good report, the commander-in-chief desires to return his deep and heartfelt thanks to the officers and soldiers under his command.

Reduced to our present position by the cowardice of some, the incapacity of others and the treachery of many, the army has yet written a page of American history which it is impossible to forget or erase. From the future, if not from the present, we may expect just judgment.

Three years before, almost to the day, the Republic of Sonora had vanished in surrender, also to the United States. And in three years, Walker had lost none of his trust in destiny. General Order No. 59 was no more the end than any of the other defeats had been the end. Accepting the terms offered by Davis, because he had no choice, he gave no thought to defeat. His mind raced ahead of the immediate moment, to plans for a return to this country and the restoration of his splendid power, which had endured for so little time.

Henningsen cannily had not mentioned the stores of war in his discussions with Commander Davis and the navy man apparently forgot them in his absorption with the more important task of disposing of Walker. Before the agreement was signed, therefore, Henningsen and his faithful gunners had destroyed what they had created for the defense of Rivas. The foundry lovingly built and tended by Captain Swingle was demolished; a dozen guns spiked, dismounted and their carriages cut up; nearly a ton of powder, 55,000 cartridges, 300,000 percussion caps flung into wells. Nothing was left, when the victorious Allies marched into Rivas, but the indestructible solid shot Swingle had fabricated from bells and belt buckles, door hinges and wheel rims.

Commander Davis and General Zavala entered the grand plaza of Rivas in the evening of May 1. Zavala was present as escort for Walker and his staff; Davis as the officer to whom the surrender was to be made. General Order No. 59 was read and Henningsen performed the routine of turning over to Davis, exhorting the filibusters to co-operate with their captors. While this was going on, Walker and his staff left, traveling over the Transit Road.

A total of four hundred and sixty-three surrendered at Rivas, divided thus:

Officers and men fit for duty................................ 164
Wounded, sick and surgical corps........................... 173
Employees and armed citizens.............................. 86
Native troops 40

The majority of these, of course, remained in Rivas after Walker left. There was much grumbling when it was learned that the General had gone off before his men; the grumbling was given point when the Allies, discovering the destruction of the arsenal, became enraged and attempted to butcher the prisoners. Davis and his marines, however, provided the protection guaranteed in the articles of surrender.

At San Juan lay the single ship of war in the Nicaraguan navy, the *Granada*. Fayssoux remained in command, the red-starred flag still flew from her masthead. It is not unlikely that Walker looked upon this ship as a last desperate hope and, even as he stood on the American vessel, contemplated some action which would restore him to power through the use of the *Granada's* two little cannon; but he was not given the chance. Commander Davis, more determined than ever to overlook nothing in the deposition of the Filibuster, demanded that she be surrendered, and advised Walker not to permit Fayssoux to resist. Walker protested, on the reasonable ground that the *Granada* had not figured in the articles of surrender, but Davis lined the *St. Mary's* rails with marines and ordered her broadside trained on the Nicaraguan ship. His messenger to Fayssoux returned with the defiant response, "I'll surrender only in the face of a superior force," and, as in the incident of the *Esk,* there ensued a belligerent, strained silence. But Walker, filled with his frustration, averted the possibility of bloodshed; in a notebook held against the side of the cabin, he wrote swiftly the last order he was to give: "Deliver the *Granada* to the United States."

In five minutes, Fayssoux, grimly furious, was aboard the *St. Mary's* and a Jamaica Negro, serving the Costa Rican forces, took command of the schooner. It was sorry solace for Walker that the Negro ran the *Granada* aground and completely wrecked her while carrying Guatemalan troops to Realejo.

Walker arrived in New Orleans on May 27, 1857.

He was, for a little time, the darling of the mob.

BOOK FIVE

Truxillo

BOOK FIVE:

Truxillo . . .

With us there can be no choice; honor and duty call on us to pursue the path we have entered, and we dare not be deaf to the appeal . . . I adjure you never to abandon the cause of Nicaragua. Let it be your waking and your sleeping thought to devise means for a return to the land whence we were unjustly brought. And, if we be but true to ourselves, all will yet end well. . . .

I

His return to the United States was a triumph. Admiring throngs met him in New Orleans; he was carried ashore on the shoulders of his most vociferous worshipers; within an hour of the time he registered in the Saint Charles Hotel he was forced to step upon a balcony and say a few words to the crowd in the street below. With no more than an idea and fifty-eight men he had captured a country, razed its proudest city and withstood for a remarkable time the assaults of four neighboring nations. There was magnificence in that story and it was more than the magnificence of legend. Statistics and the admissions of the enemy left no doubt that Walker had been a giant in Nicaragua. Henningsen, an astute and accurate military observer, said that Walker's forces in the two years he had been in Central America had totaled only twenty-five hundred men, against whom the Allies had hurled eighteen thousand. Not once was Walker able to pursue a campaign with sufficient troops. The greatest body he put into the field was at Masaya, when eight hundred marched. With such facts established, the adulation of New Orleans and New York followed

299

as a matter of course. But no hero survives on the glory of past combats alone. Decisive and successful action was required of the Filibuster, if he meant to hold the affection of the mob. He could not provide this action. He would have been a greater figure in the end, had he not surrendered at Rivas, but been annihilated, for he could not go up again, but now inevitably must go down.

He spoke many times in New Orleans (which, incidentally, had little civic memory of its one-time lawyer and journalist). The business leaders of the community felicitated him and, as Southerners, assured him that his next expedition would be handsomely fitted. To the public at large he was a reckless devil of the most admirable stamp; every schoolboy knew what he had done; crowds gathered when he walked through the streets, universally marveling that so much strength could be packed into so tiny a man.

From New Orleans he traveled to Louisville, to visit Alice Richardson, his sister; there, too, he received in full measure the plaudits of the city. He went to Washington, Philadelphia and Amboy, and from the last by boat to the Battery. He landed June sixteenth and received a reception identical with New Orleans'. He was called upon again to make a speech from his hotel balcony, and his remarks included these:

"I feel not ashamed to say that I am favored of the gods, for I feel that an overruling Providence, which has carried us so far, has not permitted us to do so much for naught. I feel that luck—as my enemies call it—or Providence—as I term it—will carry us successfully yet, and enable us to accomplish yet more for the greatness and glory of the American people."

At Wallack's Theatre, a few days later, he and General Henningsen stopped the show. Cheered thunderously, they were compelled to speak from the box they occupied with Mrs. Henningsen.

And then, as instantaneously as a snap of the fingers, the public cooled. The hero (as he had always, as he must always!) overreached himself. Cheers from the populace and the possibility of governmental encouragement on his return to Nicaragua were not enough for him. Many times in his career he lashed out blindly when he was thwarted, nor ever seemed to learn that his petulance almost invariably penalized him. Arriving in New York as the returned conqueror, he sought in Commander Davis an outlet for the rage born in him by his deposition from Rivas.

Some indication of the retaliation he meant to seek for the interference of the United States Navy already had been given after Walker's brief interview with President Buchanan when he paused in Washington on his way north. The Filibuster hinted that Buchanan sympathized with his motives and had pledged official assistance to future movements in Central America. Now, Walker sought to force Buchanan to support him. The United States, which had read garbled reports of the action in Central America, was for the first time given a complete story of Commander Davis's interference in San Juan del Sur.

The log carefully kept by Captain Fayssoux* gives as clear a picture of Davis's work as is possible to get. Early in April a body of Costa Ricans occupied San Juan. Their numbers were not such as to interfere with a retreat from Rivas had Walker chosen to make it; nevertheless, Fayssoux planned to harass them, until Davis persuaded him to agree to a truce for the protection of civilians. As soon as the truce had been arranged, the enemy began to erect barricades in the streets of the town. Fayssoux protested to Davis, who shrugged him off; and when the guns of the *Granada* were trained on shore, Davis swung his ship broadside to the schooner, warning Fayssoux that he would enforce the truce with cannon if the Filibuster attempted to violate it. No warning was sent ashore, however, and for some weeks the unfair condition was permitted to continue, with Fayssoux made impotent in the harbor, and the protected Allies working happily to secure their position.

At about the same time, Davis appears to have been counseling the officers of the Allies. On April seventeenth, for instance, Fayssoux wrote in his log:

> Mora requested Davis to go up and speak to the troops at Rivas, to get them to desert General Walker. . . . Captain Davis read me the letter from Mora.

Although the truce was still supposed to be in effect, Fayssoux entered, on April eighteenth, this fact:

---

* As quoted in *The War in Nicaragua.*

At 10 P.M. received a communication from the shore to the effect that Jerez was coming in with two hundred more troops and that they were going to fire on the schooner at daybreak. The enemy offered Michael Mars [of the *Granada's* crew] two thousand dollars to place the schooner in their hands.

The alleged attempts to obtain the *Granada* by bribery as recorded in the log were persistent and in at least one case condoned by Commander Davis, a fact which did much to win sympathy for Walker when he returned to the United States. The report of the incident given to the public by Walker or his officers was similar to that included in *The War in Nicaragua:*

Then, on Friday the twenty-fourth, we have an account of a most singular scene on board the *St. Mary's.* Fayssoux's object in permitting the interview may be readily imagined, but it is more difficult to divine why Davis should permit his ship to be made the theatre of an attempt to seduce an officer from his allegiance. The log: "I met Colonel Garcia [a Costa Rican] on the *St. Mary's.* He stated that [Maximo] Jerez had written him, by order of General Mora, to see me and try to make some arrangement to bring the war to a speedy close; that the schooner being in port under General Walker's orders, she was much dreaded and might delay the close of the war. He asked if I had any proposition to make; I told him he had sought the interview, and I was waiting to hear for what purpose. He then said they wished the schooner taken from the port, or given up to them; I asked upon what terms; he said he was not prepared to offer any, but that a commissioner would be appointed for that purpose; that his object was to see if I could be approached. I said I would listen to any proposition from General Mora; that the present interview had not effected anything; that he had not proposed any mode of closing the war; that we stood as we have previously. I acted on the above occasion with the knowledge and approval of Commander Davis . . . and at no time lost control of my temper, although seeing the full extent of the dishonor offered me and the insult of their sending such a noted thief and traitor to confer with me."

Walker maintained throughout that he would have won the war had the United States not interfered. The claim, examined against the condition of his troops in Rivas, does not at first seem reasonable; but the state of the enemy in the last days of the war was little better than his, and even President Mora, whose hatred of the Americans equaled Santos Guardiola's, was forced to admit that "cholera would have forced the Allies to abandon the war in twenty days, had Walker not surrendered." In a letter to President Buchanan, Walker protested against Davis's opposition on this ground, adding that the naval officer had acted in an "insulting, degrading and offensive manner." Of the schooner *Granada,* which had not figured in the articles of surrender and yet was seized by the *St. Mary's,* the Filibuster said that Davis offered to permit the Americans to keep the arms and ammunition on the ship, if they would give her up peacefully. This offer was refused, the letter said, because both Walker and Fayssoux felt that "not a rag or splinter should be given up except to an overwhelming force; the honor of the little vessel was in her hull and rigging and in the flag she bore, and in comparison with this the property aboard her was dross."

From June 16, 1857, when Walker arrived in New York, until June twenty-eighth, when he left, he built up his case against the government. It was a strong one. It might have gained for him the enduring affection of the masses. But he was a man who knew no restraint; he could not fight subtly. He worried the matter of Davis until it was a shred, of which the public was faintly tired. And then, to turn his plaints against him, there came into New York the U. S. S. *Wabash,* a sidewheel frigate commanded by Commodore Hiram Paulding. She carried with her the wreck of the Walker government in Nicaragua: one hundred-odd dejected survivors.

The reporters who went aboard the ship found a bitter story to write. So covered with lice were the men of Walker's army that they had infested the spotless warship, forcing her officers to bathe in rum. There were in all one hundred and thirty-nine persons on the vessel: one hundred and twenty-one men, thirteen women, five children. Almost all were sick. The men were dressed in foul rags and were gaunt from their long diet of mule meat and less. Perhaps tired of picturing Walker as a paragon of military virtue, or perhaps under orders from their owners, the gentlemen of the press wrote brutally of the condition of the rank-and-file. The first charge hurled at the Filibuster was that he had deserted his men after the surrender. The soldiers said that with Walker gone, the Allies entering Rivas had plundered wildly, without hindrance from their officers. Trunks were looted, clothing stolen from the bodies of the sick and wounded, sidearms taken from the remaining American officers. Only the presence of Davis's marines saved the entire filibuster army from execution. At Virgin Bay, to which they were taken as the first leg in the journey home, there was insufficient food. Many of the wounded used gnarled sticks for crutches, and hobbled the entire distance to Virgin Bay, to escape the menace of the drunken and bloodthirsty conquerors. From San Carlos to Greytown the voyage was a hideous nightmare; there was steady rain, the boats were overcrowded, there was no care for the sick and no food. Costa Ricans were in charge of the defeated soldiers and they treated them cruelly; the New York *Herald* quoted one soldier as saying that the gentlest man in the Allies' army was the Jamaica Negro, David Murray, to whom Davis had delivered the *Granada*.

All New York read the stories of the victims who came in on the *Wabash;* yet it was still possible for Walker to have replied to them, to have made what happened the result entirely of events instead of a creation of his own hard mind. He might have visited the sick and tired faithful; he might have turned them to his use against Davis and the government. But instead, still blind, still arrogant, he went away from New York two days after his privates came in. Their accusations went unanswered. Davis and Commander Paulding pointed out skilfully that the evidence was before the people in the men returned from Nicaragua: had the Navy not acted, Walker and all his helpers would have been slaughtered. And for the third time, the loafers of the saloons and fire-houses jeered at the Filibuster.

II

NEVER one to heed his critics, he now became even more remote. The second conquest of Nicaragua obsessed him to the exclusion of all else. Destiny, destiny ... it was in his brain like the fumes of a drug, driving him, costing him the last fragment of human feeling.

Henningsen remained in New York to look after recruiting; Lockridge (not yet disgraced for the fiasco on the San Juan, but one day to fight a duel with Walker in disagreement over the conduct of

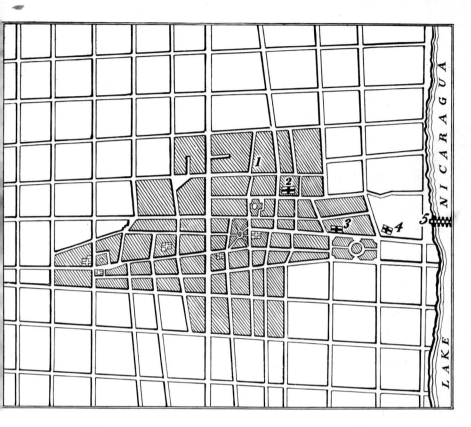

GRANADA

1. Plaza San Sebastian
2. San Francisco Cathedral
3. Esquipulas Church
4. Guadaloupe Cathedral
5. Lake Wharf

filibustering) was sent to Texas. Walker himself, needing more than
ever the money and guns the South might give him, began a tour em-
bracing Charleston and Nashville and ending in Mobile.

In the latter city, he learned that Patricio Rivas had been deposed
as the claimant to the presidency, and a military alliance had been
formed between the Democrats and Legitimists. He should have
grinned at this, for it was a perfect example of the Central American
weakness which he and his followers still hoped to exploit; but instead he went on, in his humorless way, insisting that he was the
president of the country, who had been illegally deposed by the interference of the United States. He addressed meetings, conferred with
men of substance about a new expedition and made no effort what-
soever to hide what he was doing from Washington. The government, as a result, fell into another panic.

Lewis Cass, who the year before had written a letter to a Walker
mass meeting declaring, "He who does not sympathize with such an
enterprise [as filibustering] has little in common with me" had become Secretary of State. Politics is a harsh taskmaster and because of
it Cass surrendered his splendid sympathy. He issued instructions to
every Federal officer in the ports of the South to see that no vessel
freighted with Walker's freebooters be permitted to sail. Isaac Toucy,
Secretary of the Navy, sent orders to commanders of American vessels
in Caribbean waters, containing vague suggestions for preventing the
landing of invaders on any of the coasts they patrolled.

On November tenth, at a few minutes before midnight, the United
States marshal called on Walker, who had gone quietly to New
Orleans to polish off plans for the new attempt. The affidavit the
marshal bore charged violation of the neutrality law. Walker was
taken to the Federal building and questioned about the ship *Fashion,*
suspected of carrying contraband of war for the use of the recruits
who would board it. His answers gave the authorities no satisfaction,
however, and he was released on bond to reappear later in the week
for a hearing. He went directly from the courtrooms to the *Fashion;*
on the date set for his hearing he was off the Central American coast.

Nearly three hundred men were with him. The veteran officers
included Von Natzmer, Swingle, Henry, Hornsby, Fayssoux and

Anderson. Editor John Tabor was returning to issue a revived *El Nicaraguense*. There were six of the original Immortals.

The *Fashion* skirted Greytown and ran down the coast to the Colorado River, where Anderson and a company of men went ashore to seize the Transit route. The steamer then turned and sailed into Greytown harbor, passing within a few feet of the United States sloop *Saratoga,* supposedly in harbor solely to prevent Walker from landing. Before anyone aboard the *Saratoga* knew what was happening, the *Fashion* had tied up at Punta Arenas and two hundred men were ashore on the spit, making camp. Chatard, the commander of the naval vessel, was helpless to deal with the situation: he could not fire on the *Fashion* to prevent the men from going ashore and once there they were beyond his jurisdiction. He sent for help, then, in a message addressed to Commodore Paulding, who had returned to his command of the Caribbean squadron.

The *Fashion* reached Greytown on November twenty-fourth. Walker waited for news from Anderson, without whose success on the river he was impotent. Days passed; rain fell endlessly on the flimsy shelters the men had constructed; the camp took on the look of beaten desolation so constantly a characteristic of Walker's armies. December fourth arrived without news; Walker sat by a small fire throughout the night, watching for a light at the river's mouth. He waited vainly the next day, and the next, and had all but abandoned hope when a canoe came down the San Juan River, moved swiftly to the wharf at Punta Arenas and deposited a courier. The message read:

> I send you in haste the fact that I have taken Fort Castillo Viejo at 5 o'clock this morning, with all its guns, ammunition, steamers and ten prisoners. I will send up in the morning to take the steamer *Virgen*—I am almost certain of taking her. . . .
>
> F. P. ANDERSON, *Colonel Commanding.*

An hour after dawn the *Wabash* anchored in the harbor mouth. On the seventh the U. S. S. *Fulton* came in and silently joined her two watchful sisters. The *Brunswick* and the *Leopard,* of Her Majesty's Navy, followed . . . and some of the jubilation in the camp of the filibusters began to die.

Commodore Paulding, determined that William Walker should

not foment war in Nicaragua, acted with a directness which was to force him into retirement. A letter he wrote to his wife at the time showed he was aware of the peril of his course and it is to his everlasting credit that he did not waver. He had received instructions to prevent filibustering, but they were so hedged in by the requirements of maintaining the respect for the sovereignty of other countries that he abandoned all hope of executing them satisfactorily and concentrated instead upon the filibusters alone, without regard for diplomacy.

On the evening of the eighth small boats mysteriously left the *Saratoga* carrying marines, and did not return. Walker sent Fayssoux and Hornsby to spy on them in the night. The two officers found an effective blockade had been set on the San Juan River and, when they went aboard the *Wabash* the next day to protest, they were detained by Paulding, who immediately moved three hundred marines onto Punta Arenas, in position behind the filibusters, and ordered the guns of the *Saratoga* trained on them from the front. An officer appeared in Walker's camp, carrying a written demand for surrender; and Walker, who had disbanded his army and withdrawn his sentries, accepted the inevitable.

Anderson's river steamer came into sight just as the filibusters were being herded aboard the *Saratoga;* it was seized and the handful of men aboard it added to the other prisoners taken by Paulding. Anderson himself remained upriver until he was sure Walker had been beaten again; then, after spiking the guns at Castillo Viejo, he surrendered on December twenty-fourth and was returned to the United States.

Paulding invited Walker to come aboard the *Wabash,* saying that officers and men would be quartered separately. The Filibuster sent an oral reply which in effect told the navy man that he wanted no special consideration. Paulding, irritated by his impertinence, ordered him to embark upon the warship at once, and in a letter to his wife, the commodore told of their meeting:

Upon this order he came to see me, and this lion-hearted devil, who had so often destroyed the lives of other men, humbled himself and wept like a child. You may suppose it made a woman of me, and I have had him in the cabin since as my guest. We laugh and talk as though nothing had happened, and you would think, to see him with the captain and myself, that he was one of us. He is a sharp fellow and requires a sharp fellow to deal with him. I have taken strong measures to force him from a neutral territory. It may make me President or it may cost me my commission.*

Walker traveled to Aspinwall on the *Wabash,* maintaining the pretence of geniality described in the Commodore's letter. Secretly, however, he was filled with bitterness toward his captor. When the warship reached Panama, and it was learned that no vessel bound for New York was due for a week, Walker cast off what had seemed at first a philosophical acceptance of his fate. He declined brusquely to eat another meal aboard the *Wabash.* He likewise declined Paulding's courteous invitation to live on the ship until the northbound passenger vessel arrived. Instead, giving his parole to surrender to the United States marshal in New York, he went ashore. He spent the following five days in a poor hotel, keeping strictly to himself and strolling in the afternoons to the railroad workshops, where the activity interested him.

III

WALKER had not been close to victory even at Punta Arenas, but he chose to contend that he had been. It has been shown that he knew nothing of sportsmanship; engaged in a gambler's occupation, he was a poorer loser than any of his men. In New York he stayed at the Henningsen house while the bewildered government tried to decide what to do with him. He repeated with more force, in the weeks that followed, what he had said after the surrender at Rivas, but this time it was Commodore Paulding who was his target. To the reporters who interviewed him as soon as he reached New York, he characterized Paulding's action as that of an invader on the territory of a peaceful nation, and therefore claimed that the United States must return his forces to Punta Arenas and apologize publicly for the insult to the flag of Nicaragua.

Theoretically, he was under arrest. But the marshal in New York was dubious about the action expected of him, and suggested a trip

* *Life of Hiram Paulding,* by Rebecca Paulding Meade, as quoted by Scroggs.

to Washington. In the capital, Secretary Cass tacitly disavowed what Commodore Paulding had done, by informing Walker that he was free to go until such time as formal legal proceedings, charging violation of the neutrality law, were instituted. The Filibuster accepted this as the beginning of victory and waited quietly while the tempest began to seethe.

Abolitionists hailed Paulding as the agent of a law higher than that on the statute books. The South, however, rose in its wrath, interpreting the interference as a further evidence of Northern domination. Resolutions were adopted (one at a mass meeting in New Orleans) demanding that Walker be returned to Nicaragua on a vessel of the United States and his followers be indemnified; several Southern congressmen promised their constituents to demand the same thing. President Buchanan, one of the authors of the Ostend Manifesto,* who was supposed to be a supporter of filibusterism, sent a message to Congress on December 8, 1857, denouncing Walker's activities as injurious to the country, using the words "robbery and murder" to describe the expedition to Nicaragua, and urging that every weapon be employed to prevent repetitions. On January 4, 1858, the Senate ordered an investigation into the Paulding affair, and Buchanan elaborated upon his position, calling Paulding a "gallant officer," but admitting that he had committed a "grave error." Conceding that the naval officer had exceeded the law in invading a friendly territory, Buchanan maintained that Nicaragua alone could complain; Walker, as an invader on his own account, enjoyed no rights.

Walker replied to this in a bitter open letter, defending himself as the head of a lawful expedition and announcing his determination to return to Nicaragua. His supporters denied he had violated the neutrality laws; said that he had passed beyond the jurisdiction of the United States as soon as he reached the high seas, and called the landing of the marines at Punta Arenas a clear violation of another country's sovereignty. The other side had as many charges to offer: Central American diplomats had asked for the protection of their coast and their permission was sufficient to sanction Paulding's action; the

* Drawn by the ambassadors to England, France and Spain, this document urged upon Spain the sale of Cuba to the United States and suggested that its military seizure would be both possible and justified if such a sale were declined.

government was responsible for invasions of a friendly power by its citizens; Greytown was territory in dispute, over which Nicaragua did not have clear claim.

But although the administration earned its full share of censure, what was said of it could not compare with the denunciations of Walker. Senator Hawkins, of Florida, said in debate: "I have but small faith in the star of the 'Gray-Eyed Man of Destiny,' for it shines dimmed and pale, receiving or borrowing no lustre from his civic or military talents. That he possesses uncommon personal courage, force of will and firmness under difficulties there is no doubt; but these attributes of character appear unaccompanied by the requisite knowledge of the art of war, the gift of gaining the affection of his troops, and the enforcement of a salutary discipline, save by acts of extreme and probably unnecessary severity." Senator Winslow, of North Carolina, urged the United States, if acquisition was an aim, to take Nicaragua "in manly and open warfare; let us not 'set the dog' on her." Senator Slidell, of Louisiana, called Walker "William the Conqueror," damned his bloody dictatorship, charged him with ignorance of military affairs and brought up again his ungrateful attacks on Commander Davis.

Although these attacks were from Southern congressmen, it was yet to the South that Walker turned for assistance. The responsible segment of the Southern opinion had abandoned him, however; and while he was cheered to the echo at Richmond and Montgomery and Mobile, it was by crowds unable to give any concrete aid.

Commodore Paulding, the scapegoat, was relieved from duty and remained in retirement throughout the balance of the Buchanan administration. He knew a strange fate. The government gave him in one voice both praise and blame for what he had done. Nicaragua presented him with a jeweled sword and its thanks. Half the press rewarded his gallantry; the other half denounced his high-handedness.

And Walker, never failing to advance along his chosen road, continued to work for the one end—dictatorship. At Mobile he engaged rooms on Custom House Street and while awaiting trial, executed the shrewdest latter-day trick in his fight to regain his power. He wrote *The War in Nicaragua,* which was published in the spring of

1860, by S. H. Goetzel, of Mobile and New York, and which was as
strange a mixture of truth and prejudice as any author ever penned.

IV

The War in Nicaragua remains today one of the two standard refer-
ences on the Nicaraguan campaign, from Realejo to Rivas.* It is
written in disciplined prose, refers to its author in the third person
except in a passage or two, evidences a diligence toward truth which
is both remarkable and creditable, and is shot through with queer
philosophy and bitter prophecy. It is dedicated to Walker's companions in the war, and the dedication pledges its author never to
abandon the filibuster struggle for power on the Isthmus. Introduced to the reader by a short preface, it is presented as a history
necessarily written while the events are still fresh in the public mind,
and one to be excused if the author, because he was so much part of
the action, "may not be well fitted" to write of it.

"But if the memoir writer be fair and discreet," the preface con-
tends, "he may contribute materials for future use, and his very errors
may instruct after ages. The author of the following narrative does
not expect to attain perfect truth in all things; he merely asks the
reader to give him credit for the desire to state facts accurately, and
to reason justly about the circumstances attending the presence of the
Americans in Nicaragua."

While the book is, in the main, a description of the various battles
fought in Nicaragua, sections of it are propaganda of the boldest sort,
skilfully developed and undoubtedly of great influence in the period.
The discussion of slavery, for instance, is a lengthy one arguing openly
for the support of the Southern States. Of the decree which opened
the way to slavery in the Central American Republic, the book says:

> The spirit and intention of the decree was apparent; nor did its author
> affect to conceal his object in its publication. By this act must the Walker
> administration be judged; for it is the key to its whole policy. In fact
> the wisdom or folly of this decree involves the wisdom or folly of the
> American movement in Nicaragua; for on the re-establishment of
> African slavery there depended the permanent presence of the white

* The other: *Filibusters and Financiers.*

race in that region. If the slavery decree, as it has been called, was unwise, Cabañas and Jerez were right when they sought to use the Americans for the mere purpose of raising one native faction and depressing another. Without such labor as the new decree gave, the Americans could have played no other part in Central America than that of the pretorian guard at Rome, or the Janizaries of the East; and for such service as this they were ill-suited by the habits and traditions of their race.

Walker asserted (and whether he believed this is open to question, considering his earlier convictions) that the prosperity of Cuba was due to the slave system, whereas the decline of San Domingo and Jamaica resulted directly from acts freeing the Negro. He argued further that the true conservatives of the United States existed in the South, where slavery offered a firm footing for capital because it enabled "the intellect of society to push boldly forward in the pursuit of new forms of civilization."

Turning then to Central America, the author of *The War in Nicaragua* attempted to prove that the Latin American countries had suffered from the abolition of slavery. He was hopeless that sufficient numbers of white men to furnish labor would enter the tropics and he urged that a population of Negroes owned by whites would definitely set Nicaragua and the other countries on the high road to civilization and prosperity. As a second great advantage, he foresaw the abolition of the mixed races in Central America, with a society more nearly that of the Spanish caste system and so more nearly perfect.

This policy was set before the South with the shrewd observation that the cessation of the slave trade was causing a shortage of Negro labor in the United States and the re-establishment of slavery in Nicaragua would to a degree mitigate this circumstance. And, also, he asserted that "to avert the invasion which threatened the South, it is necessary for her to break through the barriers which now surround her on every side, and carry the war between the two forms of labor beyond her own limits. A beleaguered force, with no ally outside, must yield to famine at last, unless it can make a sally and burst through an enemy that confines it."

The Regenerator asked further:

Is it not time for the South to cease the contest and fight for realities?
. . . It is only the stronger party which can afford to throw away its
force on indecisive skirmishes. At present the South must husband her
political power, else she will lose all she possesses. . . . And unless she
assumes now an entirely defensive attitude, what else is left for the
South except to carry out the policy proposed to her three years ago in
Central America? How else can she strengthen slavery than by seeking
its expansion beyond the limits of the Union? The Republican party
aims at destroying slavery by the sap and not by assault. It declares
now that the task of confining slavery is complete and the work of the
miner has already commenced. Whither can the slaveholder fly when
the enemy has completed his chambers and filled in the powder and prepared the train, and stands with lighted match ready to apply the fire?
Time presses. If the South wishes to get her institution to tropical
America, she must do so before the treaties are made to embarrass her
action and hamper her energies. . . . The South has but to resolve upon
the task of carrying slavery into Nicaragua in order that the work may
be accomplished.
Something is due from the South to the memory of the brave dead
who repose in the soil of Nicaragua. In defense of slavery these men
left their homes, met with calmness and constancy the perils of a tropical climate, and finally yielded up their lives for the interests of the
South. I have seen these men die in many ways. I have seen them
gasping life away under the effects of typhus; I have seen them con-
vulsed in the death agony from the fearful blows of cholera; I have
seen them sink to glorious rest from mortal wounds received on honorable fields, but I never saw the first man who repented in engaging in
the cause for which he yielded his life. These martyrs and confessors
in the cause of Southern civilization surely deserve recognition at its
hands. And what can be done for their memories while the cause for
which they suffered and died remains in peril and jeopardy? . . . the
true field for the exertion of slavery is in tropical America; there it finds
the natural seat of its empire and thither it can spread if it but makes
the effort, regardless of conflicts with diverse interests. The way is open
and it only requires courage and will to enter the path and reach the
goal.
Will the South be true to herself in this emergency?

Much of the honesty of the rest of the book is weakened by the
chapter on slavery, for Walker did not believe in the institution and,
by pretending that his intentions in Central America were entirely
those of a champion of bondage, he revealed pitifully that his original

idealism had given way to a heedless lusting after power. While it did material good, the book did not win for him the entire South; he continued to receive, as always, the support only of the few opportunists who were willing to gamble on the possibility of plunder. And although it is a singular fact that the Filibuster himself did not plunder, and enriched himself not at all in his campaigns, his army was composed of a species of pirate. The cry about the "brave dead who yielded up their lives in defense of slavery" is treacly; the "brave dead" were recruits from mining camps of California, the saloons of all the country, and the gutters of all the world—men who could not earn and so sought to take.

But yet there is something to be said for Walker's motives. Whether at this time he regretted the blind stubbornness which had caused him to defy Vanderbilt and so construct his destroyer is questionable; the one truth to be found in *The War in Nicaragua* is that he was willing to treat for support. His early hints of annexation had won him some men and money; with the publication of his book, he sought Southern help with definite promises.

The entire volume is built around the slavery chapter. Preceding and following it are sections devoted to the action of the Nicaraguan campaign which are fair and accurate. Sylvanus Spencer, the agent for Vanderbilt, who seized the San Juan River, blocked off Lockridge's reinforcements and was directly responsible for the surrender at Rivas, receives full credit:

It is clear that the success of Mora's movement to the San Juan River was due to the skill and daring of Spencer. The march to San Carlos with all its expense and all its fatigues would have been useless without the aid of the bold hand which got possession of the river steamers. And the success of Spencer was the result of a rashness which, in war, sometimes supplies the place of prudent designs and wise combinations. The fortune which proverbially favors the brave certainly aided Spencer much in his operations. Mora afterward attempted to deprecate the value of the services Spencer rendered him; and the brutality of the man toward the soldiers made it an object for the Costa Rican to get rid of him. But it would be difficult to overestimate the advantages of the Allies derived from the services of the base and murderous man who did not scruple for the sake of lucre to imbrue his hands in the blood of

countrymen struggling to maintain the rights of their race against a
cruel and vindictive foe.

In the section of the work devoted to actual warfare, in the period
between June, 1855, when the Immortals landed, and May, 1857,
when Davis forced surrender, there is an honest effort to be accurate.
Historians of Central America, although biased against Walker, have
inclined to accept his statistics on battles in preference to the official
reports of their own military men. Occasionally, an unnecessarily
high tone makes itself heard in *The War in Nicaragua*: this, for
example, regarding the desertions at Rivas:

> Let us pass the names of those with sorrow for the weakness of human
> nature, nor taint the air with the narration of their crimes and degrada-
> tion. There is shame and infamy enough in the world without seeking
> for them on fields where glory should be won and honor achieved.

Having finished his book and assured himself of some gain from
it, Walker turned to another trickery to further his ends. He had
been reared in a strict Protestant atmosphere, but he had belonged
to no church at any time in his life. Suddenly he was "converted" to
Catholicism. The moment he chose to embrace this religion was too
obvious; it was patently an attempt to appease the Central Americans
and to reveal himself as worthy before the peons he hoped yet to
govern. It is also possible that he hoped for aid from the large Catholic communities in Southern cities—notably New Orleans and Mobile.

And all the time, pitifully now, he labored toward that return. In
December of 1859, Anderson, Doubleday and others of the original
expedition, with more than one hundred men, sailed on a schooner
named the *Susan*. Walker was not aboard, but was to have followed
as soon as his army had established itself in Central America. The
Susan played hide-and-seek with a revenue cutter in Mobile Bay, the
filibusters' ship carrying as hostage a Federal officer who had gone
aboard with an ultimatum for surrender. Fog covered the bay and
the filibusters made for the Gulf of Mexico; suddenly the cutter appeared before them. The skipper of the *Susan* then proposed that the
two ships anchor until the fog should lift; and when the proposal was
accepted, he rattled chains in the hawse-holes so convincingly that

he managed to escape. The filibusters paused briefly in the Gulf, two days later, to transfer the revenue officer to an inbound steamer, and then proceeded, under orders to base on an island off Honduras until reinforcements should arrive.

A day's sail from Belize, the *Susan* was wrecked on a reef, and on New Year's Day, less than a month after their departure, the filibusters were back in Mobile, having been rescued by a British war vessel.

There was a new war coming—a great war. Walker was no soldier, but he might have served the Confederacy, as so many of his officers were to do. He might have rested on his Nicaraguan laurels and been remembered as the greatest of filibusters. But he could not ease the gnawing within him, and awake or asleep he could not close his eyes to the vision of his destiny.

Whatever the consequences, however pathetic the result, he had to try again.

V

HE WAS away in the spring of 1860, visiting his sister in Louisville, when a messenger came to New Orleans, with an appeal for his aid. In the midst of disappointment and reversal, this courier presented a solution to the physical difficulties preventing a new invasion of Nicaragua: he proposed to Fayssoux, in the absence of Walker, an expedition to the Bay Islands, off Honduras.

The Bay Islands—Ruatan, Bonacca, Utilla and three smaller ones— had for years occupied the same position in the British colonial system as the Mosquito Coast. Ruatan was seized in 1841, theoretically given up by the Clayton-Bulwer treaty of 1850, and in 1852 made part of the "Colony of Bay Islands." Britain claimed the islands as part of Belize (now British Honduras); the United States rejected the claim and insisted that they be restored to Honduras; and Britain declined to act except as a principal with Honduras itself. The dispute continued until November of 1859, when a treaty was signed between England and Honduras restoring to the latter the territory of the islands.

It was this treaty which gave Walker his opportunity to return to Central America. The Ruatan Islanders, loath to become citizens of Honduras, prayed Queen Victoria not to permit the ratification of the treaty. Their prayer went unheeded and in May, 1860, the treaty was ratified.

Walker, on his return to New Orleans, set to work at once, and in a few weeks had assembled another expedition.

In June, 1860, he sailed, the "Gray-Eyed Man of Destiny" again, moving doggedly against the countries that did not want him, attempting futilely to keep alive an adventure already as outmoded as the Crusades. A glance at his officers on the last, fated expedition reveals the blindness of the man and the utter lack of sympathy the United States had for his obsession. There was no Henningsen to withstand siege and still perform any task he might be given. Fayssoux declined to go, and never more would stand on the deck of a leaky schooner and damn the assembled navies of the world. There was no Swingle to make cannon shot out of whatever came to hand; no Doubleday, Anderson, Hornsby, Von Natzmer, De Brissot. All of them, men once devoted to the cause of filibusterism, were significantly absent when the Filibuster sailed away to die—perhaps they knew he was to die. Nor yet did fear alone deter them, for those who lived were in a year fighting gallantly enough for the Confederate States of America; it must have been an awakening that cost Walker his best officers, and perhaps a little shame in the breasts of some who recalled (*Agui Fué Granada!*) deeds that once seemed brave.

He had Henry, the reckless leader of a two-man charge at Masaya, the inveterate duelist, the often-wounded. He had Rudler, who for want of a better served as second-in-command. He had Dolan, another Crocker who believed William Walker to have the wisdom of God and the courage of the devil. The rest were nonentities.

Throughout April and May a trickle of recruits left New Orleans on the fruit boats. By June they reached the number Walker felt necessary—a hundred odd. Dolan and Rudler were sent, then, to the base on Ruatan Island. They sailed on the schooner *Clifton,* carrying miscellaneous cargo for Belize and "machinery and farm implements" for William Walker's army. The *Clifton* went no farther than to Belize, where a British officer inspected her, discovered that boxes traveling on the manifest as merchandise contained powder and shot, and denied her a clearance.

Meanwhile, Walker and Henry had reached the vicinity of Ruatan aboard another schooner—the *Taylor*—and waited for the *Clifton* to make the rendezvous so they could be at their hostilities. Rudler and Dolan, bringing men but no supplies, arrived near the contested island a few days after Walker, to report their loss in Belize; but even then it did not seem that the expedition need necessarily fail. Another vessel out of New Orleans was expected, carrying still more supplies, and Walker decided to wait until it reached him before directing any attack. Because the British authorities were suspicious of the number of strangers "visiting" Ruatan, the recruits sent ahead were taken aboard the *Taylor* and the entire party transferred to an uninhabited island, Cozumel, almost within sight of the port of Truxillo.

The rainy season was at its worst and the army had a poor time of it. Rude structures of branches and leaves failed to keep off the rain. Throughout July the men huddled on the island, watching to the north for the ship they expected. Day followed rainy day and still there was no sign. The men grumbled; not alone in officers was Walker poor, for the rank-and-file had none of the calm acceptance which had distinguished the Immortals. And Walker himself was as impatient as the most regretful private; pacing the beach, studying his maps, pretending to keep the meticulous muster rolls and other documents in which he had taken such great pride when his title was Commander-in-Chief of the Armies, the cancer of dissatisfaction grew within him. By August first he was finished with waiting. He allowed less than a week to pass and, when the supply ship failed to appear on the horizon, he conferred in the cabin of the *Taylor* with Rudler and Henry.

He then went ashore to address the men. He told them that the expedition no longer could remain idle on the little island and he offered them their choice of the two alternatives: a return to New Orleans or an assault on Truxillo. How nearly unanimous the vote for Truxillo was it is not possible to say. The Honduran city was garrisoned and had a fort; against it Walker planned to lead about a hundred irregulars, armed with a rifle each and about forty rounds of cartridges. He had no artillery and no better equipment than he had had in Sonora, barely seven years before.

On the evening of August fifth the *Taylor* ran across to Truxillo, passed the town without lights and anchored in a cove three miles up the bay. The company landed after midnight, formed in the light of a waning moon and set out boldly for the city. Walker and Henry led the main column, Rudler followed with the reserve. They came upon the city as the first streaks of dirty gray stained the eastern sky. The old fortress, walled with great blocks of stone laid down by Cortez's filibusters, was alert; guns frowned from the embrasures and sentries called shrilly when the attacking army came into sight. The column halted; six volunteers were sent to draw the fire of the garrison while the main attack was prepared. They ran forward with something of the Immortals' zeal, into a storm of grape, cannister and musket-shot; three died before they neared the walls and the other three were wounded. Behind them, in a second wave, trotted every man but Rudler's tiny reserve. They reached the wall while the Hondurans were reloading and formed pyramids, one man on the shoulders of two others, to reach the inside of the fort. The Hondurans incontinently fled; in fifteen minutes Truxillo was taken and "the President of Nicaragua" was planning his next move.

Six men were killed in the attack. Walker, having no surgeon, cared for the half dozen or so who were seriously wounded. In a matter of minutes the fortress was established under its new banner, with Henry commandant of the garrison and a man named Ryan as chief of artillery. The prize Walker had won was on an eminence, dominating the town, and contained thirty-six guns, mostly obsolete but still serviceable. Two appeared to have been cast from silver and bore plates engraved *Seville, 1800.* The buildings of the fort were made of adobe, with huge timbers holding the roofs; they swarmed with gigantic lizards, a foot or more long. There were many rooms, some barred for prisoners and others cemented to the ceiling for the storage of powder. A good supply of ammunition and food was discovered and taken in charge by the quartermaster; in the magazine many casks of powder, a few opened, were stacked against the walls.

On August seventh, the day after the capture of the fort, Walker issued a proclamation addressed to the people of Honduras. It read:

More than five years ago I, with others, was invited to the Republic of Nicaragua and was promised certain rights and privileges on the condition of certain services rendered to the state. We performed the services required of us but the existing authorities of Honduras joined a combination to drive us from Central America. In the course of events the people of the Bay Islands find themselves in nearly the same position as the Americans held in Nicaragua in November, 1855. The same policy which led Guardiola to make war on us will induce him to drive the people of the Islands from Honduras. A knowledge of this fact has led certain residents of the Island to call upon the adopted citizens of Nicaragua to aid in the maintenance of their rights of person and property; but no sooner had a few adopted citizens of Nicaragua answered this call of the residents of the Islands by repairing to Ruatan than the acting authorities of Honduras, alarmed for their safety, put obstacles in the way of carrying out the treaty of November 28, 1859. Guardiola delays to receive the Islands because of the presence of a few men whom he has injured; and thus, for party purposes, not only defeats the territorial interests of Honduras but thwarts, for the moment, a cardinal object of Central American policy. The people of the Bay Islands can be ingrafted on your Republic only by wise concessions properly made. The existing authorities of Honduras have, by their past acts, given proof that they would not make the requisite concessions. The same policy which Guardiola pursued toward the naturalized Nicaraguans prevents him from pursuing the only course by which Honduras can expect to hold the Islands. It becomes, therefore, a common object with the naturalized Nicaraguans, and with the people of the Bay Islands, to place in the government of Honduras those who will yield the rights lawfully required in the two states. Thus, the Nicaraguans will secure a return to their adopted country and the Bay Islanders will obtain full guarantees from the sovereignty under which they are to be placed by the treaty of November 28, 1859. To obtain, however, the object at which we aim, we do not make war against the people of Honduras, but only against a government which stands in the way of the interests, not only of Honduras, but of all Central America. The people of Honduras may therefore rely upon all the protection they may require for their rights, both of person and property.

Between August sixth, when the city fell to him, and August twenty-second, when he moved down the coast toward Nicaragua, the Filibuster suffered twice, once from his own blunders and again from the weakness of the men serving under him. He abolished customs duties, declaring Truxillo a free port, which was the blunder; and he lost Colonel Thomas Henry, his bravest aide.

The Hondurans had permitted cannon and other equipment to lie untended and uncleaned; Walker saw to it that everything the fort offered for defense was placed in the best condition. During these

From *Frank Leslie's Illustrated Newspaper.*

EXPLOSION OF THE *Scott*

labors, Henry one day returned from the town, where he had found liquor. He was a fighter; his entire character is summed up in that word. In Nicaragua he had fought several duels, and in New Orleans just before the departure of the expedition he, as well as Walker himself, had challenged Lockridge. At least eight Allied bullets had hit him in the Nicaraguan war and he was the despair of surgeons because of his obstinate refusal to remain in hospital when there was fighting to be done.

Trinidad Cabañas, the Honduran revolutionary who was among the first to accept Walker as a deliverer, and who will be remembered as having become a bitter opponent when the Filibuster denied him aid, again was attempting to overthrow the government of Honduras, now as before in the control of Santos Guardiola, the Butcher. Henry had been sent to confer with Cabañas in the back country. Whether he saw him is not known; but on his return, Henry stopped in the town to drink. He was in an evil mood when he returned to the fort. In the magazine a squad was preparing charges for the cannon. Henry entered the magazine, which was carpeted in spots with loose powder, smoking a cigar. The officer ordered him out. There was a struggle; Henry was shot in the jaw.

Walker personally treated Henry's wound, a ghastly thing that had destroyed the entire lower part of his face. For days the wounded man lingered, unable to speak and communicating all his wishes with words painfully scrawled on a slate. He could not possibly live without more adequate treatment than could be given him and yet he clung to life, for a week and then for two.

Meanwhile, the British warship *Icarus,* commanded by Norvell Salmon, came into the harbor. Walker was alone and unsupported; the Englishman knew this. He knew, too, that the Filibuster was as great a thorn in the side of the United States as he was in England's. Salmon's intentions were the same, with less of fear to stay them, as Commander Davis's had been at Rivas. He sent a message ashore, informing Walker that the customs duties of Truxillo were mortgaged to British interests for a debt, demanding the return of some two thousand dollars said to have been taken from the customs house and suggesting that the Americans lay down their arms and abandon the coast. Walker replied in a conciliatory tone, regretting the loss of the

custom money while denying all knowledge of it and evading, with
a request for particulars on Salmon's actions in that event, the suggestion that he evacuate Truxillo.

Late in the afternoon of August twenty-first, Salmon's reply was
received. Because he had been petitioned for protection by the residents of Truxillo and other Honduran coast points, he said, he must
require that Walker leave, at his own expense, aboard one of the two
ships then in harbor which might be chartered. He held Walker
personally responsible for the money taken from the customs house.
And, finally, he regretted that no further explanations of his intentions appeared necessary to him, inasmuch as Walker was lawlessly
warring upon the people of an accepted government.

Walker asked to be allowed to consider the demands until morning. He inspected what he could see of his situation and found it
hopeless; in addition to the *Icarus,* there were seven hundred Honduran troops massed just outside Truxillo. Surrender was the only
wise course. But the Filibuster had become more desperate than
he had ever been before. Failure after failure brought him no nearer
Nicaragua than this; and he was determined that he would go nearer.
He resolved then to give up the fort and retreat southward. He
believed that he might manage to cut his way through the jungles
into Nicaragua, of which he was still, in his own stubborn mind,
president.

In the account of Walter Stanley, survivor of the last expedition,* we have a vivid picture of the scene in which this decision was made. Henry, who had been to Walker what Crocker
had been in Sonora and whose recklessness in the past had swung
the balance from defeat to victory, was of no value to Walker now.
He lay, a speechless hulk, in great agony. Worms had eaten away
the rottenest part of his face and but for his living eyes one would
have thought him dead. He could reveal to Walker no gleam of
hope, not even when the Filibuster had written his problem on
the slate and held it before his eyes.

Henry picked up the slate, scratched the pencil across its face
and made a single word. He handed the slate to Walker, who read
it, sat still for more long minutes. Then, with a shrug, the Filibuster

* Quoted in *With Walker in Nicaragua.*

touched the shoulder of the dying Henry with one thin hand and went out into the darkness of the old fort.

Once long before, a successful *Yanqui* had sailed in the night and taken a city named Granada. He had sailed as the savior of Central American democracy; and to his prize had come a fervent, believing patriot, Trinidad Cabañas. But the successful *Yanqui* had turned the old man away, because to ally with him would not have furthered the vast dreams of conquest which had driven him from New Orleans to San Francisco, and to Sonora, and to Nicaragua. And now, face up on the blanket, lay a slate with a single word of bitterest irony; the only possibility of help Henry could see for Walker's extrication: the name "Cabañas."

Presently Henry forced himself upright. He took from the table beside him a tin cup filled with lemonade and dumped into it the full contents of a bottle of morphine. He stirred his mixture and poured what of it he could into the shattered cavity that had been his mouth; then he lay back and turned his face to the wall, and pulled the blanket up about him. The morphine killed him quickly.

VI

Gone was pride. Dead (almost) was hope. There remained only one possibility: to find Cabañas if he could; to plead for help from one to whom he had denied it; to try and cut his way through jungle and blood and bone to the chair of the President of the Republic of Nicaragua. Some dampening of the spirit, some consciousness of the wrongs he had done, must have been forced upon William Walker by the mere coincidental presence of Cabañas. What he had done to Cabañas and Kinney and Goicouria must have accused him, as he set out upon his last and most dogged march.

Spiking the fort's cannon, destroying the surplus rifles and pouring casks of powder into the well, Walker abandoned Truxillo and started on his last march south. It was midnight when he left, abandoning to the possible protection of the English five wounded men. A guide, said to know where Cabañas might be found, led him through an orange grove at the edge of the town and into the jungle.

The first night's march was swift and silent and marked by only one engagement—at a place on the Roman river, where the vanguard of the Honduran pursuit caught up with Walker's sixty-five and withered the stragglers with musket fire. Twenty were wounded there, but the march did not halt; when the pursuers had been driven off the guide led on, over trails in places wide enough for only one man.

At sunrise on the twenty-third, at a banana plantation called Lima, the Hondurans attacked again. They were driven back after a brief engagement and Walker seized canoes for the passage down the Rio Negro. Carrying hands of bananas for food, he drifted with the current to within four miles of the coast, where Cabañas was supposed to be waiting.

The guide had disappeared; when the army reached the camp its leader knew why. There was no Cabañas, no great army of Honduran revolutionaries to give the Americans strength, nothing but empty rifle pits. And fewer than fifty men remained in the filibuster ranks, many wounded.

For more than a week William Walker held the barricades Cabañas had left. There was a never-ending exchange of fire, the men had no rest. The country for miles around was a swamp, vaporous, humid and as full of death as a pest house. The men lay in the rifle pits under rain or sun for fourteen of the day's twenty-four hours. In time they forgot that there were days and nights and dazedly loaded and fired their pieces; two who were careless, and walked for water along the top of the trenches, died under the accidentally good marksmanship of the Hondurans.

The phrase had failed him; William Walker was no longer the "Man of Destiny." Ridden with fever himself, indefatigable, inevitably calm, he went about his duties, moving in the pits for hours longer than any of his companions. What he hoped for in this moment is not known; but what he had traveled to was clear for him to see. The firing squad he had summoned for so many of his opponents now waited for him, for there was no victory here, as there had been at Granada; no retreat, as there had been at Rivas; no American naval vessel for haven, as there had been at Punta Arenas.

On September 3, 1860, Commander Salmon appeared off the camp with two boatloads of his sailors. He came ashore and brusquely demanded surrender. In their conference Walker asked twice to whom he surrendered, and both times was told, "to her Britannic Majesty."

He returned from the beach, where he had talked with Salmon, and gave his last order: for his men to lay down their arms and claim the protection due citizens of the United States.

The men were carried down the river and went aboard the *Icarus,* in little groups of two and three. Walker was the last to go aboard. He regained here some of the arrogance he had lost in the three years of his futile striving: he said, when the officer listing names asked his:

"I am William Walker, President of Nicaragua."

Only one of his men, Rudler, abandoned with the Filibuster the claim to citizenship; and the two stood together, Nicaraguans by their own claim, as the *Icarus* went smoothly back to Truxillo.

VII

To HAVE retained that arrogance, to have stood by his boldness in saying, "I am the President of Nicaragua"—that would have been a grand ending for the Filibuster. But the struggles he had endured, the failures, the dwindling of his fame, all had made him petty. He whined when he lost.

At Truxillo a reporter for the New York *Herald* came aboard. Walker talked with him and gave him the correspondence with Salmon. He declared that Salmon now planned to turn him and Rudler over to the Hondurans, for the death they would certainly decree for them; and he dictated, without mentioning his brazen claim when the deck of the *Icarus* was beneath his feet, this statement:

September 5, 1860.

I hereby protest before the civilized world that when I surrendered to the Captain of Her Majesty's steamer *Icarus,* that officer expressly received my sword and pistol, as well as the arms of Colonel Rudler, and the surrender was expressly made in so many words to him, as the representative of Her Britannic Majesty.

This was the last document from his pen. He had pledged death
to his enemies, he had written flamingly of rights and the courage
of men who die for them, he had played for a little more than five
years of his life the part of a regenerator aware of the risks he took
and glad, because of his mission to humanity, to take them. And
then, a few days short of the dignity of death, the pent-up bitterness
at his loss of power, and the obstacles placed in the way of regain-
ing it, found voice in a "protest to the civilized world."

They put him in the powder magazine, where Henry had died,
and for six days he sat there, watching the back of the indolent guard
in the corridor, moving to avoid the lizards on the stone walls,
thinking his thoughts. Priests attended him and found him altogether calm; what he said to them is not known. Outside his men
were quartered on the shore, closely guarded from the Hondurans
by the United States marines who would see them safely back to
the States. Other filibusters had been captured and shot at once:
but Walker was a devil, Walker was an extraordinary case; to kill
Walker required time. It was six days in all, because it took the
courier that long to return from Tegucigalpa with the order of execution. And the man who affixed that signature must have guffawed
loudly as he wrote, for he was Santos Guardiola, the Butcher of
Honduras.

Walker is said to have spent the last six days of his life in medita-
tion and prayer. One can doubt the sincerity of the prayer and yet
pity the man for turning to it in his last hours. And one can wonder
of what he thought as he waited for the bad marksmen of Honduras to dispatch him thence.

Did he remember the wild welcome at Leon? The inauguration?
The celebration after Fayssoux's *Granada* blew up the *Once de Abril?*

Did he think of the stature he had grown in five short years? Of
the legends built up about him: the blood-red parrot which (the Costa
Ricans said) had screamed throughout the second battle of Rivas,
"Hurrah for Walker!"; the widespread tale that he was a disgraced
aide-de-camp of the Duke de Nemours, who in the last year of the
reign of Louis Philippe had been caught cheating at cards, and had
gone off as William Walker to conquer in the New World; or the
stories which pictured his officers and himself dining nightly at

Granada, brave in evening dress, on the finest of wines and viands?

Or, just possibly, did he watch the ghosts of all the men he had killed stand with the lizards in the corners of the room and look upon him with the great pity of the dead for the living?

VIII

A squad of barefooted, brown men led him from his prison to an open field near the beach. He walked firmly, his mincing boot-heels loud on the paving of the corridor. In one hand he carried a crucifix, and he murmured to the priest who walked beside him.

They fired raggedly, with their clumsy muskets, and did not quite kill him. An officer peered nervously into the unconscious face, then shot into it blindly with a pistol, the bullet tearing away part of the jaw and giving to the man who never smiled a clown's grin.

The natives went away hurriedly, even now not quite sure that the terrible one was gone. The priests remained, to bury the Fili-buster in a shallow grave soon to be obliterated by the sea.

The date was September 12, 1860. On that day there was in San Francisco a celebration of the anniversary of California's admission into the Union. Edmund Randolph spoke and what he said may well have been said in the same moments that the guns were sounding in Truxillo:

"You cannot tell today which pine sings the requiem of the pioneer. Some have fallen beneath their country's flag; and longings still unsatisfied have led some to renew their adventurous career upon foreign soils. Combatting for strangers whose quarrels they espoused, they fell amid the jungle of the tropics. . . .

"And fatted the rank soil there, with right precious blood."

THE END

AUTHORITIES...

MATERIAL on the life of William Walker is limited, scattered and, in many cases, inaccurate. With the exception of Walker's memoirs, contemporary publications are generally biased and unreliable. Indubitably the best reference is Dr. Scroggs's work, to which too much credit cannot be given for its value in the preparation of this book. Many quotations (notably those at the beginning of each section of *The Filibuster*) have been taken from the Walker text; with the exception of a few relatively unimportant phrases, all unidentified quotations are from that source.

BOOKS

Abdullah, Achmed [with T. Compton Pakenham], *Dreamers of Empire;* New York, 1929.

Allen, Merritt Parmalee, *William Walker, Filibuster;* New York, 1932.

Bancroft, Hubert Howe, *History of Central America;* San Francisco, 1887.

Bell, Horace, *Reminiscences of a Ranger;* Los Angeles, 1881.

Clapp, Theodore, *Autobiographical Sketches;* Boston, 1858.

Crowe, Frederick, *The Gospel in Central America;* London, 1850.

Crowther, Samuel, *The Romance and Rise of the American Tropics;* New York, 1929.

Davis, Richard Harding, *Real Soldiers of Fortune;* New York, 1906.

Doubleday, C. W., *Reminiscences of the "Filibuster" War in Nicaragua;* New York, 1886.

Dunn, Henry, *Guatimala, or the United Provinces of Central America;* New York, 1828.

Hall, A. H., *The Manhattaner in New Orleans;* New Orleans, 1851.

Hittell, Theodore H., *History of California;* San Francisco, 1885-1897.

Jamison, James Carson, *With Walker in Nicaragua;* Columbia, Mo., 1909.

Manning, William R. [Editor], *Diplomatic Correspondence of the United States;* Washington, 1932.

North, Arthur Walbridge, *Camp and Camino in Lower California;* San Francisco, 1910.

Officer in the Service of Walker, *The Destiny of Nicaragua;* Boston, 1856.

Oliphant, Laurence, *Patriots and Filibusters;* London, 1860.

Powell, E. Alexander, *Gentleman Rovers;* New York, 1913.

Roche, James Jeffrey, *The Story of the Filibusters;* London, 1891.

Scroggs, William O., *Filibusters and Financiers;* New York, 1916.

Shuck, Oscar T. [Editor], *Representative and Leading Men of the Pacific;* San Francisco, 1870.

Simmons, William E., *The Nicaragua Canal;* New York, 1900.

Soule, Gihon and Nisbet, *The Annals of San Francisco;* San Francisco, 1855.

Squier, E. G., *Nicaragua;* New York, 1852.

Stout, Peter F., *Nicaragua;* New York, 1859.

Thomas, Jane H., *Old Days in Nashville, Tennessee;* Nashville, 1897.

Truman, Benjamin Cummings, *The Field of Honor;* New York, 1884.

Walker, William, *The War in Nicaragua;* Mobile, 1860.

Warren, T. Robinson, *Dust and Foam;* New York, 1859.

Wells, William V., *Walker's Expedition to Nicaragua;* New York, 1856.

Other Sources

El Nicaraguense.
Harper's Weekly.
Leslie's Illustrated Weekly Newspaper.
Louisville *Times.*
Mobile *Register.*
Montgomery *Advertiser.*
New Orleans *Commercial Bulletin.*
New Orleans *Delta.*
New Orleans *Picayune.*
New York *Atlas.*
New York *Herald.*
New York *Sun.*
New York *Times.*
New York *Tribune.*
Sacramento *Daily Democratic State Journal*
San Francisco *Alta California.*
Tennessee Historical Magazine.
Wheeler Scrapbooks [Collection of five, in Library of Congress, dealing
    with Walker and other contemporary personages and including news-
    paper and magazine articles and manuscript notations].

INDEX

tort

Pindray, Marquis de, leader of a
Sonora expedition, 28
Pollard, E. H., exalted the Filibuster,
200
Price, renegade, urged men to desert
Henningsen, 257
Price, Rodman, Governor of New
Jersey, exalted Walker, 200
Principal, storehouse in Leon, 195
Pueblo Nuevo, Martinez's victory at,
110
Punta Arenas
recruits at, 283
Walker's second expedition to
Nicaragua encamped at, 306
Purdy, Deputy Sheriff, and the *Vesta*,
63-64

Queen of the Pacific, Transit ship,
108
Quitman, General John A., and the
Cuba filibuster, 24

Ramirez, Nicaraguan colonel, 66
and Walker
at Rivas, 73*ff*
desertion, 79, 85, 95
Randolph, Edmund
and Goicouria, 222
and Walker
and the Transit charter, 161*ff*,
189
defended, 46
didn't send supplies, 105
sought loan in New York, 220
speech at San Francisco on requiem
of pioneer, 327
Raousset-Boulbon, Gaston Raoul de,
leader of an expedition to Sonora,
28
Realejo, 81, 85, 86, 87, 92
description of, 66-67
history of, 65
Rivas ordered fortifications of dismantled, 196

Reminiscences of a Ranger, 167n.
Rescue
bought by Lockbridge, 264
rescued remainder of San Juan
River expedition, 288
sick carried aboard, 288
Resolute, tug, 64
Richardson, Alice Walker, 22
visited by Walker, 300
Richardson, doctor with Walker's expedition, 35
Rivas, Nicaragua
appearance of, 269
battles of
first, 72*ff*, 85, 95
second, 180*ff*
third, 272, 276-277, 280*ff*
commanded Transit Road, 269
Corral in, 107*ff*
evacuated by Walker, 179
Rivas, Patricio
and Walker
approved court-martial for Corral, 131
as President, 123, 190
peace proclamation of, 190
defection from, 195*ff*
manifesto quoted, 203-204
fled Leon, 196
gained courage, 175
opposed to new election, 193
trap in Leon, 195-196
treaty of alliance with other
Central American Republics,
205-206
deposed as claimant to presidency,
305
Robellero, Colonel, 32
Robert, Charles Frederick, native
chief,
coronation of, 139-140
gave grant to Samuel and Peter
Shepherd, 140
Rogers, William K.

Titus, Colonel H. T.
  failed to take Castillo Viejo, 286
  life and characteristics of, 285-286
Tola, 74
"Topsy-Turvy"
  see Rivas, Patricio
Toucy, Isaac, Secretary of the Navy,
    ordered prevention of invaders,
    305
Trajuanna, Hacienda, 17, 20
Tribune, New York, quoted on Walk-
    er's appearance, 210
Truxillo
  declared free port, 320
  description of, 319
  taken by Walker, 319

Ugarté, Francisco, hanged by Walk-
    er, 188
Utilla, one of the Bay Islands, 316

Vallé, José Maria
  and President Rivas's defection,
    197ff
  captured at Chinandega, 231
  in battle of Virgin Bay, 99
  in first battle of Granada, 108ff
  joined American Phalanx, 94
  put down Legitimists of Segovia,
    190
Vanderbilt, Cornelius, 21, 314
  and Goicouria, 219ff
  and Law, 238
  and the United States government,
    177
  and Walker
    contrast between, 183-184
    co-operated with Mora against,
      264
    message to Birdsall, 183
    negotiated with President Rivas
      against, 263
    signed requisitions for tickets,
      165

Vanderbilt—Cont.
  suspended service, 177
  built Accessory Transit Company,
    137
  demanded protection of Transit,
    167
  Garrison associate of, 96
  gave Minié rifles, 284
  regained Transit, 267
Vesta, 62, 75, 81, 82, 84, 85, 86, 95
Vijil, Padre Augustin
  and Walker, 114ff
  deserted, 235
  Minister to Washington, 199
  presided at inauguration of Ri-
    vas, 126
  return from Washington, 214
Virgin Bay, 57, 81
  description of inhabitants of, 102-
    103
  First Infantry at, 242
  Hornsby at, 240-241
  massacre of, 120
  men moved to because of cholera
    in Granada, 190
  taken by Mora, 268
  victory of, 105
Von Natzmer, Bruno
  on first Nicaraguan expedition, 87,
    88
  advanced against Cabañas on
    Transit Road, 241
  and the Rivas-Salagar trap in
    Leon, 195-196
  in capture of Granada, 108ff
  on second Nicaraguan expedition,
    305-306

Wabash, U. S. S.
  at Punta Arenas, 306-307
  survivors of Walker's government
    on, 303
Walker, James, brother of William
  Walker, 22

Walker—*Cont.*
   see Walker, William, decrees of
   flag of, 31
   march to Sonora, 42*ff*
   mutiny in, 38-39
   poor generalship, 38-39
   surrendered to United States, 20
   on trial for filibustering, 46*f*, 305
   recruiting activities of, 224
   refused to reply to stories of victims, 304
   stories about, 326
   toured and addressed meetings, 305
   visited Alice Richardson, 316
Wallerstein, Edward, Costa Rican Consul General, letters quoted, 169-170
War in Nicaragua, The
   accuracy of, 314, 315
   evaluation of, 311
   gave facts of second battle of Rivas, 185
   quoted on
      Fayssoux's encounter with Sir Robert McClure, 274
      Fayssoux's encounter with Davis, 301-302
      O'Neal, 272
      slavery issue, 311-312, 313
      Spencer, 314, 315
   writing of, 310-311
Waters, Major John P.
   at Masaya, 231, 232, 233
   led foragers at Rivas, 281
   recruiting activities, 280
   went to relief of Granada, 260*ff*
Watkins, Henry
   arrested and fined, 41, 46, 47
   law partner of Walker, 26
   recruiting officer, 34
Webster, William R. C., in campaign that captured San Juan River, 264*ff*

Wheat, General Robert Cheatham
   at Punta Arenas, 283
   and Captain Cockburn, 284
   helped take Hipp's Point, 285
   planned to reach Walker from Pacific side, 287
Wheeler, John H., United States Minister to Nicaragua, 61
   and Walker
      extended recognition of United States to Walker, 214
      Mayorga in custody of, 121
      obtained release of Livingstone, 216
      report to Washington of conference with Cabañas about Walker, quoted, 148-150
      supported Walker, 111, 116
      threatened by Estrada's army, 235
   recalled by State Department, 237
   reprimanded by Washington, 143
Wilson, Colonel Billy
   joined Walker at Granada, 151
   With Walker in Nicaragua, 322n.
Wilson, W. F., helped found New Orleans *Crescent*, 24
Winslow, Senator, criticism of Walker quoted, 310
Wool, Brevet Major John E.
   enforced neutrality laws, 41
   approved Castellon grant, 60

Xatruch, General Pedro, 116
   at Masaya, 131
   Corral's letter to, 129

Yrena, Niña, Legitimist of Granada, 115

Zavala, General
   escort for Walker, 295
   spy for Allies, 257